The Sacred Grove, *by J. Rulon Hales*

RETURN

Endsheets: *The Purpose of Life,* by Robert Oliver Skemp.
© Intellectual Reserve, Inc. Used by permission.

Library of Congress Cataloging-in-Publication Data

Hales, Robert D., 1932–

    Return : four phases of our mortal journey home / Robert D. Hales.
       p. cm.
    Includes bibliographical references and index.
    ISBN 978-1-57008-769-1 (hardbound : alk. paper)
  1. Plan of salvation (Mormon theology) 2. Christian life—Mormon authors.   3. The Church of Jesus Christ of Latter-day Saints—Doctrines. 4. Mormon Church—Doctrines.   I. Title.
    BX8643.S25H35 2010
    234—dc22   2010011474

Printed in the United States of America
Publishers Printing, Salt Lake City, Utah

10   9   8   7   6   5   4   3   2   1

To Mary,
my eternal companion, and
our eternal family

For behold, this is my work and my glory—
to bring to pass the immortality and
eternal life of man.

Moses 1:39

CONTENTS

ACKNOWLEDGMENTS

I could not have written this book alone. For many years, I had the concept for this book in mind and appreciate the encouragement from friends and associates to complete it.

Mary Berrey has been my faithful secretary, editor, and friend for twenty-six years. She carefully reviewed each word of the manuscript with a cautious eye, questioning every unwarranted use of a superlative or absolute statement. When I had a hard time getting to work on the manuscript, Mary's masterful use of reminder notes helped me get back on task.

Rob Eaton's input has been invaluable. He is familiar with the talks I have given over the years, and he has helped me organize my thoughts for this book. Perhaps more important, he helped persuade me to include here some stories that I have never shared before to illustrate the doctrines I teach.

I appreciate Jim Bell's early assistance as well. Among other things, Jim conducted hours of interviews with me that proved an invaluable resource. His work served as a catalyst that helped me to really begin this project.

I am grateful to Henry J. Eyring, who encouraged me to write this book, and also to David Warner, who provided useful feedback on the manuscript and assisted with the editing.

Cory Maxwell and Sheri Dew of Deseret Book Company have been supportive with me over the years. Few editors and publishers would patiently support an author for more than a decade as they have. I also deeply appreciate their trusting me enough to allow me to take a rather unusual approach in this book.

Many others behind the scenes at Deseret Book have helped in important ways. Suzanne Brady has carefully edited the book and suggested important clarifications. Richard Erickson's creativity and sensitive eye have enhanced its appeal and appearance. It has likewise benefited from Tonya Facemyer's attention to detail as she did the typesetting.

I am indebted to more mentors than I can name. The thoughts we write in books are shaped by the experiences of our lives. My life has been richly blessed and my thoughts have been profoundly influenced by my parents, the prophets with whom I have served, my colleagues in the Quorum of the Twelve, and many other leaders and friends I have been blessed to know.

No one has shaped and blessed me more than has my dear wife, Mary. Our marriage has been a true partnership through the years; she is, without doubt, my better half. We were blessed with two fine sons, Stephen and David, and our grandchildren, who have enriched our lives. There is no question in my mind that I would not be the man I am today without Mary's loving influence in my life. To the extent that this book is a reflection of any progress I might have made, it is also a reflection of her constant dedication and inspiration that have helped me become a more complete disciple of Christ.

Mary is also the best editor a writer could have. She is

always kind, but she never holds back. Both this book and my talks through the years are better because of her wise suggestions.

Finally, I am reluctant to take credit for the ideas developed here. Any ideas that were worthwhile came through the Spirit from a loving Heavenly Father. That is not to suggest that every word of this book is inspired, however. Even though I have labored over it carefully and was helped in its preparation, I alone am responsible for the views it expresses. It is not an official statement of Church doctrine.

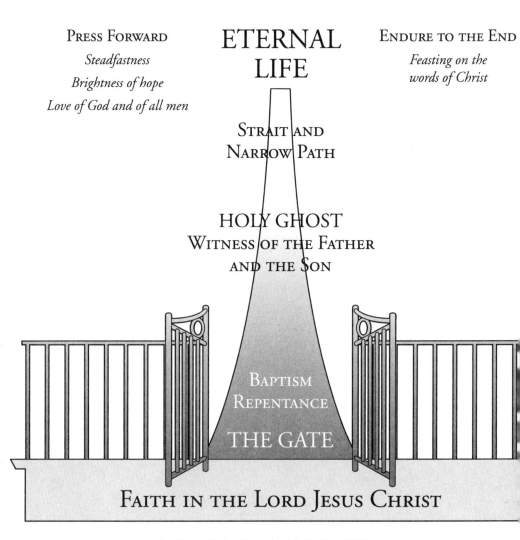

PRESS FORWARD

Steadfastness

Brightness of hope

Love of God and of all men

ETERNAL
LIFE

ENDURE TO THE END

*Feasting on the
words of Christ*

STRAIT AND
NARROW PATH

HOLY GHOST
WITNESS OF THE FATHER
AND THE SON

BAPTISM
REPENTANCE

THE GATE

FAITH IN THE LORD JESUS CHRIST

THIS IS THE WAY

2 NEPHI 31:17–21

INTRODUCTION

WHILE SERVING OUR mission to England, Sister Hales and I continually thought about how to teach the gospel to our brothers and sisters. Our missionaries and their investigators needed more than information—more than just terms and concepts. They needed a deep personal understanding of the essential truths of our existence: who we are, where we came from, why we are here, and where we are going. They needed to know that all of us are on our journey home.

In those days we identified five steps to help them, based on the first principles and ordinances of the gospel. These steps we described as a bridge from this world into the kingdom of God: faith in the Lord Jesus Christ, the gate of repentance and baptism, receiving the Holy Ghost and a witness of the Father and the Son, the strait and narrow path of obedience, and the goal, eternal life.

As you can see, the steps across the bridge were simple enough for the missionaries to remember and for their investigators to understand. So simple, in fact, that they could have been

"Burma-Shave"[1] signs to lead them along! In talking about a bridge, we were teaching them: "These are the important things that every member of the Church needs to know to return to Heavenly Father with honor. These are the essential truths of the gospel, and this is why they apply to you."

Later, while serving as the Presiding Bishop, I had the opportunity to expound on these steps, using those little advertising signs I remembered from my childhood. I wanted to teach, in a visual way, that progress along the path to exaltation is supported by our progress in becoming self-reliant (see pages 4 and 5).

Why did I use these modest illustrations? Among other things, I wanted to make it clear that the gospel truly is simple. There are just a few key steps we need to take now and throughout our lives in order to have all the blessings Heavenly Father has promised us. I also wanted to reassure my brothers and sisters that living the gospel is a process, like walking down a path. In contemplating my own life, I remember what my father used to say to me: "How did Hannibal cross the Alps? One step at a time, and the rest of the army followed." In the same way that we would cross a bridge or follow a path, we live the gospel *one step at a time*—"line upon line, precept upon precept" (2 Nephi 28:30). The more steps we take, the more clearly we understand that life on earth is, in fact, a journey to a familiar destination. We have been in the presence of our Heavenly Father and His Son Jesus Christ *already*. We have felt Their love and we have loved Their

---

1. If you are too young to remember, let me explain: Burma-Shave was a popular brushless shaving cream advertised by a sequence of little red signs along the highway. These held one-liners that led you step by step to the desired conclusion. Here's one example from 1933, submitted through a regional contest held during football season and posted along the highway: "Within this vale / Of toil / And sin / Your head grows bald / But not your chin / Burma-Shave." When I was a child, our family would drive from New York to Utah and discuss these signs. Along the way we eagerly looked for the next set of signs to appear. See http://eisnermuseum.org/_burma_shave/signs_of_the_times.html; accessed 25 February 2010.

light *already.* And now we are walking in that light—following that light—back to Them.

What is the path that will lead us back to Their presence? Our Divine navigational aides are found in the scriptures and the temple, and we can obtain individual guidance through prayer, fasting, and the continual promptings of the Holy Ghost. But to know the path itself—that winding lane through the valley, the bridge across the stream, the narrow trail leading to the rugged mountain peak, the sweeping vista—requires a friend who has walked the path before. As I have had such friends in my life, this book is an expression of my friendship for you. It provides an eternal perspective of this journey from our premortal life through the various decades of our mortal sojourn upon the earth. It is not a compilation of previous talks; rather it is personal, practical advice combined with selected teachings and stories from my years as a General Authority. Some of these experiences I have never shared before. They are organized into the four phases of life: the *Decades of Preparation,* the *Decade of Decision,* the *Decades of Serving and Pressing Forward,* and the *Decades of Serving and Enduring to the End.* Through every page and in every thought the beautiful doctrines of the gospel, taught in the scriptures and words of living prophets, lead us to the source of wisdom and understanding. These are offered to bless fellow travelers as they hold to the rod and stay on the path to the end.

I bear my witness that our travel through this life can bring us great happiness. Ultimately, that happiness is possible because of our Savior and His atoning sacrifice. He is our greatest, truest friend. He is the one who has walked the path of mortal life before us. And because He suffered all things for us, He is the Holy One who can understand us, succor us, comfort us, heal us, and strengthen us. I testify that He lives, and because He lives we can have the joy of returning with honor back into His presence. May that joy be ours today as we continue in our glorious journey home.

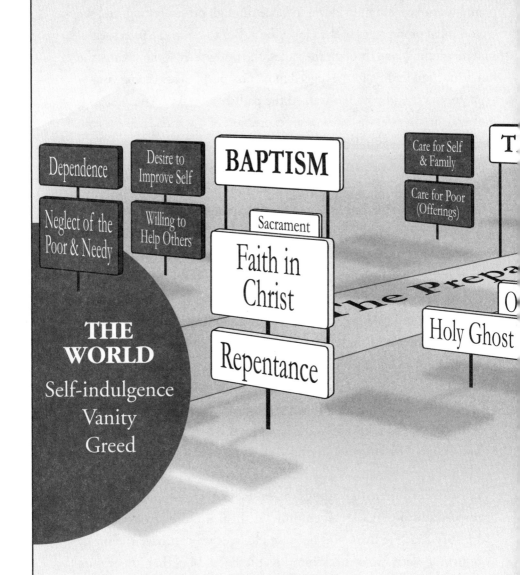

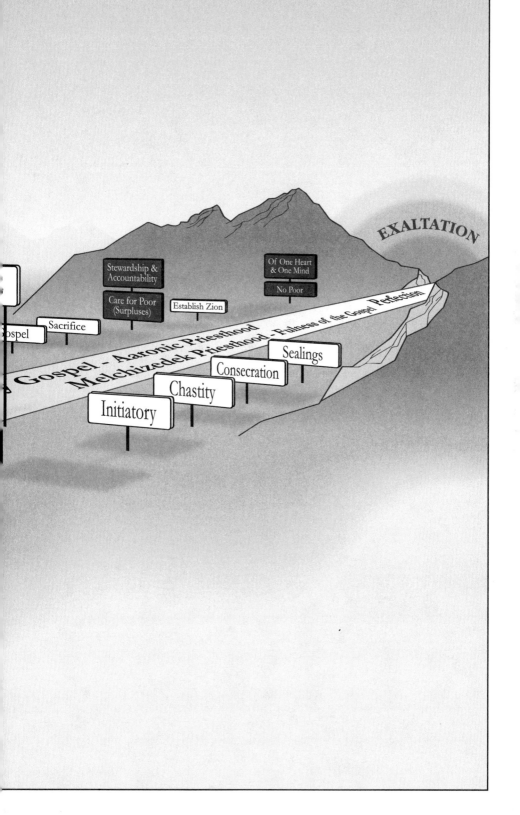

We will make an earth whereon these may dwell;
and we will prove them herewith, to see if they will do all things
whatsoever the Lord their God shall command them.

ABRAHAM 3:24–25

CHAPTER ONE

Our Journey Home

THIS EARTH IS LITERALLY a proving ground. Each of us chose to come here to experience mortality and to prove ourselves in a test of trials and tribulations, joys and sorrows. Our goal is to endure faithfully to the end in righteousness and return to the presence of God, our Heavenly Father and His Son, Jesus Christ. "And this is life eternal, that they might know thee the only true God, and Jesus Christ, whom thou hast sent" (John 17:3). How will we make our journey back to them?

Return with Honor

As a young man, I had the opportunity to serve in the United States Air Force as a jet fighter pilot. Each unit in our squadron had a motto that would inspire its efforts. Our unit motto—displayed on the side of our aircraft—was "Return with Honor." This motto was a constant reminder to us of our goal: to return to our home base with honor after expending all efforts necessary to complete our mission successfully.

Having left Heavenly Father's presence to come to earth, we too must determine to return with honor to our heavenly home. Our aim is to receive eternal life, "the greatest of all the gifts of God" (D&C 14:7). To do this we must remember where we came from, why we are here, and where we desire to go when we leave this life.

When I think of the four stages of life, I am reminded that one of the most difficult missions I flew as a jet fighter pilot occurred while I was stationed in Albany, Georgia. I was selected for a special mission called High Flight. Our task was to ferry some of our older models of the F-100 jets to Spain. We were basically giving jet hand-me-downs to one of our NATO allies. I asked the squadron leader why he chose me to be his wingman, especially since I was younger than most other crew members. He replied, "Because I know you are always sober."

These jets had limited range, so flying them across the Atlantic Ocean was not easy. We first flew to Newfoundland, where we waited for a shift in the weather, after which we headed on to the Azores, beautiful little islands that could serve as a way station en route to Spain. We had just enough fuel to make the flight from Newfoundland to the Azores. The winds were against us, so in this case we waited about thirty days for favorable conditions.

During those thirty days, we were supposed to prepare for our trip. We got up every morning at 6:00 for drills. If we had to eject over the North Atlantic, we would probably survive the frigid water just long enough to inflate and climb into the life raft attached to our seat. So we prepared by jumping off a diving board into a pool of freezing water and cinching our flight suits tight around our necks and ankles. As we hit the water, we would pull a cord to inflate the raft and then climb in. We could not simulate the swells of ten to fifteen feet we would probably have experienced in the North Atlantic, but at least the test helped us know how to inflate our rafts and climb into them in freezing water.

We would then study the *Dash-1,* a manual that explained

practically everything about our airplane—every part, every function, every emergency procedure. Exceptional pilots knew the essential chapters and pages by memory. These pages had the answers that could save us in an emergency. With these answers in our minds, *Dash-1* could relieve us of the anxiety we would otherwise have had.

The training got old fast. It was hard to prepare so much when what we really wanted to do was fly. But in time the day for our departure came. The weather was still marginal; however, because of the demands of our assignment, we could not wait any longer. We took off for the Azores, flying our single-seat fighters in two formations of four planes each. Like the Holy Ghost, Navy ships below provided navigational direction for us as we crossed the Atlantic Ocean.

It wasn't until we reached No Man's Land—about halfway between Newfoundland and the Azores—that one of the pilots first started having problems. "Something's wrong with my fuel pump," the lieutenant said over the radio. "My fuel isn't feeding properly. My gauges are not giving me the right information." Our squadron leader got on the airwaves to talk him through the problem, but the lieutenant became more and more worried. "I'm losing a lot of fuel out of one tank. I don't understand what's going on."

So our squadron leader said, "Hales, will you get up there and see if you can see any loss of fuel outside the plane?" I flew up six to eight feet beneath the troubled plane, bouncing around in the turbulence of the North Atlantic air, but I couldn't see any signs of a leak. Back in formation, I reported my findings.

At this point the lieutenant said, "My fuel warning light is on." We were still a long way from the Azores, but we were past the point of no return. Then he started to panic. The rest of us became fairly excited, and we all started giving him advice at once over the radio.

Our more experienced squadron leader—who had been an ace in

the Korea conflict—took control of the situation and calmly began reviewing our options. He asked some of the other pilots to review their *Dash-1* manuals to see what they could learn about the fuel pumps. This leader, who had done his homework and was well prepared, told us how we could determine whether the problem was a broken gas gauge or a faulty fuel pump not drawing fuel from one of the tanks. We soon determined that the problem was the failure of one of the pumps. The engines were not getting any fuel from one of the tanks.

Our leader, based on the *Dash-1* and his own experience, came up with a plan. It nearly scared the lieutenant to death, but frankly, it was his only chance. Our leader told him to turn off *both* his pumps, including the one that was working, to try to determine whether he could get the fuel to flow using gravity by "porpoising," or rapidly changing altitude. The idea was to use gravity to get the fuel flowing naturally—the aeronautical equivalent of siphoning.

Of course, we barely had enough fuel to make it to the Azores as it was, so using precious fuel to fly up and down seemed like the last thing a pilot would want to do. The poor lieutenant about lost it. He said, "I'm not gonna win either way. I'll go in, one way or the other. I'll just chance it." He had convinced himself he was not going to make it and that he would have to bail out.

Then the squadron leader ordered him to porpoise. "The temperature of that water, Lieutenant, is a lot better where the Azores are than where you are right now. Will you please do what I say?" It came down to whether the lieutenant was going to listen, despite his fear. Finally, he decided to follow the orders from the seasoned veteran who was leading us. That may have been one of the most important decisions of his life.

But making the decision wasn't enough. This pilot was understandably rattled, yet he still had to fly in formation and carry out the order. Together we all flew up one or two thousand feet, came down, became weightless and then pulled back up to increase gravitational forces, forcing the fuel to flow. It worked, and our squadron leader had the lieutenant turn on his good pump again. Because of the lieutenant's emergency training, he had pulled himself together and pressed forward.

When we finally reached the Azores, we were ready to be back on the ground safely. But we still faced an obstacle—a huge cumulonimbus cloud rising from the islands thirty thousand or forty thousand feet into the atmosphere, with lightning coming out on all sides. The thunderstorm was right over the Azores, and it wasn't going anywhere. We didn't have any reserve fuel, so we could not circle and wait for the storm to pass or dissipate. However, with determination we found a little clearing in the middle, and we went in.

Our fuel was low, so we landed in formation, two at a time. We were landing in the wind and rain; we could barely see the runway. We came in hot—faster than our normal speed. The pilot on my wing was inexperienced, so he pulled the chute on his plane early. It came out and went right off the plane, and he shot past me. Panicking, he slammed on the brakes, his tires blew, and he skidded in front of me on his rims. I had to decide quickly whether to pull up and come around again for a clean landing alone or try to finish. But there just wasn't enough fuel to risk going around again. This was my one chance. So I deployed my chute and somehow kept from hitting the plane. He crashed into the cable barrier at the end of the runway and his plane caught fire, but he got out without getting hurt. Of course, he had to fly back on a commercial flight—something no pilot ever wants to do. But we had arrived safely, despite all the challenges we had faced.

OUR MISSION IN MORTALITY

Can we see the parallels to our own experience on the earth? Our squadron had had thirty days to do nothing but get ready for our

Lieutenant Hales beside his F-100 aircraft

mission—a preparatory period. We practiced in a pool to prepare us to face real-life crises, and we were supposed to carefully study flight manuals. Certainly it would have been more relaxing to play rather than to prepare; some of us used this time better than others. In our lives, we begin with a season I call the *Decades of Preparation*. This is the time when we first experience agency, enter into our baptismal covenant, study God's word, learn about His commandments and standards for us, and learn how to use the great navigational gift of the Holy Ghost—as essential to our well-being as the Navy ships that guided us across the ocean. Those who use this period best are always most prepared for the challenges that follow.

When my fellow pilot discovered the problem with his fuel, we had some critical decisions to make. Turning to the flight manual

The crest and motto of the 308th Fighter-Bomber Squadron

enabled us to diagnose the problem. Our seasoned leader then had an inspired solution, but acting on his direction took real faith. The lieutenant had to overcome his feelings of despair and his fear that he was going to have to bail out. Ultimately, he had to choose whether to do what came naturally—trying to save his fuel by flying level—or to trust our squadron leader and follow his directions. My pilot buddy saved his life by making the right decision and following his leader.

In our lives it is not just one decision but many that will determine whether we make our journey home and inherit eternal life. We face an unusual number of these critical choices in the *Decade of Decision,* when we determine the direction we will take the rest of our lives and throughout eternity. We decide whether to serve missions, whom to marry, and what educational and career goals to pursue. For those who marry, we begin to establish patterns that will determine what kinds of marriages and families we will have. As we study and learn the words of Christ and hearken to the counsel of His prophets, we will find the wisdom and strength to chart the right course home.

On our mission to the Azores, once we diagnosed the problem and decided on a solution, we still needed to carry out our plan. In our mortal journey, as we emerge from our *Decade of Decision,* most of us still have decades of the journey ahead of us. During this time most of us become parents or mentors to help others stay on the course that leads home to Heavenly Father. Inevitably we encounter obstacles but discover that even life's ups and downs can serve an important purpose. We may feel overwhelmed and full of despair at times, doubting that we really can complete our journey. But as we exercise faith and obey our leaders, we gain the strength to carry on. I call this season of life the *Decades of Serving and Pressing Forward.*

After all the stress we had had on our flight to the Azores, we might have hoped for an easy landing, but it was not to be. Instead, we were faced with one of the most difficult landings I have ever had to make. Even after preparing, making good decisions, and carrying out our squadron leader's plan, had we lost our focus after finally reaching the Azores, we would not have successfully executed the landing—and our journey would have been in vain. That's how it is in life. Even after preparing well, making good decisions, and serving faithfully during the *Decades of Serving and Pressing Forward,* to return to Heavenly Father with honor we must endure well to the end. The storms we face at the end of our lives include the deterioration of our bodies and sometimes even our minds. Many suffer from loneliness as loved ones pass on before them. And some struggle to find the will to continue to serve as their physical or mental capacity is diminished or as the opportunities for service move from center stage to behind the scenes. This stage of life, the *Decades of Serving and Enduring to the End,* is the time when seasoned Saints shine.

THE WAY—THE *ONLY* WAY

A single book about all the decades of life may be unusual in a day of finely targeted marketing geared to narrowly defined demographic groups. Yet stepping back and seeing our entire mortal journey in the context of our Heavenly Father's plan may be just what we need, wherever we are on life's path. My hope is that this book will be of value to inquisitive youth, concerned parents, those in the sunset of their lives, wise Church leaders, and earnest truth seekers of any age or faith.

What makes this book different from other books about the journey of life? The restored gospel of Jesus Christ helps us understand all the dimensions of our journey: We have a loving Father in Heaven who provided the opportunity for each of us to come to earth and experience mortality as a part of our eternal progression. His plan enables us to become like Him and return to His presence. As part of that plan and out of His pure love for us, He sent His Only Begotten Son to earth to voluntarily atone for the sins of every one of us. Even with diligent preparation, the best of decisions, and faithful obedience, we would never be able to return with honor were it not for that atoning sacrifice.

Through His Atonement, Jesus Christ provided the way back. More literally, He *is* the way back, "and there is none other way . . . whereby man can be saved in the kingdom of God" (2 Nephi 31:21). He is also "the truth, and the life"—even eternal life (John 14:6). Without Him, it would be impossible for us to complete our journey home. I know He lives. In Him I have unwavering faith that all of us can return to our Heavenly Father with honor and live with Him forever.

PART 1

DECADES OF PREPARATION

*Prepare ye, prepare ye for that
which is to come.*

DOCTRINE & COVENANTS 1:12

This life is the time for men to prepare to meet God;
yea, behold the day of this life is the day for men to perform
their labors. . . . This day of life . . . is given
us to prepare for eternity.

ALMA 34:32–33

CHAPTER TWO

Always Preparing

I HAD A DEAR FRIEND who was an all-American football
player. His team earned the opportunity to play in the Orange
Bowl. Before one hundred thousand spectators and a large television audience, his team lost by a huge score. It turned out that he
and other members of his team had not listened to their coach and
learned the lessons he had tried to teach them, and they paid a dear
price for it. They had to live with the consequences of losing a big
game with a very embarrassing final score.

A few years passed. Two members of this same football team
were in my flight-training class. As we sat in the cockpits of our
flight simulators, our instructor would teach us about emergencies
that could occur while flying a jet fighter at the speed of sound. For
each emergency, we were taught the procedures for avoiding disaster. We would practice each procedure over and over, so that when
a real emergency came we had developed automatic or conditioned
responses. In other words, we would be able to respond instantly
without having to discuss, reason, research, or even decide on the
appropriate course of action. For instance, we learned in advance

exactly what to do if the fire-warning light lit up or if the panel indicated some other technical failure onboard. We even predetermined the safe altitude at which we would bail out if the plane were on fire or out of control.

One of the men who had been on the losing Orange Bowl team was an exemplary, well-disciplined student—a model pilot who had learned the lesson of preparation well from his failure in the bowl game.

The other man, however, had not learned to listen to those with more knowledge and more experience. As a result, when it came time for learning emergency procedures and preconditioning his own mental and physical responses, he would put his arm around our instructor and say with a winning smile, "Check me off for three hours of emergency procedure, will you?" Then, instead of going to train in the flight simulators, he would go to the swimming pool, pistol range, or golf course. Later our instructor said to him, "What are you going to do when there is an emergency and you are not prepared?" His answer: "I am never going to have an emergency."

I went on to fly single-seated fighters, and my friends went on to fly multiengine bombers, which required both a pilot and a copilot. A few months later, on an evening mission, fire erupted in the quiet sky over Texas. When my friend's plane dropped to five thousand feet in flames, the young, well-disciplined pilot did what he had prepared to do months earlier. He said, "Let's get out of here." With centrifugal force pulling against him, he bailed out with a parachute that barely opened before he slammed to the ground. This pilot received serious injuries but survived.

However, my friend who had not trained or prepared stayed with the airplane and died in the crash—a terrible price for not listening to those who knew more. I will never forget the feelings my wife and I had when we drove from Big Spring to Lubbock, Texas, to see his young widow. My friend's recklessness had not only cost him his own life but caused incredible grief and pain for his wife and their newborn child.

A couple of years later I learned firsthand the importance of those laborious hours of learning emergency procedures in the flight simulator. While my plane was on takeoff row, the fire-warning light came on. I remember my crew chief saying to me, "I have never seen a man get all the switches off and be out with his parachute and raft in less than ten seconds." I answered, "Have you ever been in a burning plane?"

But fear of a fire is not what got me out of the plane successfully. It was the preparation and preconditioning to act, without having to think in the moment, under stress, about what I should do to save my life.

The Decades of Preparation

Like pilots in training, all of us have the opportunity to train for the great decisions that will serve as the foundation of our lives. For members of the Church participating in Primary, Young Men, Young Women, and Sunday School, this training takes place during the twenty or so years before young adulthood—the *Decades of Preparation;* however, members of all ages can and do elect to prepare themselves to choose the right. For new and returning Church members, this preparation often occurs during an intense period of learning the gospel and awakening to the influence of the Spirit of the Lord. The ongoing process of conversion naturally leads to making commitments and developing preconditioned responses to temptation and other challenges of mortality.

All of us live in a world that is just as spiritually challenging as flying in the cockpit of a fighter jet. When fire-warning lights come

Lieutenant Hales, 1955

on in our lives, it is imperative that we are already trained to make righteous choices. For youth throughout the world, the standards in *For the Strength of Youth* are a core part of this training. These standards are so simple and so helpful that members young and old benefit from learning and living them. For example, one standard reads:

"Have the courage to walk out of a movie or video party, turn off a computer or television, change a radio station, or put down a magazine if what is being presented does not meet Heavenly Father's standards. Do these things even if others do not. Let your friends and family know that you are committed to keeping God's standards."[1]

---

1. *For the Strength of Youth: Fulfilling Our Duty to God* (Salt Lake City: The Church of Jesus Christ of Latter-day Saints, 2001), 19.

The scriptures, coupled with these clearly stated, inspired standards, help all of us to be ready to respond to the adversary. And when we are prepared for "all the fiery darts of the adversary" (D&C 3:8), he will not triumph over us.

Be There

Wherever we are in life, *we are always preparing* for greater opportunities to learn, grow, and serve others, *we are always preparing* to return with honor to the presence of our Heavenly Father, and *we are always preparing* to be more devoted disciples of Jesus Christ, which means accepting His invitation to "come, follow me" (Luke 18:22). This is the decision we made in our premortal lives. Now we must make it again here in mortality, every day, in every situation, by taking the Savior's name upon us, remembering His atoning sacrifice, and keeping His commandments. This we covenanted to do when we were baptized, and we have the opportunity to renew those covenants each week as we partake of the sacrament.

We are always preparing to have the Holy Ghost as our constant companion. This means doing what the prophets have taught us to do—following the promptings of the Spirit, studying the scriptures, praying morning and night, attending Church meetings, fasting monthly, paying a full tithe, being honest in our dealings with others, being worthy of the priesthood, attending the temple, and always, always living the standards revealed by prophets in the booklet *For the Strength of Youth.*

As youth and young single adults, *we are always preparing* to be worthy of a righteous, eternal companion to whom we can be sealed in the temple. Our peer group can inspire us to do great things or tempt us into strange and miserable paths. In everything we do, we are preparing to be the kind of person a righteous companion can choose to be with forever. We should always ask ourselves, Am I the kind of person I want my eternal companion to be?

Whether we are young or approaching the golden years of life, *we are always preparing* to preach the gospel. Depending upon our individual circumstances, we may be able to serve a full-time mission. A mission is a priceless opportunity to keep temple covenants by living the law of consecration—giving all of your time, gifts, and talents to the Lord and serving Him with all your heart, might, mind, and strength. I have always felt that the two years young men serve is a tithing of time on the first twenty years of their lives. But even if we are not able to serve a full-time mission, we can prepare ourselves to share the gospel with others and then do so every day.

We are always preparing for the future by learning and developing our talents. Our diligence in school and other educational and training programs is the way we keep prophetic counsel to get all the education we can. We must decide now to do our best in school and at work. Then, when opportunities knock, we are ready to open the door and take advantage of them. "To every man is given a gift" (D&C 46:11), the Lord reminds us, and we are commanded to develop our gifts and talents and to seek learning by study and also by faith. As members of the Church of Jesus Christ, all of us are expected to continually prepare ourselves for greater opportunities and more responsibility in the future.

We are always preparing by using our time properly. "This life is the time for men to prepare to meet God" (Alma 34:32). Our time on earth will be sufficient if we learn to use it wisely, beginning in our youth. "O, remember, my son, and learn wisdom in thy youth; yea, learn in thy youth to keep the commandments of God" (Alma 37:35).

We are always preparing to safeguard our birthright. Nearing the end of his life, the Old Testament prophet Jacob gave a father's blessing to each of his sons. Reuben was the firstborn and should have had the birthright—special blessings intended just for him. But in his blessing to Reuben, his father said, "Thou art . . . unstable as water, thou shalt not excel" (Genesis 49:3–4). Think for a moment about what the phrase "unstable as water" means. When water gets hot, it evaporates. When it gets cold, it freezes. When it is unchanneled, it causes erosion and destroys whatever may be in its path.

As members of the Church, we are charged to not let our resolve dribble out and our commitment to follow the Savior evaporate. We must be firm as a rock in living the gospel. None of us knows all the blessings that await us. The only way we lose those blessings is to give them up through disobedience. We must prepare ourselves to hold on to our divine heritage as sons and daughters of God. By our obedience we prepare now to honor, protect, and receive our glorious birthright.

We are always preparing by making correct decisions, because these decisions become seeds of future opportunities. "Whatsoever ye sow, that shall ye also reap" (D&C 6:33). Contemplating the glorious harvest ahead—eternal life—we should ponder how we make decisions. The law of the harvest offers a valuable pattern. We prepare the soil through prayer, knowing that we are children of God. We plant the seeds by counseling with those who can give sound advice; then we seek the guidance of the Holy Ghost. We let the seeds of inspiration grow. These budding ideas need tending. They need time to mature. The light of inspiration will bring the spiritual harvest, which comes when we ask our Heavenly Father in prayer if we have made a correct decision. As we follow that light, the darkness will vanish and the light will grow "brighter and brighter until the

I have a work for thee, Moses, my son.

Moses 1:6

CHAPTER THREE

REMEMBER WHO YOU ARE

P RESIDENT NATHAN Eldon Tanner grew up on a family farm in Aetna, Canada, near Cardston. He did not come from a wealthy family. Their family cow, which provided them sustenance, was their most prized possession. One day Nathan's father was preparing to go into town and asked Nathan to care for the cow. His father stressed the importance of milking her so she wouldn't go dry. Nathan agreed, but after his father left, Nathan's friends arrived and soon they were all caught up in an impromptu rodeo, including riding the cow. Fortunately his father came back early enough to discover that the first milking had been missed and the second was fast approaching. Even though the cow was in danger, Nathan's father didn't yell at him or strike him. Instead, he sat his son on a fencepost and said, "Nathan Eldon, you are a Tanner." This reminded young Nathan what was expected of him. His father also reminded him that he held the priesthood. Finally he spoke the words that President Tanner so often repeated to us: "Remember who you are and act accordingly." President door" (Genesis 4:7), as the scriptures say. But in everything we do, in every decision we make, we can exercise our agency to choose the Savior instead and to humbly walk the path of obedience that leads us to Him. The adversary must depart if we tell him to depart. He cannot influence us unless we allow him to do so, and he knows that!

When we remember who we are, we can understand, in a deeply personal way, that the power is in us to act for ourselves—to act and not to be acted upon (see 2 Nephi 2:26). The more we understand that we are truly God's spirit children, the more we desire to use our agency to choose the path of our Savior Jesus Christ and to return to our heavenly home with honor.

ACCOUNTABILITY

As we remember who we are, our understanding of other essential principles deepens, including the principle of accountability.

In 1976 Johnny Miller, a member of the Church, won the prestigious British Open golf tournament, one of the major championships in professional golf. The following year, Sister Hales and I were presiding in the London England Mission when Brother Miller came back to play in the same tournament. Before the event began, he promised that after the final round of play he would speak to a gathering of youth from several stakes in our mission.

Because of Brother Miller's earlier victory, Britain's national media covered his visit with great fanfare. Unfortunately, he missed the cut and did not qualify for the last two rounds of the championship. Banner headlines trumpeted his failure to defend his title, and some expected he would quickly board an airplane and retreat home. But Brother Miller had made a commitment. He had promised to testify to hundreds of youth, and he felt accountable to them to keep his commitment.

I clearly remember this world-renowned Hall of Fame golfer standing before the youth. He gripped the pulpit, white knuckles showing. After a long pause, controlling his emotions, his voice cracked as he said, "I don't know why a person thinks he or she can go through life without a scorecard." It was an unforgettable teaching moment for me and everyone else in attendance.

Have you ever wondered what it would be like to have your failures printed in the morning paper for everyone to see? As a professional athlete, Brother Miller recognized that his golfing was the source of enjoyment for millions, and their interest in his playing made it possible for him to earn a living as a golfer. Therefore he was accountable to the public for how he performed in the game.

As we remember and understand who we are, we begin to realize that our lives are of supreme importance to our Heavenly Father. As His literal spirit children, our well-being matters more to Him than anything else. And because we have been bought with the price of the Savior's blood, we are not our own (see 1 Corinthians 6:20)—we are accountable to Him for how we live our lives. We are accountable for our sins and mistakes, even though no one else on earth may know about them. The adversary does not want us to assume this accountability. Instead, he wants us to blame others and our circumstances. He wants us to feel powerless to act for ourselves and evade responsibility, rationalizing and excusing ourselves for whatever actions we take. But we can choose to be accountable.

As a young boy, I learned this principle from my older brother. We loved to play baseball. When I was about ten or eleven years old, I hit a home run—all the way over the fence and into the greenhouse of a woman who was well known to all of us. She was the woman who never gave our baseballs back. We said she ate them.

As soon as we heard the crash of the glass, everyone ran. I was left with the bat and my glove and my brother. "You have two choices," my brother said. "You can run, and then the phone will ring, and Dad will ask why you didn't face up to it." (I wondered how my brother got so smart, and later I realized he had learned the same lesson by his own experience.) "Or," he said, "you can go see her right now. You can own up to it."

So I went over and rang the doorbell. Through her plate glass window I could see our baseballs lined up one after another along the sill. "I'm sorry," I confessed. "I really hit that one, didn't I? Do you think I could have it back?"

No one had ever asked her to give a ball back before. "If you'll come and do a few chores for me," she said, "we can work this out." Over time, we got all our baseballs back, and I learned how good it feels to accept responsibility for our own actions. As we do, our understanding of who we are increases.

Regaining Agency

Accepting accountability and responsibility is challenging when we are living with the painful consequences of unrighteous choices. These consequences often include diminished power to act for ourselves (see 2 Nephi 2:16). But through the Atonement, Heavenly Father can help us regain the use of our agency. Through His Spirit, we can be assured that we faithfully exercised our agency before we came to this earth, and we can do so again.

This fact is especially important when we are struggling to overcome the thick darkness of addiction. If we have fallen into the cycle of destructive, addictive behaviors, we may feel we are spiritually in a black hole. As with the real black holes in space, it may seem all but impossible for light to penetrate to where we are. How do we escape? How do we reclaim our agency? How do we begin again to exercise the power to choose and receive the light again?

The world offers many strategies for finding ourselves and

Robert, about age ten

regaining a sense of self-control. But ultimately, because we are children of God, the only way to fully regain our agency is to choose faithfulness—to choose to be obedient to Him. As we do so, our power to make right choices increases. Here are a few suggestions for some of the first choices we can make in order to regain our agency:

Choose to accept—truly accept—that you are a child of God, that He loves you, and that He has the power to help you.

Choose to put everything—literally everything—on the altar before Him. Believing that you are His child, decide that your life belongs to Him and that you will use your agency to do His will. You may do this multiple times in your life, but never, never give up.

Choose to put yourself in a position to have experiences with the

Spirit of God through prayer, in scripture study, at Church meetings, in your home, and through wholesome interactions with others. When you feel the influence of the Spirit, you are beginning to be cleansed and strengthened. The light is being turned on, and where that light shines, the darkness of evil cannot be.

Choose to obey and keep your covenants, beginning with your baptismal covenant. Always remember Him for His atoning sacrifice. This you do as you continually live worthy to partake of the sacrament and then do so in a sacrament meeting each week.

Choose to prepare to worthily attend the temple, make and renew sacred covenants, and receive all of the saving ordinances and blessings of the gospel.

Finally, and most importantly, choose to believe in the Atonement of Jesus Christ. Accept the Savior's forgiveness, and then forgive yourself. "Behold, he who has repented of his sins, the same is forgiven, and I, the Lord, remember them no more" (D&C 58:42). Because of His sacrifice for you, He has the power to "remember them no more." We must each do likewise.

The Spirit Is the Key

In all our choosing, following the Spirit of the Lord is the key. That Spirit can bring about a mighty change in our hearts so that "we have no more disposition to do evil, but to do good continually" (Mosiah 5:2). When spiritual promptings come, they will not generally stop us in our tracks, for the Spirit of God does not speak with a voice of thunder. The voice will be as soft as a whisper, coming as a thought to our minds or a feeling in our hearts. By heeding its gentle promptings, we will be protected from the destructive consequences of sin.

With Father Lehi, I testify of the blessings of agency. Agency allows us to be tested and tried to see whether or not we will endure to the end and return to our Heavenly Father with honor. Agency is the catalyst that leads us to express our inward spiritual desires in outward Christlike behavior. Agency permits us to make faithful, obedient choices that strengthen us so we can lift and strengthen others. Agency used righteously allows light to dispel the darkness and enables us to live with joy and happiness in the present, look with faith to the future, even into the eternities, and cease to dwell on the things of the past.

Because of the way we used our agency before we came to this earth, we have been given the supernal blessing of becoming Heavenly Father's spirit children in mortality. This is "who we are," to use the words of President Tanner's father. To "remember who we are and act accordingly" is to continue to be obedient in following Heavenly Father's plan—to faithfully use our agency to obey, to be accountable for our sins and mistakes, and where necessary, to regain our agency by choosing again to keep the commandments of our Heavenly Father and His Son, our Savior Jesus Christ. To remember who we are is to always remember Them and use our agency to return to Their presence with honor.

CHECKPOINTS

✓ How well do I remember my divine heritage and potential?

✓ How well do I cherish the gift of agency?

✓ Do I take responsibility for my own actions?

Faith is a gift of God. As we seek for faith through prayer, it will be granted unto us. Then we can teach others how to gain faith, and we will have our faith with us always. The Apostle Paul wrote to the Romans, "Faith cometh by hearing, and hearing by the word of God" (Romans 10:17). We hear God's word when we read it, when we listen to His servants, and when we feel the promptings of the Spirit. The first step to finding faith in the Lord Jesus Christ is to let His word—in whatever form—penetrate our hearts.

But it is not enough merely to let His word wash over us, as if the words of the prophets alone could transform us. We must do our part. Or as the Savior Himself said, "He that hath ears to hear, let him hear" (Matthew 11:15). In other words, hearing requires an active effort. "Faith without works is dead" (James 2:26). It means taking seriously what is taught, considering it carefully, studying it out in our minds, and applying it in our lives.

As the prophet Enos learned, it means letting others' testimonies of the gospel sink deep into our hearts. Let us review some of the elements of Enos's profound, faith-building experience:

Enos heard the gospel truths from his father, just as many of us are hearing them in our families from our parents or siblings or in our personal study.

Enos let his father's teachings about "eternal life, and the joy of the saints" sink deep into his heart (Enos 1:3).

Enos was filled with a desire to know for himself whether these teachings were true and where he himself stood before his Maker. To use Enos's words, "My soul hungered" (Enos 1:4).

Enos qualified himself, through his intense spiritual appetite and worthiness, to receive the Savior's promise: "Blessed are all they who do hunger and thirst after righteousness, for they shall be filled with the Holy Ghost" (3 Nephi 12:6).

Enos obeyed the commandments of God, which enabled him to be receptive to the Spirit.

Enos records, "I kneeled down before my Maker, and I cried unto him in mighty prayer and supplication for mine own soul; and all the day long did I cry unto him; yea, and when the night came I did still raise my voice high that it reached the heavens" (Enos 1:4).

It wasn't easy. Faith did not come quickly. In fact, Enos characterized his experience in prayer as a "wrestle which I had before God" (Enos 1:2). But faith did come. By the power of the Holy Ghost, he did receive a witness for himself.

We cannot find Enos-like faith without our own wrestle before God in prayer. I testify that the reward is worth the effort. Remember the pattern:

- Hear the word of God, spoken and written by His servants.
- Let His word sink deep into our hearts.
- Hunger in our souls for righteousness.
- Obediently follow gospel laws, ordinances, and covenants.
- Raise our voice in mighty prayer and supplication, asking in faith to know that Jesus Christ is our Savior.

If we do these things sincerely and unceasingly, the words Christ spoke to His disciples will be fulfilled in our lives: "Ask, and it shall be given you; seek, and ye shall find; knock, and it shall be opened unto you" (Matthew 7:7).

THE TRIAL OF FAITH

Only through a *trial* of our faith can we receive the miraculous blessings we seek for ourselves and our families. In fact, we were told before we came to this mortal probation that we would have trials of our faith, but after the trials of our faith, blessings would be poured out upon us, depending upon how we endured the tests (see Abraham 3:24–25).

There will be times when we don't understand our trials. I have read the book of Job a number of times in my life. Consider his example of faithfully enduring the most severe trials we can imagine: the loss of material possessions, health, children, and the regard of spouse and friends. Even as he was being tested, he exclaimed, "Blessed be the name of the Lord." And then, in the next verse, it is recorded that "in all this Job sinned not, nor charged God foolishly" (Job 1:21–22). How often, when we are tested or when we are called upon to sacrifice, do we charge God foolishly and ask, Why me?

Sometimes our greatest tests are when loved ones suffer and we cannot do anything to relieve or reverse their pain and sorrow. In such cases, it is often the afflicted one who humbly accepts the trial and increases in faith while family and friends resist and resent the trial, and find their faith diminished.

Faith in the Lord is trust in the Lord. When in prayer we say, "Thy will be done," we are expressing trust that His will is going to be accomplished. We are also acknowledging that we will endure whatever He allows to happen to us. Part of enduring well is to thank Him "in all things" (D&C 59:7). This means that we express our gratitude for the good things we enjoy and also for the opposition and challenges that give us experience and fortify our faith. We put our lives in His hands, realizing that whatever transpires will be for our experience and for our good.

As we put our faith in the Lord and keep our focus on the eternities, we will be blessed to be able to accept whatever trial we are given, for life on earth, as we know it, is only temporary. As Paul taught, "For which cause we faint not; but though our outward man perish, yet the inward man is renewed day by day.

"For our light affliction, which is but for a moment, worketh for us a far more exceeding and eternal weight of glory;

"While we look not at the things which are seen, but at the things which are not seen: for the things which are seen are temporal; but the things which are not seen are eternal" (2 Corinthians 4:16–18).

If we endure our afflictions well, the Lord has promised us, "and, if you keep my commandments and endure to the end you shall have eternal life, which gift is the greatest of all the gifts of God" (D&C 14:7). When we honor the Lord by placing our faith and trust in Him, ultimately "[our] sorrow shall be turned into joy" (John 16:20).

FAITH AND SELF-ESTEEM

It has become apparent to me that many with low self-esteem lose faith. And many who lose faith may also lose self-esteem. When we are marred spiritually or physically, our first reaction is often to withdraw into the dark shadows of depression, to blot out hope and joy—the light of life that comes from knowing God loves us and from loving Him by keeping His commandments. Such retreat ultimately leads to the darkening influence the foundation upon which all gospel truths rest. Because of our Savior's Atonement, in death's darkness there is no sting; in death's depression there is no victory. His resurrected light dispels the darkness, defeating the prince of darkness, with a brightness of eternal hope.

I invite all those whose souls are hungering for faith "to seek this Jesus of whom the prophets and apostles have written" (Ether 12:41). Let their witness that the Savior gave His life for us sink deep into your heart. I testify that as we seek a witness of the truth through the Holy Ghost in prayer, we will see our faith strengthened as we joyfully meet the challenges of this mortal life and prepare for eternal life.

Jesus Christ is *my* Light, *my* Redeemer, *my* Savior—and yours. He did come. He did live. And He will come again. This I know; of this I give my special witness and testimony.

Checkpoints

✓ How firmly am I built on a foundation of faith in Christ?

✓ Do I let God's word sink into my heart, or does it merely wash over me?

✓ How much do I hunger and thirst after righteousness?

✓ Do I wrestle for faith in prayer or just go through the gospel motions?

✓ Do I have enough faith to trust the Lord, even in affliction?

✓ Do I let my fears and frustrations overwhelm my faith and drive me into isolated darkness?

✓ Is my faith centered in Christ and His atoning sacrifice?

✓ What am I doing to keep the light of faith alive in my life?

Lieutenant Hales entering the cockpit of his F-100 aircraft

had wrecked it. The instructor was horrified, and so was I. I never went back to take another lesson.

At that point, one would ordinarily be washed out. But I wanted to be a jet fighter pilot. Somehow I had to get over this phobia, this paralyzing fear from my first crash. Later, in Florida, as I got into my first jet fighter, I couldn't get the image of crashing that first plane out of my mind. But somehow I managed to move past my first experience to become combat-ready. The only way I was able to let go of the fear was to embrace my goal of becoming a fighter pilot.

There will be times when we have embarrassing crashes. The adversary will try to replay those images in our minds to keep us from progressing. We must learn to forgive ourselves. How thankful I am for the doctrine of repentance. Only through the gift of repentance can we receive the forgiveness we need to resume our journey home and become who our Heavenly Father wants us to become.

FORGIVENESS IS PART OF REPENTING

The Savior teaches that we will be forgiven to the same degree that we are able to forgive others. We will not be able to be forgiven or forgive ourselves for our mistakes if we do not overlook others' transgressions against us (see Matthew 6:15).

Most of us recognize the importance of forgiving others, but many of us forget the most difficult part—forgiving ourselves. One of the adversary's greatest tools is influencing us not to forgive ourselves. We are taught to abhor the sin but not the sinner—a principle that applies even when we are the sinner. When we do not follow this principle, we do not allow the Spirit of the Lord to come into our lives to guide us.

After we have repented, it is often true that the Lord has forgiven us long before we forgive ourselves. The Savior taught that we should put our hand to the plough and not look back (see Luke 9:62). Paul, who had a past of his own to forget, described his approach this way: "This one thing I do, *forgetting those things which are behind, and reaching forth unto those things which are before,* I press toward the mark for the prize of the high calling of God in Christ Jesus" (Philippians 3:13–14; emphasis added).

So what do we do when we realize we've made a mistake, willfully done something wrong, or failed to do what is right? We recognize it. We acknowledge it to ourselves, before God, and to others we have injured intentionally and unintentionally. And then we don't do it again. We confess to the Lord, and we also confess to the bishop when necessary. When we have done these things, we focus on forgiving others and ourselves and then engage ourselves have experienced the miracle of repentance, I like to ask them, "What about the others who are still back dragging Main Street?" Sometimes, after we return to the strait and narrow, we forget those who, because of us, may still be "wandering in strange roads" (1 Nephi 8:32). Do we have any responsibility for them? Have we truly repented if we have gone our way without regard for the consequences of our actions in the lives of others? Do we have any responsibility for those we have injured? Could we go back and lift them by writing them a sincere letter seeking forgiveness, encouraging them to turn around, and bearing our testimony to them?

THE NEED FOR REPENTANCE IS ONGOING

Sometimes we think of repentance as something we do in our youth. But we must continually repent.

To be an Apostle of the Lord is a process—a process of repentance and humility, of looking inward and asking for forgiveness and strength to be what I should be. Unfortunately, I am not a perfect man, and infallibility does not come with the call. Therefore, I have had to ask for forgiveness from Heavenly Father for things I have done that are less than perfect and ask forgiveness of anyone I might have offended, knowingly or unknowingly, because of my personality or style.

As children of our Heavenly Father, we have been brought to earth that we "might repent while in the flesh." Our state is one of probation while here in mortality, "according to the commandments which the Lord God gave unto the children of men. For he gave commandment that all men must repent; for he showed unto all men that they were lost, because of the transgression of their parents" (2 Nephi 2:21).

The Savior promises all of us forgiveness through repentance. I testify that repentance has the power to bring all of us back from the depths of sin and despair and to help us return to our heavenly home with honor.

CHECKPOINTS

- ✓ How well do I take advantage of the extraordinary gift of repentance?
- ✓ Do I engage in real, life-changing repentance, or do I merely have regrets?
- ✓ Do I exercise faith in the Savior so that my heart can be changed?
- ✓ How well do I do everything in my power to make amends for my sins, including reaching out to help those I may have led astray?
- ✓ How willing am I to let go of my sins and look forward to Christ without looking back?
- ✓ How well do I let go of my sins and forgive myself when the Lord has forgiven me?
- ✓ Do I realize the need for ongoing repentance in my life, or do I see it as a one-time exercise in my youth?

*The gate by which ye should enter is repentance
and baptism by water; and then cometh a remission of
your sins by fire and by the Holy Ghost.*

2 NEPHI 31:17

CHAPTER SIX

THE GATE OF BAPTISM

J ESUS TAUGHT, "MY KINGDOM is not of this world" (John 18:36). Baptism takes us out of the ways of this world and into the kingdom of God. When we understand what our baptism really means, it forever changes the way we live.

No event has had greater significance in setting my life's course than my own baptism. It is indelibly etched on my spiritual memory as though it happened yesterday. It took place in Brooklyn, New York, at the only font available for wards and branches in the New York City area. I can still see the room, the baptismal font, and those who participated. My father performed the ordinance, and as I came out of the font, my mother motioned me to sit next to her on a little metal chair. She asked me what I was feeling just then. I replied that a warm feeling came over me when I came out of the water, and I felt happy and clean. She then said to me that in a short while I would be confirmed a member of the Church and receive the gift of the Holy Ghost and that I could have that feeling with me throughout my life if I would remain faithful and obedient.

That is a moment I have never forgotten. It has sustained me rewards us whenever we obey. The commandments enable us to avoid so many foolish mistakes and so much needless heartache in our lives. They guide and protect us and allow us to return to the presence of our Heavenly Father.

The irony is that those who choose to ignore God's commandments because they are worried about exercising their freedom are ultimately led "by the neck with a flaxen cord, until [Satan] bindeth them with his strong cords forever" (2 Nephi 26:22). Those "who live without God in the world" (Mosiah 27:31) limit their options and their liberty as they become addicted to wicked ways that can never bring happiness. Keeping the Savior's commandments means humbly answering His invitation, "Follow thou me." And, as Nephi taught, "Can we follow Jesus save we shall be willing to keep the commandments of the Father?" (2 Nephi 31:10).

The Book of Mormon teaches us that our baptism is a covenant that includes a promise "to stand as witnesses of God [and His kingdom] *at all times and in all things, and in all places* that ye may be in, even until death, that ye may be redeemed of God, and be numbered with those of the first resurrection, that ye may have eternal life" (Mosiah 18:9; emphasis added). Our effort to stand as a witness means that wherever we are and whatever we do, we demonstrate that we are His true followers.

As true followers of Christ, we are part of His flock. We are His lambs and His sheep, and we desire "to *come into the fold of God,* and to be called his people" (Mosiah 18:8; emphasis added). This promise becomes especially important whenever we stand at a crossroads in life and have to decide which path to take. Some paths lead to the great and spacious building that represents the world and its worldly ways. One strait and narrow path leads to eternal life. Of course we cannot walk both paths at once and arrive at our desired destination, although sometimes we try! By choosing to come into the fold of God, we are choosing to separate ourselves from the world. As Elder Bruce R. McConkie stated, "His people cannot have one foot in the kingdom and the other in the world and expect to survive spiritually."[2] We must choose, as suggested in Robert Frost's classic poem "The Road Not Taken." Our choice makes all the difference.

To come into the fold of God, we have to take the road that is not traveled by the world. Our dress will be modest, our thoughts pure, our language clean. The movies and television we watch, the music we listen to, the Web sites we visit, and the books, magazines, and newspapers we read will be uplifting. We will choose friends who encourage our eternal goals, and we will treat others with kindness. We will shun the vices of immorality, gambling, and using tobacco, liquor, and illicit drugs. Our Sunday activities will reflect the commandment of God to remember the Sabbath day and keep it holy. We will follow the example of Jesus Christ in the way we treat others. We will live to be worthy to enter the house of the Lord. We will be examples "of the believers, in word, in conversation, in charity, in spirit, in faith, in purity" (1 Timothy 4:12).

We know we are in God's fold whenever we keep the promise to "bear one another's burdens, that they may be light; yea, and are willing to mourn with those that mourn; yea, and comfort those that stand in need of comfort" (Mosiah 18:8–9). When we return to our Heavenly Father, we will discover that none of us returns alone. Those who return with honor will recognize and appreciate the many, many others who have helped them along the road of life. That is the gospel plan.

When our Air Force squadron selected as its motto "Return with Honor," we knew that motto applied to all of us—to every

---

2. Bruce R. McConkie, *The Mortal Messiah* (Salt Lake City: Deseret Book, 1980), 2:252.

member of our flight team, both individually and collectively. We flew jet fighter planes in a fingertip formation. For a moment, fold your thumb under your hand and look at the back of your hand with your fingers extended. Your fingers represent a grouping of four planes with a leader and three wingmen. In this formation they can watch out for each other and help each other. We all knew and were taught from bitter experience that a "loner" out of formation was unprotected and would surely be destroyed. Why then do many of us "go it alone" and deny those who love us most the joy and blessings of helping us? They need those blessings just as much as we do. This beloved Scottish proverb describes how both baptized members of the Church and those who help them will find their way home with honor and also how my own eternal companion and I are making our way along life's path:

> *Thee lift me, and I'll lift thee*
> *And we'll both ascend together.*

When we keep our baptismal covenant and all of the promises associated with it, we qualify ourselves to *have a mighty change of heart.* Adult converts to the Church often recognize this best because coming into God's kingdom as an adult generally requires a greater change in attitude and lifestyle. But regardless of our age and life experience, what Paul taught is true: Entering by the gate means walking in a "newness of life" (Romans 6:4). This newness is possible because a mighty change of heart is possible, which liberates us from the disposition to do evil and instills in us a desire to do good continually.

I testify that baptism and confirmation are the way we leave the worldliness of this world and enter God's kingdom. Baptism frees us from sin (see Romans 6:7) and allows us, like those who were baptized in the Waters of Mormon, to come to the knowledge of our Redeemer (see Mosiah 18:30). Regardless of how old we are or how long ago we were baptized, when we understand baptism and confirmation, they are etched in our spiritual memories to sustain us through life's temptations, challenges, and times of personal discouragement. As we reflect on the incomparable blessings of our membership in the Church, we recognize and rejoice that we have come in by the gate and have taken the first step along the "strait and narrow path which leads to eternal life" (2 Nephi 31:18).

Checkpoints

✓ How well do I really understand my baptismal covenant?

✓ How well have I taught my children, grandchildren, or investigators about the baptismal covenant?

✓ How seriously do I take my baptismal covenant?

✓ What more can I do to take the Savior's name upon me and always remember Him?

✓ How valiant am I as a witness of Christ?

✓ Do my actions show that I have left the world and entered God's kingdom?

✓ How well do I reach out to others and allow others to help me?

✓ Is my faith centered in Christ and His atoning sacrifice?

✓ Have I truly experienced a mighty change of heart?

*For behold, again I say unto you that if ye will
enter in by the way, and receive the Holy Ghost, it will show
unto you all things what ye should do.*

2 Nephi 32:5

CHAPTER SEVEN

THE GIFT OF THE HOLY GHOST

ONE EVENING, SHORTLY after I was transferred to England as a young executive, my wife and I invited some of our company's other executives to our home in London for dinner. I was new to my position and a foreigner, and I was eager to get home from work in plenty of time to meet our guests.

As I left work that day, the Spirit whispered to me that I needed to stop by the home of an older sister whom I had recently been assigned to home teach. I was reluctant to follow the prompting for fear of being late for our party; I knew how hard my wife was working to prepare dinner. But the prompting was clear.

When I knocked on her door, there was no answer. This was unusual, since this sister had always been home before. I walked around to her back door, which was open. When I entered, I found her on the floor, unconscious from a heart attack. I called for emergency assistance, and she was rushed to the hospital, where doctors were able to save her life.

I was late for dinner, but when I told my new colleagues why I was late, they were very understanding. My most important job that day was not being an executive but being a home teacher. In that role, it was my right and responsibility to receive promptings from the Spirit that were critical to the life of this good sister. How vital it is that we listen to and obey the promptings of the Spirit—always.

We are all entitled to receive promptings from the Holy Ghost, and those promptings are often critical to our eternal welfare and the welfare of those for whom we are responsible. Having entered in at the gate of baptism, we are not isolated from the challenges of life. Striving to walk on the strait and narrow path that leads home to our Father in Heaven, we will continue to be bombarded with ugly things of this world. To have the strength to resist evil and stay on that path, or, when necessary, repent and return to the path, we need the Holy Ghost as our guide.

With the analogy of the path in mind, we also need the Holy Ghost to help us make better choices at the crossroads of daily decisions—choices that will help us prepare for eternal life with our Father in Heaven and His Son, Jesus Christ. But to realize the benefit of this remarkable gift, we must learn to seek and recognize the still, small voice of the Holy Ghost and then have the courage to follow its gentle, essential promptings.

THE NATURE OF THE GIFT

Each of us has the Light of Christ within us. "I am the true light that lighteth every man that cometh into the world," the Savior said (D&C 93:2). It is "the light which is in all things, which giveth life to all things" (D&C 88:13). This light which "inviteth and enticeth to do good continually" is "given to every man, that he may know good from evil" (Moroni 7:13, 16).

By using the Light of Christ to discern and choose what is right, we can be led to an even greater light: the gift of the Holy Ghost.

Through the restoration of the gospel and the holy priesthood of God, disciples of Jesus Christ in these latter days have the power to give the gift of the Holy Ghost. It is bestowed by the laying on of hands by those who have the authority of the priesthood, and it is received by those who have followed the principles of faith and repentance and have received the ordinance of baptism by immersion for the remission of sins.

The Holy Ghost is the third member of the Godhead, "a personage of Spirit" (D&C 130:22). He is the Comforter, the Spirit of God, the Holy Spirit of Promise. He testifies of Jesus Christ, His work, and the work of His servants upon the earth. He acts as a cleansing agent to purify and sanctify us from sin (see Alma 13:12; 2 Nephi 31:17).

The primary purpose of the gift of the Spirit is to guide us, protect us, comfort us in our mortal probation, and prepare us for our eternal destiny after our test here in our earthly probationary state is complete. When temptations come our way, if we will listen, the Holy Ghost will remind us that we have promised to remember our Savior and obey the commandments of God. The gift of the Holy Ghost, given to us when we are confirmed, helps us to discern the difference between the ways of the world and the ways of God's kingdom. The Holy Ghost gives us the strength and courage to conduct our lives in the ways of God.

The Holy Ghost is also the source of our testimony of the Father and the Son. As the Savior taught, "But when the Comforter is come, whom I will send unto you from the Father, even the Spirit of truth, which proceedeth from the Father, he shall testify of me" (John 15:26). And Moroni promised, "By the power of the Holy Ghost ye may know the truth of all things" (Moroni 10:5).

The Spirit comforts us and brings peace to our souls. With the Holy Ghost dwelling in us, we feel a love for God and all His children. Paul declared that "the fruit of the Spirit is love, joy, peace, longsuffering, gentleness, goodness, faith, meekness, temperance: against such there is no law" (Galatians 5:22–23).

The Spirit can function as a kind of antenna that allows us to discern the feelings of others whom we love and for whom we are responsible. Oftentimes such discernment comes in our callings and in our dealings with others, including when we choose friends and eternal companions.

The Spirit also prompts us with insights customized for each situation of our lives, whether we are counseling, speaking, or teaching. "Neither take ye thought beforehand what ye shall say; but treasure up in your minds continually the words of life, and it shall be given you in the very hour that portion that shall be meted unto every man" (D&C 84:85). As we treasure up in our minds continually the words of life by studying the scriptures and praying, the Spirit can inspire us with thoughts and words to share with others. While we always prepare diligently for talks and other assignments, the Spirit will sometimes prompt us to set aside our prepared remarks and speak the words that He brings to our minds and hearts.

The right to the constant companionship of the Spirit is among the greatest gifts we can receive in mortality, for by the light of His promptings and His cleansing power, we can be led back into the presence of God. As we obey the will of our Father in Heaven, this priceless gift of the Holy Ghost will be with us continually.

RECEIVING THE LIGHT OF THE SPIRIT

Do you remember being afraid of the dark when you were a child? When you became frightened, you probably turned on the light—in fact, you lit every light in the house! When your parents came home later in the evening, they would ask, "Why is every light on in the house?" And then they would proceed to give you a lecture about the family budget and the cost of electricity.

You learned, however, that by turning on the light you could push back the darkness and overcome fear. In this ordinary experience, you learned an extraordinary law of nature, which is also a spiritual law: Light and darkness cannot occupy the same space at the same time.

Light dispels darkness. When light is present, darkness is vanquished. And darkness cannot conquer light unless the light is diminished or withdrawn. When the spiritual light of the Holy Ghost is present, the darkness of Satan must depart.

We are engaged in a battle between the forces of light and darkness. If it were not for the light of Jesus Christ and His gospel, we would be doomed to the destruction of worldly darkness. But the Savior said, "I am come a light into the world" (John 12:46). "He that followeth me shall not walk in darkness, but shall have the light of life" (John 8:12). The Lord is our light and, literally, our salvation (see Psalm 27:1). Like the sacred fire that encircled the children in 3 Nephi (see 3 Nephi 17:24), His light will form a protective shield between us and the darkness of the adversary as we live worthy of it. We all need that light.

To keep the light of the Holy Ghost with us requires more than a one-time exercise of faith. A few years ago I had the opportunity to learn more about my lungs. I became very aware that we cannot store oxygen. We need to breathe, and we cannot save up in reserve the air we need no matter how hard we try. Moment by moment, breath by breath, our lives are granted to us and we are renewed. Each breath is a gift of life—a gift of God. As King Benjamin taught his people, the Lord is "preserving you from day to day, by

Young Robert with his older brother and sister

lending you breath, that ye may live and move and do according to your own will, and even supporting you from one moment to another" (Mosiah 2:21).

So it is with spiritual light. When I was a boy, I used to ride my bicycle home from basketball practice at night. I would connect a small pear-shaped generator to my bicycle tire. Then as I pedaled, the tire would turn a tiny rotor, which produced electricity and emitted a single, welcome beam of light from the bicycle light on the handlebars. It was a simple but effective mechanism. But I had to pedal to make it work! I learned quickly that if I stopped pedaling, my bike would come to a halt, the light would go out, and I would be in darkness. I also learned that when I was "anxiously engaged" (D&C 58:27) in pedaling, the light would become brighter and, with the illumination, the darkness in front of me would be dispelled.

Spiritual light must be generated in us by our daily "spiritual pedaling." It comes from praying, studying the scriptures, fasting, and serving—from living the gospel and obeying the commandments. "He that keepeth his commandments receiveth truth and light," said the Lord (D&C 93:28), "and he that receiveth light, and continueth in God, receiveth more light; and that light groweth brighter and brighter until the perfect day" (D&C 50:24). That "perfect day" is when our light so shines that we can abide the light of celestial glory and dwell in the presence of God and Jesus in the eternities.

Retaining the Light of the Spirit

Beyond receiving the Spirit by our efforts to live righteously, we want to keep that Spirit with us. We do this by continuing to be obedient to the laws, principles, and ordinances of the gospel and to live as the Savior would. The Holy Ghost cannot be with us if we are angry in our hearts, contentious with our companions, or critical of the Lord's anointed. He departs whenever we are rebellious or immoral, dress or act immodestly, are unclean or profane in mind or body, are slothful in priesthood callings and duties, or commit other sins, for "the Spirit of the Lord doth not dwell in unholy temples" (Helaman 4:24).

As we retain the Spirit, we will be able to avoid temptation and evil. President Spencer W. Kimball, in an area conference, explained that when jungle dwellers happen upon a python egg, they step on it and break it so it will not hatch. His message was clear—if we stop the little things (python eggs) from developing into big things (thirty-foot pythons), we need not be concerned about having the spiritual life squeezed out of us.

WITH ALL OUR HEARTS

Receiving and retaining the Holy Ghost takes a whole-souled effort. Some people expect to have one foot in the world and one foot in the kingdom of God and still be able to move forward on the path to eternal life. Unfortunately, that is not possible. Why? To use our earlier analogy, it is because spiritual pedaling takes both feet! Unless we are fully engaged in living the gospel—living it with all of our heart, "mind, might, and strength" (Alma 39:13)—we cannot generate enough spiritual light to push back worldly darkness. As the Savior said, "No man can serve two masters: for either he will hate the one, and love the other; or else he will hold to the one, and despise the other. Ye cannot serve God and mammon" (Matthew 6:24).

The need to cultivate light becomes more clear when we realize that in this world, the darkness is never far away. In fact, it is always just around the corner, waiting for an opportunity to come in. "If thou doest not well," the Lord said, "sin lieth at the door" (Genesis 4:7).

It is as predictable as any physical law: if we let the light of the Spirit flicker or fade by failing to keep the commandments or to partake of the sacrament or to pray or to study the scriptures, the darkness of the adversary will surely fill the void. "That wicked one cometh and taketh away light and truth, through disobedience" (D&C 93:39). In the scriptures we read that some individuals "grope in the dark without light" and "stagger like a drunken man" (Job 12:25). So often we, too, feel our way along, tentative and unwilling to move forward with conviction, as if we were afraid in the dark. Stumbling along, we may become accustomed to the dimness of our surroundings and forget how glorious it is to walk in the light. It is so much better to turn on the light of faith and move ahead with energy and commitment.

The covenant we make at baptism and renew as we partake of the sacrament—to take upon ourselves the name of Jesus Christ, always remember Him, and keep His commandments—brings His promise that we will always have His Spirit, that we will always have that light to be with us (see D&C 20:77). The emblems of the Savior's Atonement remind us that we need not stumble in darkness. We can have His light with us always. When we live the commandments, our countenance is filled with gospel light. With this spiritual light, we no longer wander in the strange and darkened paths of the adversary, becoming lost, discouraged, depressed, and fearful. Walking in the light of the gospel, we keep our eternal goals in sight and move forward with joy and gladness.

Pondering the Path of Life

Sin is not the only thing that keeps us from enjoying the guiding light of the Holy Ghost. Sometimes we simply fail to make room in our busy lives to seek and recognize the delicate promptings of the Spirit.

My father was a commercial artist for a large advertising agency in New York City. On one occasion he was under tremendous stress to produce an advertising campaign. He had come home on a Friday evening and worked most of the night. Saturday morning, after a few hours working in the yard, he retired to his studio to create the advertising campaign for a new product. My sister and I found great delight in chasing each other round and round the dining room table, which was situated in a room directly over his head. He had told us to please stop at least twice but to no avail. This time he came bounding up the steps and collared me. He sat me down and taught a great lesson. He did not yell or strike me, even though he was very annoyed.

He explained the creative process—the spiritual process, if you will—and the need for quiet pondering and getting close to the Spirit for his creativity to function. Because he took time to explain and help me understand, I learned a lesson that has been put to use almost daily in my life. It seems to me that the Lord does not communicate with His children through bullhorns and billboards. That is why we need to take time to tune out the things of the world and tune in to the promptings of the Spirit.

Perhaps the most powerful means of tuning in is pondering. This pondering lifts our thoughts from the trivial things of the world and brings us closer to the "still small voice" of the Holy Ghost (1 Kings 19:12; 1 Nephi 17:45; D&C 85:6). In the Doctrine and Covenants, the Lord spoke to David Whitmer: "Your mind has been on the things of the earth more than on the things of me, your Maker . . . ; and you have not given heed unto my Spirit" (D&C 30:2). As we listen to the Spirit, we will understand the profound invitation in Proverbs to "ponder the path of life" (Proverbs 5:6)—to listen to what the gentle hand of our Maker would guide us to, and what He would have us do to take the next steps.

Even the Savior took time during His ministry to draw Himself apart from those He served to pray and draw close to His Father in Heaven. Luke records that He "went aside privately into a desert place" (Luke 9:10). Matthew notes that "when he had sent the multitudes away, he went up into a mountain apart to pray: and when the evening was come, he was there alone" (Matthew 14:23). After the Holy Ghost was poured out on His disciples in the Americas, "Jesus departed out of the midst of them, and went a little way off from them and bowed himself to the earth" and thanked His Father for giving the Holy Ghost to those whom He had chosen (3 Nephi

19:19–20). After His disciples were then blessed in an extraordinary way so their countenances shone, "he turned from them again, and went a little way off and bowed himself to the earth" and poured out His heart in gratitude to His Father again (3 Nephi 19:27). He then conversed with His disciples and smiled on them. Finally, a third time we read that "he went again a little way off and prayed unto the Father" (3 Nephi 19:31). Please don't think it selfish, on occasion, to go a little way off from the things of the world to ponder your needs and blessings and seek guidance.

What keeps us from pondering? Often it is the demands of our worldly occupations and activities, but sometimes we can even become too caught up in the good things we are trying to do to take time to ponder. For example, Bishop John Wells was a hard worker with an eye for detail; he served as a counselor in the Presiding Bishopric for many years. In 1915, his son was killed in a railroad accident. It was not clear from the circumstances whether foul play was involved. Sister Almena Wells was understandably grief-stricken. One day in her despair, her son appeared to her to let her know that his death was an accident and that she did not need to worry about him. He also told her that he had tried to convey this same message to his father, but Bishop Wells had been so busy that his son could not reach him.

Are we too busy to hear the guiding and comforting promptings of the Holy Ghost? By pondering the things of the Lord—His word, His teachings, His commandments, His life, His love, the gifts He has given us, and His Atonement for us—we draw near to Him and are prepared to hear the word of His Spirit. He promised, "Draw near unto me and I will draw near unto you" (D&C 88:63).

The temple is an especially effective place to put worldly things away and draw near to Him. Learning God's eternal plan, making covenants with Him, and remembering the divine role of our Savior, we ready ourselves to receive the guidance of His Spirit. When Sister Hales and I go to the temple, we always take the time to ponder the path of our lives. If we have an important decision to make, we begin by studying the matter out in our minds. Then we are ready to consider the matter as part of our temple worship. We take time there to remember our blessings, express our love for each other, listen to the guidance of the Holy Ghost, and share impressions of how our family can better follow the Savior.

WHAT WE MOST DESIRE

As with baptism, many fail to appreciate the extraordinary nature of the Holy Ghost, the supernal gift given to us by a loving Heavenly Father. When we understand that gift more fully, we will become like the Savior's disciples of old: "And they did pray for that which they most desired; and they desired that the Holy Ghost should be given unto them" (3 Nephi 19:9).

As our desire for the steady companionship of the Holy Ghost grows, so will our commitment to honor His sacred promptings. I testify that each of us can live so that we always have the Spirit to be with us as we follow those promptings that will keep us on the strait and narrow path and bring us joy. The Holy Ghost truly is our personal guide for the journey home, for through it the Savior's promise is realized: "I will not leave you comfortless: I will come to you" (John 14:18).

CHECKPOINTS

✓ What am I doing to be worthy of having the Holy Ghost as my guide for my journey through life?

✓ What am I doing that might be driving the Spirit away?

✓ What more can I do to invite greater light into my life?

✓ How well and how often do I take time to ponder the path of my life?

✓ What am I doing to generate spiritual light in my life by actively pedaling? Or am I letting the light go dim by spiritually coasting?

*Behold, I testify unto you that I do know that
these things whereof I have spoken are true. And how do ye
suppose that I know of their surety? Behold, I say unto you they are
made known unto me by the Holy Spirit of God.*

<small>ALMA 5:45–46</small>

CHAPTER EIGHT

PERSONAL REVELATION

I GREW UP ON LONG ISLAND in New York State. When I was a deacon, my father invited me to go on a trip to the Baseball Hall of Fame in Cooperstown, New York, though his real purpose was to take me to the historical sites of the Restoration. I was excited to see my boyhood heroes in Cooperstown, but it was what I saw and felt in the other places that had a profound impact on the course of my life. The trip proved to be one of the most memorable experiences of my youth.

As we stood on the banks of the Susquehanna River in Pennsylvania, my father related to me the story of the restoration of the Aaronic Priesthood on May 15, 1829, when John the Baptist bestowed that authority on Joseph Smith and Oliver Cowdery in this dispensation of time. Later we arrived at our real destination, the Sacred Grove. It was here that my father introduced me to those who were to become my true heroes. We saw the grove where Joseph Smith, at fourteen years of age, knelt in prayer and was given instructions to join none of the churches in his community but to prepare himself for a mission to bring forth the Church of Jesus Christ in these latter days. Joseph was worthy and in time completed his mission, bringing forth the translation of the Book of Mormon and organizing The Church of Jesus Christ of Latter-day Saints.

As a deacon, understanding this story, being in the Sacred Grove, and hearing my father's testimony awakened feelings in me that have continued to have a great impact in my life. At that time my father and I also made a few promises and goals, including a promise to keep the commandments and a goal to return to the presence of our Heavenly Father with our family. That goal has never changed. When we returned home, he painted a picture of the Sacred Grove, which I have treasured through the years and which now hangs in my office.

Why was this experience so formative for me? At a young age, I learned for myself that there is a God, a personal God. He wants us to pray, and He responds through personal revelation. Some may wonder, What is personal revelation? It is the way we know for ourselves the most important truths of our existence: the living reality of God, our Eternal Father, and His Son, Jesus Christ; the truthfulness of the restored gospel; and God's purpose and direction for us. It is the means by which They communicate with us and help us return to Their presence. Every Church member, if faithful, has the right to receive personal revelation for his or her own blessing. As faithful children, youth, parents, teachers, and leaders, we may receive personal revelation more frequently than we realize. The more we receive and acknowledge personal revelation, the more our testimonies grow.

How Do You Know?

Our testimony comes by the gift and power of the Holy Ghost. It is received and carried within us, enabling us to keep perspective and hold a steady course in times of prosperity and to overcome fear

The Sacred Grove, *by J. Rulon Hales*

and stay on the path in times of adversity. Regardless of the length of time we have been members of the Church, we are blessed to know and remember what a testimony is, how we obtain it, how it grows, and what Heavenly Father expects us to do with the testimony we have been given.

A testimony of Jesus is the spirit of prophecy (see Revelation 19:10). It is a personal revelation from God, revealing the truthfulness of the gospel of Jesus Christ. A testimony comes through the Holy Ghost and makes a deep and lasting impression on the soul. It is as "true north" on our spiritual compass—a point of reference on which we can always rely. It is a moving force that cannot be seen but is truly felt.

Wherever I have traveled in the course of serving the Lord,

people have asked me, "How do you know? How can you know that God lives and that Jesus is the Christ?" There is no formula, but there is a discernible pattern. Gaining a testimony and becoming converted begins with desiring to know the truth; study, prayer, and pondering in our hearts; living the gospel with patience and persistence; and inviting, waiting upon, and following the Spirit with constancy and commitment.

A DISCERNIBLE PATTERN

Paul counseled the Saints to rely on the Spirit rather than the wisdom of the world (see 1 Corinthians 2:11–16). To obtain that Spirit and the testimony it brings, consider that every major event of the Restoration—the First Vision, the appearance of Moroni and the coming forth of the Book of Mormon, the restoration of the priesthood, and the appearance of Jesus Christ following the dedication of His holy temple—has been preceded by a prayer of inquiry, by asking in faith.

The answers that come plant the seed of testimony, yet these answers are provided in the Lord's time and season. For some, this seed is planted quickly. For others, it happens gradually over months and even years. Often our faith is tried by the length of time Heavenly Father allows us to wait before the answer comes. When President David O. McKay was a young man herding cattle, he sought a witness, but it did not come until years later while he was serving his mission in Scotland. He wrote, "It was a manifestation for which as a doubting youth I had secretly prayed . . . on hillside and in meadow. It was an assurance to me that sincere prayer is answered 'sometime, somewhere.'"[1]

Prayer and patience provide the foundation for personal

---

1. Quoted in Francis M. Gibbons, *David O. McKay: Apostle to the World, Prophet of God* (Salt Lake City: Deseret Book, 1986), 50.

revelation and testimony. But more may be required. As the Lord reminded Oliver Cowdery, "Behold, you have not understood; you have supposed that I would give it unto you, when you took no thought save it was to ask me" (D&C 9:7). In addition to asking in faith, answers come and testimony grows as we strive to be obedient, study the scriptures, pray, ponder, and follow the prophets and our priesthood leaders. Our testimony grows as we reach out to help, lift, and strengthen others and serve the Lord in our assignments and callings.

Generally speaking, and as President McKay's experience suggests, the full strength of our testimony comes over time and through life's experiences. To understand that process, it may be helpful to consider how a nondigital photograph is developed into a printed image. Powerful impressions of the Spirit come like flashes of light on receptive photographic film. Like the chemicals needed to develop the picture, certain spiritual conditions and experiences are needed in our lives for our personal testimony to develop into a certain truth and knowledge. And, as with a photograph, a testimony must be carefully preserved or it will fade with time. It must be constantly nourished, expressed, and defended, or it will waste away. We can strengthen our testimonies through study, prayer, and living the gospel. Ultimately, there is no greater way to strengthen our own testimony than to share it with others—to bear our testimonies of the Savior to the world.

WHAT ABOUT DOUBTS?

As we grow in the gospel, it is natural to have questions and sometimes even doubts. Genuine questions can actually fuel our spiritual growth. As we study and seek answers, doubts about matters of religion that arise from a lack of knowledge can be constructively resolved.

We might ask, How do we question without becoming suspicious and losing our desire to believe? At various times in our lives, questions arise on policies, procedures, and even principles. Our attitude, or how we ask the question, is vitally important. If we demand an answer on our terms, we may not see the answer the Lord is providing for us. Or if we have strong feelings about a matter and become unwilling to listen, we may not understand the answer when it is given. To receive answers to our genuine questions, seeking with a humble heart and an open mind is the first step. Then, sincere study and prayer and counseling with priesthood leaders give us opportunities to increase in understanding. As we do, our faith grows, our testimony is strengthened, and our doubts begin to flee away.

USING OUR AGENCY AND SEEKING CONFIRMATION

At various times in our lives, we want answers to questions and problems to be given us directly, in a manner that would take away our agency and the blessings that come from exercising faith and waiting upon the Lord. Some think it would be nice to have "spiritual fortune cookies" to give us the answers to life's most vexing challenges. Heavenly Father, however, wants to help us grow. Therefore, He allows us to be engaged in seeking answers for ourselves.

For example, when choosing an eternal companion, we do not present a list of names to the Lord and ask Him to decide. Instead, we exercise our agency by participating in dating experiences. We get to know the other person's inner attitudes and outward behavior. Then we make a decision and take it to the Lord for confirmation. In this way, we become accountable for our decisions and responsible to prayerfully resolve any challenges that may arise.

Sometimes we feel that answers to our prayers and our pleading for guidance and direction should be given through dramatic manifestations, such as a voice from heaven or a visitation by an angel or a heavenly host. My personal experience is that answers to our prayers often come slowly over an extended period of time. As we act upon the feelings of our hearts, feelings of peace, comfort, and confirmation grow within us, and we know that we are on the right course.

I learned this truth as a Regional Representative of the Twelve, while traveling with President Marion G. Romney to a stake conference for the selection of a new stake president. We had been driving in a car for over an hour, discussing the Church and priesthood administration. Along the way I asked President Romney a question and realized, in the moment I asked it, that it was not appropriate. The question was, "What is the most spiritual experience you have had as an Apostle of the Lord?" There was a pause. He answered, "I believe what Joseph Smith and Brigham Young taught, that if we would keep our most sacred spiritual experiences to ourselves, many more spiritual experiences could be shared with us." There was a period of silence after he spoke, and then he said, "I owe you a better answer." He explained that the greatest spiritual experiences of his life had been when he had been on assignment from the President of the Church or the President of the Quorum of the Twelve, as we were that day. He said, "We will interview twenty-five or thirty priesthood brethren, and there will be more than one who will be qualified to be the stake president. But after we have done all we can do, we will get on our knees and pray to our Heavenly Father. We will tell Him of our feelings of who the new stake president ought to be and the reasons why. We will tell Him of the needs of the stake at this time. Then He will give us confirmation."

Through the years I have come to treasure those feelings of

confirmation, feelings that come after sincere effort on our part. In the work of finding a new stake president, confirming feelings follow much preparation and deliberation. However, revelation comes on the Lord's timetable. In our daily lives we are often required to move forward in faith, even though we haven't received all the answers we want or think we need.

I was assigned to help reorganize a stake presidency under the direction of then-Elder Ezra Taft Benson. After praying, interviewing, studying, and then praying again, Elder Benson asked if I knew who the new president would be. I said I had not received that inspiration yet. He looked at me for a long time and replied he hadn't either. However, we *were* inspired to ask three worthy priesthood holders to speak in the Saturday evening session of conference. Moments after the third speaker began, the Spirit prompted me that he should be the new stake president. I looked over at Elder Benson and saw tears streaming down his face. Revelation had been given to both of us—but only by continuing to seek our Heavenly Father's will as we moved forward in faith.

In His Due Time

On another occasion I accompanied Elder Marvin J. Ashton of the Quorum of the Twelve to select a new stake president. He suggested that after we had concluded our interviews and prayed, we each write down the name of the man whom we thought the Lord wanted to serve as the president of that stake.

However, after the last man had been interviewed and our prayers had been offered, I still had no answer. I didn't know what to do, and I wondered to myself why I wasn't receiving an answer. Finally, the Spirit prompted me to just leave the paper blank, fold it, and put it on the table. Elder Ashton folded his paper and put it on the table too. He asked if I'd like to pray again, and we did. Once again, I received no direction about whom the Lord wanted to serve as president of the stake. I was feeling the pressure, but once again I nervously placed my blank piece of folded paper on the table next to Elder Ashton's.

"Do you want to look at them?" he asked. I believe he was testing me, and I wasn't enjoying it. But sure enough, when we opened each of the papers we had folded, they were all blank.

Just then the currently serving stake president knocked on the door. A brother who had recently moved into the stake had just stopped by to see the stake president. Though he hadn't been on our list of people to interview, the stake president felt that perhaps we should talk with him. We quickly agreed. As soon as I shook this brother's hand, the Spirit made it powerfully clear that he was to be the new stake president. I watched Elder Ashton anxiously as he shook the man's hand, and tears came to his eyes as the Spirit testified to him, too, that we had found the new stake president.

What if we had simply called the man who was the most logical choice? Clearly we would not have found the man the Lord desired to have serve. In our daily lives, perhaps we are too often impatient for an answer, or lack the confidence that we are able to receive an answer, and therefore we do not allow the Lord to reveal sacred truths to us "in his own time, and in his own way, and according to his own will" (D&C 88:68).

RECEIVING REVELATION FOR OURSELVES

We often receive wise counsel from Church leaders about how to serve in our Church leadership callings. Yet sometimes we underestimate our right and capacity to receive revelation ourselves, for any calling we may hold, and for every aspect of our lives. I once received a call from Johannes Wondra, president of the Vienna Austria Stake at the time. He had a list of ten very good questions for me. I listened carefully to his list of questions and replied, "If I knew the answers to those questions, President, I would be the president of the Vienna Austria Stake." President Wondra understood my point and later used it as an Area Seventy in teaching other priesthood leaders about their ability to receive inspiration for themselves.

There are, however, limits to the revelation we are entitled to receive. We are privileged to receive inspiration for our own callings, our own families, and our own lives. But we do not have the right to receive revelation for people or situations beyond the limits of our stewardship. For example, one bishop is not entitled to receive inspiration regarding another bishop's ward. And only those we sustain as prophets, seers, and revelators are entitled to receive revelation for the whole Church. As we will discuss later, this same principle applies to receiving answers about whom we should marry.

FOLLOWING THE PATTERN OF THE PROPHETS

If we are struggling to receive personal revelation, it is a great relief to acknowledge and follow the pattern of the prophets—a pattern that is exceptionally clear in the life of Joseph Smith and the unfolding of the Restoration. Turn to the scriptures. Kneel in prayer. Ask in faith. Listen to the Holy Ghost. Learn that your name and needs are known by our Heavenly Father, just as Joseph's were. Live the gospel with patience and persistence. I promise that if "ye will . . . ask [the Lord] in faith, believing that ye shall receive, with diligence in keeping [His] commandments, surely these things shall be made known unto you" (1 Nephi 15:11).

As we follow this pattern and act upon the answers we receive by the Spirit, we will come to recognize the promptings of the Spirit in our lives with greater confidence.

I testify that whether on the hillside or in the meadow, in the grove or the closet, now or in the eternities to come, the Savior's words to each of us will be fulfilled: "Ask, and it shall be given you; seek, and ye shall find; knock, and it shall be opened unto you" (Matthew 7:7; see also 3 Nephi 14:7).

While we are commanded *not* to seek after signs, we *are* commanded to "seek . . . earnestly the best gifts" (D&C 46:8). These gifts include the Holy Ghost and personal revelation. That revelation will come "line upon line, precept upon precept," as the Savior said, and "unto him that receiveth [the Lord] will give more" (2 Nephi 28:30).

CHECKPOINTS

✓ Do I have a real testimony from the Holy Ghost?

✓ How patient am I in seeking revelation? Do I impose my timetable on the Lord?

✓ What do I do to nourish my testimony?

✓ How well do I do my homework before seeking revelation, or do I simply ask the Lord to solve my problems for me?

Choose you this day whom ye will serve; . . .
but as for me and my house, we will serve the Lord.

JOSHUA 24:15

CHAPTER NINE

CHOOSING FRIENDS WISELY

THERE IS A MARVELOUS lesson to be learned from those who live in the islands. When they catch crabs, they place them in a small, flat basket. If you place one crab in the basket, it crawls right out; if you place two crabs in the basket, every time one crab starts to crawl out, it is pulled back in by the other crab.

This method is one way—and a very effective way—that Lucifer accomplishes his work. His mission statement is to make all men "miserable like unto himself" (2 Nephi 2:27). As we strive to become spiritually strong and escape the sins of this world, he strives to hold onto us and keep us within his grasp.

Knowingly or unknowingly, sometimes our friends participate in this kind of behavior. Sin likes company, and when a friend is taking a detour from the strait and narrow path, he or she will be naturally inclined to bring us along. For this reason, among the most critical decisions we make during our decade of preparation is who our friends will be. Our most important choices will be influenced by them. Wherever they go, we will be tempted to go with them. Whoever they are is a good indication of who we may be becoming.

TRUE FRIENDS

My mother taught me this principle when I was about ten. One of my friends was of concern to her, so she took me down to a pond, and we fed bread to the swans. She said to me, "Do you see any vultures or birds of prey among those beautiful, peaceful swans? There are only swans! Why? Because birds of a feather flock together!" Her message was simple. Our friends will reflect what kind of person *we* are. And good friends, true friends, will help us stay on the gospel path and become better than we are now.

True friends do not try to make us choose between their ways and the Lord's ways. True friends don't hold us back spiritually or pull us down when we're trying to rise and progress. True friends protect us. True friends help us be better than we would be on our own. True friends make it easier for us to live the gospel by being around them.

Sometimes we stay with friends because they have something we want or can give us something we think we need, such as a feeling of belonging or the social status of being in their company. But if they deviate from the correct path and lead us astray, it does not matter what kind of cars they drive, who their parents are, how effective they are on the football field or the basketball floor or the baseball diamond, or where they placed in a beauty pageant. If being in their circle means staying in the basket of worldliness, the benefit is not worth the price. And so we ask ourselves, Does this friend inspire me to live the standards of the gospel? Does this friend help me rise out of the basket of past challenges and motivate me to reach higher than before? Will this friend help me get to a better place? Ultimately, a true friend is the one who will help us live God's plan and return with honor. A true friend helps us succeed on our journey home.

Sometimes carefully chosen friends surprise us by making wrong choices. Every one of us needs to know when to walk or run away from those who have ceased to do the works of righteousness and embraced sin. Joseph recognized the evil in Potiphar's wife and ran from it (see Genesis 39:7–12). We too must recognize evil and flee from it. Paul's counsel is most succinct: "From such turn away" (2 Timothy 3:5).

If your present friends are taking you down the path of wickedness or apathy toward spiritual things, depart from them now. As the Savior instructed His disciples, "Wherefore if thy hand or thy foot offend thee, cut them off, and cast them from thee: it is better for thee to enter into life halt or maimed, rather than having two hands or two feet to be cast into everlasting fire" (Matthew 18:8). The Joseph Smith Translation makes the Savior's meaning unmistakably clear: "And a man's hand is his friend, and his foot, also; and a man's eye, are they of his own household" (JST Matthew 18:9).

Aron Ralston was hiking alone in a Utah canyon when the boulder from which he was hanging shifted, pinning his arm underneath it. He found himself trapped with no way to get help. After five days of doing everything he could to extract himself, he realized he faced a terrible decision: to cut off his own arm or die pinned under the boulder in the middle of the desert. Painful as it was to cut off his arm with only the knife in his pocket, Aron chose to do that and live rather than keep his arm and die.

Like Aron, we must make hard choices if our friends are leading us away from the path that leads to eternal life. We may be reluctant to leave behind such friends because we are afraid to be without friends. Young people have told me, "I'd rather starve than not have a friend. I'll do anything for a friend." But doing anything to get or keep a friend means having friends who could require anything from us—even things that may hurt us. When we are more worried about what our friends think than what our Heavenly Father thinks, we are vulnerable indeed.

A simple commandment will help us: "Choose you this day whom ye will serve" (Joshua 24:15). We have the power to decide whom we will serve and whom we will have by our side. The mocking, pointing fingers of those in the "great and spacious building" (1 Nephi 8:26) cannot cause us to choose friends who will weaken us or entice us off the path. Friends who encourage us to compromise our principles generally use us to benefit themselves. We may want to ask ourselves, Why are they my friends? Is it because they really support who I am and what I believe, or is it because they like the company (and tacit support) I provide in the wrong choices they make?

Sometimes when we know who we are and stand up for what we believe, we pay a price. This, I believe, is part of a sacred test. We should not think we are going to go through this life without such tests. In facing tests with faith, we are strengthened and we demonstrate before ourselves and the Lord how strong we will be in standing for truth and righteousness throughout our lives.

In choosing to be a true friend and to surround ourselves only with true friends, we may be choosing to be lonely for a time. Spiritual leadership in this world is often lonely. But the power is in us to stand alone. Short-term loneliness may be our key to eternal blessings, and such loneliness will not last forever. Standing up for what is right will be observed by others who want to do the same. Eventually they will come to us as true friends, respecting who we are and wanting to help us be even better.

OUR TRUEST FRIEND

The Savior is our friend—a true friend who laid down His life for us, His friends. In following His example of true friendship, we have the opportunity to help others, to love them, and to prepare them for the Second Coming of Jesus Christ.

As children of God in this dispensation, we are not here by accident. We are here to lift. Yet we know how hard it is to lift somebody if we're standing in the mud or, even more, how hard it is to lift somebody if we're standing on their shoulders, weighing them down. I testify that the Savior's greatest desire—indeed His work and His glory—is for us to return home with honor.

CHECKPOINTS

✓ How do my friends influence me? Do they lift me up or push me down?

✓ Am I more worried about the approval of God or of my friends?

✓ What kind of friend am I?

Upon you my fellow servants, in the name of Messiah
I confer the Priesthood of Aaron, which holds the keys of the
ministering of angels, and of the gospel of repentance, and
of baptism by immersion for the remission of sins.

DOCTRINE & COVENANTS 13:1

CHAPTER TEN

THE PREPARATORY PRIESTHOOD

WHEN I WAS A YOUNG man, my father and my bishop both helped me learn an important lesson: the Aaronic Priesthood is not just an activity or something we receive because we have grown to a certain age. The priesthood is the power of God, which is given to man to act in His name. Honoring this priesthood and fulfilling our duty to God prepares us for the critical decisions we must make in the decade of decision that follows our youth. And just as my father and my bishop helped me appreciate the significance of the Aaronic Priesthood, parents, bishops, and youth leaders throughout the Church today take special care to help young men during this preparatory period.

When I was thirteen, I was the president of my deacons quorum in the Queens Ward in New York City. Our ward met in the Citizen's League Hall, and the sacrament table was on the main floor right in front of the stage. After sacrament meeting each Sunday, the deacons would remove the sacrament trays and take them up some stairs to the back of the stage where we put them away. I can still remember one Sunday when we were putting away the sacrament trays, running and jumping off the stage each time we went to retrieve another one. As I came sailing off that stage, our new bishop was standing right there. He caught me in flight. To defend myself I said, "Well, everyone else is doing it."

"Yes," he said, "but you are the president of the deacons quorum." The bishop said he wanted the sacrament taken care of properly, with reverence, and I knew in my heart he was right.

My parents also taught me to honor the Aaronic Priesthood by their example. We passed the sacrament using stainless steel sacrament trays which, as a result of spilled water, were often dulled with hard water spots. As a holder of the Aaronic Priesthood, I was responsible for helping to prepare the sacrament. My father asked me to take home the trays, and together we cleaned them with steel wool until they sparkled. We washed and wiped each one of the individual sacrament cups, which were made of glass. (We didn't have disposable sacrament cups back then.) We would take home the cloths for the sacrament table, and my mother would launder them each week. They were cleaned, starched, and pressed; there wasn't a wrinkle in them. When I saw those cloths on the sacrament table and the sparkling trays and glasses each Sunday, I knew my parents loved the Savior and that the sacrament was sacred to them. And I knew I had done my part to invite reverence for the sacrament.

SACRED DUTIES

Filled as I am with gratitude for the Aaronic Priesthood, I continually hope the young men of the Church understand the importance of reverently preparing, blessing, and passing the sacrament to their fellow Church members. As emblems of our Savior's flesh and blood, the bread and water represent His atoning sacrifice. It is an awesome thought—the sacrament our young men administer each week is in remembrance of the Atonement.

What is the purpose of this sacrament? First, it is a remembrance of the Savior's physical offering in our behalf. Second, it is a witness to our Heavenly Father that we are willing to take upon us the name of the Savior. And third, it is our commitment to remember Him and obey Him.

In return, consider the great promise our Heavenly Father gives to us: "That [we] may always have his Spirit to be with [us]" (D&C 20:77). I believe this is the greatest promise we can have in this life, because if we honor it, we will never lose our way. This is the reason we attend sacrament meeting each week: to renew the covenants we made at baptism so we can have the Holy Ghost to be with us and thereby remain on the strait and narrow path that leads us to eternal life—to return with honor.

In light of this great purpose, I would ask all young deacons, teachers, and priests: Are you worthy to officiate in preparing, passing, and blessing the sacrament? Are you worthy to partake of the sacrament and prepared to do so in a meaningful way? If you are a priest, can you recite the sacrament prayer with meaning, understanding the significance of what you are saying? Or do you read it mechanically, as if you were reading a foreign language whose words you do not really understand?

If you are a teacher or deacon, can you fulfill your responsibilities to administer and partake of the sacrament with clean hands and a pure heart? All who serve in the Aaronic Priesthood should know that the members of the Church look to them as examples and continually observe their conduct. When I was a bishop interviewing youth, some of the young women would ask me about whether certain young men should be passing the sacrament because they knew how these young men were conducting their lives. Young men should understand that their behavior can affect a young woman's view of the sacrament and of the priesthood. If young men who are unworthy participate in administering the sacrament, the impact goes beyond themselves. (That is true of priesthood holders of all ages.) Their parents might not know, their priesthood leaders might not know, but they know, and God knows whether they are worthy. Every member in the congregation should be able to look toward the sacrament table and trust that the members of the priesthood are worthy to perform the ordinances of the Lord.

The Preparatory Priesthood

To fully appreciate the Aaronic Priesthood, it is important to understand that it is the preparatory priesthood, given for a preparatory period of life. During the Aaronic Priesthood years, young men prepare themselves to follow higher laws and make such covenants as obedience, sacrifice, service, chastity, and consecration of time and talents. These preparatory years are also critical for preparing to worthily enter the temple. Young men who successfully prepare for their endowment emerge from the house of the Lord "armed with [His] power" (D&C 109:22) to be valiant missionaries, caring eternal companions, and devoted fathers.

How young men bear the Aaronic Priesthood now prepares them not only for entering the temple but also for making the most important decisions of their lives. These decisions include receiving the Melchizedek Priesthood and temple ordinances, serving a mission, choosing an eternal companion and being sealed for time and all eternity, getting an education, and selecting an occupation. Learning and diligently fulfilling Aaronic Priesthood responsibilities now safeguards the ability to make these future decisions wisely.

Faithfully bearing the Aaronic Priesthood also prepares young men to avoid the inevitable onslaught of temptation directed at youth and especially at young men. As young men do their duty, they are trained to keep their focus on what matters most, and they develop preconditioned responses to emergency conditions—just as fighter pilots do. Then, when warning lights go off, alerting them that temptations abound and "sin lieth at the door" (Genesis 4:7), they do not waffle in their response. They are able to say *no* to disobeying commandments and *yes* to keeping them, almost without considering any other alternative.

To the young men of the Church, I would caution that in the decade ahead, your time for preparation will be limited because temptations will come quickly. You will want to develop now your own preconditioned responses to the challenges and decisions that you will soon face. For example, decide now not to use alcohol, tobacco, and drugs. When you use these substances, you become their slave, and your moral agency is thereby limited. Decide now to keep the law of chastity. Decide now to do all in your power to receive and retain the Spirit of the Lord, allowing Him to guide you and direct you back to our Heavenly Father with honor. Decide now that making no decision in a difficult moment could be just as deadly as making the wrong decision. Decide now to choose the right—always.

Fulfilling Our Duty to God

For many years the First Presidency and the Quorum of the Twelve Apostles have had great concerns for the welfare of our youth in these troubled times. Yet there has never been a time like now, when this message is being brought forward so strongly by the General Authorities and general officers of the Church. They know that parents, along with bishops and priesthood and auxiliary leaders, can make a difference in helping young men (especially those without strong families) understand who they are and what they can become—not only here in mortality but in the eternities to come.

As parents and leaders, we also need a clear understanding of who we are. As we are exemplary in following the Savior and obeying His commandments, we will have a powerful influence in the lives of youth. Our fervent plea to all who are associated with them is this: Let us strive to do our very best. As we *are,* so they will be inspired to *become.*

To the young men in particular, I hope you will get on your knees each day and express to God the desires of your heart. He is the source of all wisdom and will give us answers to our prayers. Be humble and willing to listen to the whisperings of the Spirit. Read the scriptures daily. Strengthen your testimony. Pay tithes and fast offerings. Remember and keep the covenants you made when you were baptized, and renew those covenants each week when you worthily partake of the sacrament. Keeping your baptismal covenants now will help you prepare for the temple covenants you will make in the future.

During the preparatory period of life it is important that you cultivate spiritual growth, physical growth, personal and educational development, readiness for a career, citizenship, and social skills. Obtaining strength in these areas is part of becoming a fully capable priesthood holder, prepared for a life of service to others.

That is the essence of our duty to God. By fulfilling that duty, in body and soul, you young men will be prepared to call down blessings upon your own head and also upon the heads of many, many others.

For now, every boy has a calling and responsibility to become a noble young man—to grow in strength and righteous power and to influence others for good. Young men, along with young women, are the future of the Church. The choices you make today will directly influence the number and kinds of opportunities each of you will have in the future. Each daily decision will either limit or broaden your opportunities. As you make righteous decisions during this preparatory period, you will be ready to make righteous decisions in the future.

SHEPHERDS OF YOUTH

I hope parents and youth leaders will understand that the young men and young women for whom they have responsibility have been prepared to come to earth at this particular time for a sacred and glorious purpose. Bishops, you are the president of the Aaronic Priesthood and priests quorum. You are a shepherd of the Lord's lambs—of Primary children, young men, young women, and the young single adults. What an awesome responsibility that is! It cannot be fulfilled without the hard work of your counselors. Staying close to these youth, week in and week out, will be the consuming interest of a faithful bishop and his counselors.

Aaronic Priesthood holders and young women, understand that the bishop is called to be your shepherd. Your leaders are like his sheepdogs. From his position he can see the big picture—where you need to go—and he trusts your advisers and other leaders to respond to his direction to help you get there. Through his regular personal contact, he will also personally see you through this, the most crucial preparatory decade of your lives—a decade of constant transition and momentous decision. With all the care of the Good Shepherd, he will lead you from Young Men and Young Women into the elders quorum and Relief Society and on to the work you will do in your own home and family.

Young men, love your parents and bishops and express appreciation to them for all they do on your behalf. Have the courage to seek and follow counsel from them. When your parents and bishops correct you, it is because they love you. "For whom the Lord loveth he chasteneth, and scourgeth every son whom he receiveth. If ye endure chastening, God dealeth with you as with sons; for what son

Who knoweth whether thou art come to the
kingdom for such a time as this?

ESTHER 4:14

CHAPTER ELEVEN

DAUGHTERS OF GOD

M UCH OF WHAT I HAVE written about the young men applies to the young women as well. In this chapter, however, I would like to focus on issues and concerns unique to the young women of the Church.

EDUCATION AND CAREERS

Years ago, Camilla Kimball, the wife of President Spencer W. Kimball, asked my wife about her views on higher education and women. (At the time, not nearly as many women obtained a college education as they do today.) After my wife explained why she thought it was a good idea for women who had the interest and the opportunity to obtain an education to do so, Sister Kimball said, "You are so right." Her daughter's husband was losing his sight, and her daughter needed to work to help support the family. She was in a much better position to do so because she had received an education.

No young woman knows for sure what lies in her future. Even

when we get married, we do not know what is coming down the road for us mentally, physically, spiritually, and emotionally. That is one of the many reasons education or vocational training is so important: it prepares young women for any eventuality.

Years ago we joked that some girls went to college just to obtain an MRS (Mrs.) degree; their only aim, to get a husband. Today, most young women understand that striving only to get a husband while pursuing their education or vocational training means missing an important opportunity. Some young women in the Church will be fortunate enough to marry and be in an economic situation where they are able to be full-time mothers rather than employees in the workforce. But even then, a good education is helpful, as mothers may use what they have learned at school to do everything from establishing a budget for provident living, to preparing taxes, to overseeing their families' finances, to shopping wisely, to creating nutritionally sound meals, to diagnosing diseases, to researching the purchases of cars and major appliances, to tutoring their children in algebra and calculus. Almost everything a wise and educated mother learns at a college, university, or vocational school can be used to bless her family in some way, even if she is never paid a formal wage for her services. The rewards for her developed gifts and talents are priceless—no amount of money could repay her.

Today, the odds are higher than ever that at some point in their adult lives, women in the Church will need to work outside the home to help support themselves or their families. In the proclamation to the world on the family, the First Presidency and Quorum of the Twelve stated the ideal and recognized some exceptions when it comes to fathers providing for their families: "By divine design, fathers are . . . responsible to provide the necessities of life and protection for their families. Mothers are primarily responsible for the nurture of their children. . . . Disability, death, or other circumstances may necessitate individual adaptation."[1]

Speaking to young women, President Thomas S. Monson noted: "We do live in turbulent times. Often the future is unknown; therefore, it behooves us to prepare for uncertainties. Statistics reveal that at some time, for a variety of reasons, you may find yourself in the role of financial provider. I urge you to pursue your education and learn marketable skills so that, should such a situation arise, you are prepared to provide."[2]

Some who plan to marry may discover that the blessing of marriage does not come until later than they had planned or it may not occur until the next life. Others who do marry may lose their husbands to death or divorce. Others who remain married may find that their economic situation or other factors necessitate that both husband and wife work to provide for their family. And some who have been full-time mothers will have a desire to work outside the home when their children have been raised, perhaps to help support children on missions or in college or to use their talents to bless others outside their own family. In each of these scenarios, happy is the woman who has made the most of her opportunities for education or vocational training!

Few things in this life are more tragic to me than a woman who finds herself trapped in an irreversibly unfaithful or abusive marital relationship solely because she feels unprepared or unable to provide for herself and her children without her husband. Education or vocational training can be the path out of dangerous and destructive

---

1. "The Family: A Proclamation to the World," *Ensign,* November 1995, 102.

2. Thomas S. Monson, "If Ye Are Prepared Ye Shall Not Fear," *Ensign,* November 2004, 116.

situations, providing a woman with security and a measure of independence.

In developing independence, one emotional benefit of obtaining at least some education before marriage is the opportunity to go to school away from home. In the home of my youth, we watched a robin build a nest every year in the drain pipe on our roof. Each year the chicks would come, and the mother robin would nourish them for a season. But eventually the time came when they had to fly away from the nest. I would watch the mother use her wing to nudge her chicks out of the nest and into the air three stories above the ground. Sometimes they struggled, and I would run down below and pick up the young bird from the ground. Then I'd run inside and upstairs, crawl out the window, and put the little bird back in the nest. But a few days later the mother would try again. And eventually those little birds did learn to fly.

To move away from home and live on our own can be an important part of the maturing process. While leaving home to obtain an education may not be right for everyone, moving out of the nest will help most young women gain independence and confidence that can prepare them for the next stage of their lives. Both a new bride and groom are blessed when they have had the opportunity to live away from home before marriage and assume responsibility to make decisions on their own.

Education does far more than improve our economic and emotional circumstances; education also elevates our minds. Women have greater self-esteem and more happiness in their marriages when they cultivate their minds. A good education provides a solid foundation that enables equally yoked wives and husbands to grow in step as they read and learn and talk together.

In my own marriage, I have been richly blessed by the knowledge my wife has gained. An avid reader, she shares with me what she learns from her reading, so my mind is enlightened and my spirits are lifted. Her own formal education and learning have given her the confidence to strengthen me intellectually and professionally. In fact, she advocated our taking a position overseas, which opened up many opportunities for us to serve in the Church and in my chosen career. I will never forget what she once said to a group of wives of MBA students when asked what advice she could give to them to assist their husbands in their careers: "I have always made sure that I never stood in the way of my husband's progress, and he has never stood in the way of my progress."

Finally, unlike so many other activities on which we can spend our time, education is an investment we will never regret, since "whatever principle of intelligence we attain unto in this life . . . will rise with us in the resurrection" (D&C 130:18). Every young woman should prayerfully ponder how she can best develop her talents and abilities through the education and vocational training opportunities available to her. Education is an important part of preparing for motherhood and for making a home.

Missions

Many young women struggle with the very personal decision of whether to serve a mission. Each young woman's situation is unique, which is why no one can prescribe a simple answer that fits all of the young women who would like to serve.

Unlike young men, young women do not have a priesthood responsibility to serve full-time missions. No young woman should ever feel pressured into full-time missionary service or guilty because she has not served. For young women, missions are an option to consider, not an obligation to fulfill.

Moreover, a full-time mission is not a prerequisite for sisters to live faithful, dedicated, consecrated lives. Nor should any young woman ever feel that she needs to serve a mission to somehow make up for past mistakes in life. Most importantly, a mission is also no place for a young woman to go simply to escape the romantic advances of young men. And a young woman who is seriously dating a worthy young man should pray long and hard and receive clear inspiration before deciding to serve a mission.

Having said that, as a mission president I absolutely loved the young women with whom I was privileged to serve. In fact, they were so effective in sharing the gospel that I asked the Missionary Department to send me as many sisters as they could. Those sisters who served in my mission brought a great maturity and love to the work that was a blessing to all they taught. For those young women who feel inspired to serve, a mission can be a great blessing. "And if it so be that you should labor all your days in crying repentance unto this people, and bring, save it be one soul unto me, how great shall be your joy with him in the kingdom of my Father!" (D&C 18:15).

Notice that the Lord's promise in that verse is not limited to men. Nor is it limited to full-time missionaries. Name tags are not required to share the gospel with our neighbors. The most effective missionaries are any members—male or female—who take seriously their covenant "to stand as witnesses of God at all times and in all things, and in all places that [we] may be in" (Mosiah 18:9).

None of us can fulfill such covenants merely by praying for friends and loved ones on full-time missions; we must stand as witnesses ourselves. That is why young women should prepare just as diligently as young men to share the gospel. Like all members of the Church, young women should be prepared to respond to Peter's charge to "be ready always to give an answer to every man that asketh you a reason of the hope that is in you" (1 Peter 3:15).

In preparing to do that, a young woman's approach is quite

similar to the approach a young man takes to prepare for a full-time mission. Both should study the scriptures and attend seminary regularly. Both should learn to love and serve others. Both should obtain a testimony for themselves of the truthfulness of the restored gospel. Both should learn to understand and explain the key concepts of the gospel, including our Heavenly Father's plan, the Atonement, the Apostasy, the Restoration, the Book of Mormon, and the commandments. Both should learn to overcome fears in order to talk with others about the gospel. And both should live the gospel in such a way that the light of Christ will be reflected in their countenances. Any young woman who does these things will be prepared to stand as a witness of God, whether at home or abroad as a full-time missionary.

DATING AND MARRIAGE

Later we will discuss how individuals should approach the decision about whether and whom to marry—one of the most important decisions we make in this life. Here let me simply address a few concerns that apply especially to young women when it comes to dating and marriage.

One of my greatest concerns for the young women of the Church is that they will sell themselves short in dating and marriage by forgetting who they really are—daughters of a loving Heavenly Father. The social pressures and temptations directed at youth can be devastating to young women's sense of their divine identity. The desire to be accepted and acknowledged here and now by someone—anyone—can be enormous. Unfortunately, a young woman who lowers her standards far enough can always find temporary acceptance from immature and unworthy young men.

The first step on this sad path is usually not action but attitude. When a young woman's desire to be liked by a boy or loved by a

Elder and Sister Hales leaving the
Oquirrh Mountain Utah Temple, August 2009

man is greater than her desire to be loved by the Lord, she is in immediate and severe danger. Such young women may rationalize, telling themselves that one evening out with a boy of questionable character will do no harm. But all too often one date turns into several, which leads to a relationship. And for a young woman who has yearned for acceptance, even the worst relationship can be hard to leave behind.

How tragic it is when a young man then takes advantage of a young woman's low self-esteem and asks her to "show her love" for him by joining him in breaking one of God's most sacred commandments—and she consents because she is afraid of losing her relationship with him. To succumb to such desires is to sell our very bodies for the pottage of short-term acceptance—pottage that always comes with a bitter aftertaste (see Genesis 25:29–34). As Alma taught his son, "Wickedness never was happiness" (Alma 41:10). Young women of wisdom know their true value and do not sell themselves short, even if it means being lonely for a season. They are more concerned about being accepted by Heavenly Father for eternity than about being accepted by a boyfriend for the moment.

At their best, daughters of God are loving, caring, understanding, and sympathetic. This does *not* mean they are also gullible, unrealistic, or easily manipulated. If a young man does not measure up to the standards a young woman has set, he may promise her that he will change if she will marry him first. Wise daughters of God will insist that young men who seek their hand in marriage change *before* the wedding, not after. (I am referring here to the kind of change necessary to worthily enter the temple, not the kind of change that will be part of the lifelong growth of every disciple.) He may argue that she doesn't really believe in repentance and forgiveness. But one of the hallmarks of repentance is forsaking sin. Especially when the sin involves addictive behaviors or a pattern of transgression, wise daughters of God insist on seeing a sustained effort to forsake sin over a long period of time as true evidence of repentance. They do not marry someone because they believe they can change him. Young women, please do not settle for someone unworthy of your gospel standards.

On the other hand, young women should not refuse to settle down. There is no right age for young men or young women to marry, but there is a right attitude for them to have about marriage: "Thy will be done" (Matthew 6:10; 3 Nephi 13:10; D&C 109:44). For some, through no fault of their own, marriage may not come in their twenties or thirties. But when young single adults postpone marriage for selfish reasons, such as pursuing career or travel interests, they may be forgetting the counsel from Ecclesiastes: "To every thing there is a season, and a time to every purpose under the heaven" (Ecclesiastes 3:1). The time to marry is when we are prepared to meet a suitable mate, not after we have done all the enjoyable things in life we hoped to do while we were single. Obtaining an education is excellent preparation for functioning in the divinely appointed roles of wife and mother when the time is right.

Of course, there is no perfect age at which all members of the Church should marry, since opportunity, maturity, and preparation vary from individual to individual. But as we see the average age for marriage increasing both inside and outside the Church—and the average family size decreasing right along with it—I am concerned that some are foregoing blessings they might have received had they counseled "with the Lord in all [their] doings" (Alma 37:37). When I hear some young men and young women set plans in stone which do not include marriage until after age twenty-five or thirty or until a graduate degree has been obtained, I recall Jacob's warning, "Seek not to counsel the Lord, but to take counsel from his hand" (Jacob 4:10).

Preparing for the Temple

From a young age, many young women in the Church plan to get married in the temple. This is a wonderful and appropriate goal. But the temple is much more than just the right place to get married and a beautiful backdrop for wedding photos. The temple is a place where we prepare to enter into the presence of God, and this includes receiving personal, individual ordinances.

While some young women will attend the temple and receive their endowment in conjunction with being sealed to their husbands, others will do so in preparation for their missions. Yet other sisters will receive their endowment when they are single and feel, in consultation with their parents and priesthood leaders, that the time has come for them to make sacred covenants found only in the house of the Lord. As mature young women come to think of the temple as more than just the ideal place to be wed, they can prepare themselves more fully to receive their endowment and other ordinances.

Living worthy of a temple recommend throughout their teenage years is one of the most important steps young women can take to be ready to receive their endowment when the time comes. Such preparation will include better understanding and honoring the baptismal covenant they have already made with the Lord. Regularly attending the temple to perform baptisms for the dead is another wonderful way to prepare to receive additional ordinances in the temple. Studying what prophets have written about temples and seeking out relevant passages of scripture can help make the temple experience much more meaningful.

Young women can also prepare for the temple by remembering that their own bodies are temples and treating them accordingly. "Know ye not that ye are the temple of God, and that the Spirit of God dwelleth in you? . . . The temple of God is holy, which temple ye are" (1 Corinthians 3:16–17).

Our bodies are the temples of our spirits. Additionally, our bodies are the means by which we bring souls from the presence of God into this world. When we recognize our bodies as the gifts they are and when we understand the missions they help us fulfill, we protect and honor them by how we act and dress.

In everyday living, immodest clothing such as short shorts, miniskirts, tight clothing, shirts that do not cover the stomach, and other revealing attire are not appropriate. All men and women—including young men and young women—should wear clothing that covers the shoulder and avoid clothing that is low cut in the front or back or revealing in any other manner. Tight pants, tight shirts, excessively baggy clothing, wrinkled apparel, and unkempt hair are not appropriate. All should avoid extremes in clothing, hairstyle, and other aspects of appearance. We should always be neat and clean, avoiding sloppiness or inappropriate casualness.[3]

Modesty is at the center of being pure and chaste, both in thought and deed. Because it guides and influences our thoughts, behavior, and decisions, modesty is at the core of our character. Our clothing is more than just covering for our bodies; it reflects who we are and what we want to be, both here in mortality and in the eternities that will follow.

Have you ever considered why the majestic architecture of a temple is surrounded by beautiful plants and reflecting pools? They give an outward presence and feeling that prepare us for the sacred ordinances that await us inside the temple.

Our clothing is equally important. It is the "landscaping" for presenting our bodies as temples. Just as the temple grounds portray the sacredness and reverence for what takes place inside the temple, so our clothing portrays the beauty and purity of our inner selves. How we dress portrays whether we have proper respect for temple ordinances and eternal covenants and whether we are preparing ourselves to receive them.

This is especially true on our wedding day. There will be no more significant occasion in your life than your wedding day. Your marriage will be one of the most sacred events of your life, and hopefully it will take place in the holy temple—Heavenly Father's most sacred edifice here on earth. If you truly understand the nature of the covenants that you will be making there, you want to reflect that understanding in your dress. Brides, you would choose a white temple dress with a bodice and sleeves that are appropriate for

3. See *For the Strength of Youth: Fulfilling Our Duty to God* (Salt Lake City: The Church of Jesus Christ of Latter-day Saints, 2001), 14–16.

the wearing of temple garments. You would do this because of your respect for the endowment ceremony and the covenants you took upon yourself in preparation for your sealing ceremony.

Before you attend the temple, whether it is to be married, to receive the endowment, or to perform work for the dead, you should pause for a moment and ask yourself these questions: "If the Lord were to be at the temple today, how would I dress? How would I want to present myself to Him?" Of course, the answer is clear. We would want to look and feel our best.

MOTHERHOOD

A young woman from Brigham Young University once called Sister Hales to get some information to introduce her at a speech she would be giving. The student asked what Mary had done. Mary said that she had earned her degree at BYU and that she was a mother. The young woman could not hide her disappointment that my wife's list of secular accomplishments was not longer. "Is that all you've done?" she asked.

On the other side of the veil, I trust my wife's accomplishments will be greeted quite differently. One of the greatest privileges and responsibilities given to us on this earth is that of being a parent, helping to bring to earth children of God and having a sacred responsibility to love, care, and guide them back to our Heavenly Father. Perhaps that is why one of the most ennobling characteristics of womanhood is motherhood. Whenever a mother exercises her influence—as a nurturer, a counselor, a teacher, a helper, a friend—she is about our Father's business.

I am thankful for my own mother, who was devoted to her husband and children—a mother who taught by example. She taught me from the time I was a toddler until she passed away decades later. I am the eternal beneficiary of her sacrifice and her faithfulness.

The world needs good mothers. The children of God need women who exercise the divine characteristics of motherhood. Just as great missionaries are not magically produced simply by attending the Missionary Training Center, so great mothers are not magically produced simply by attending the temple. Being a great mother requires a lifetime of preparation, part of which should be a good education or vocational training. My prayer is that the young women who are the mothers of tomorrow will take seriously the opportunities they have to prepare for that sacred calling today.

So often we judge each other by outward appearances and other things that do not matter eternally. The Lord sees us differently: He judges our hearts (see 1 Samuel 16:7). As we read in the Doctrine and Covenants, those who are exalted "see as they are seen, and know as they are known" (D&C 76:94). It is my earnest prayer that the young women of this Church will be able to see themselves as they are seen by God—as noble daughters with divine potential and a glorious future, trusted with the most sacred of all tasks our Heavenly Father has given to His children.

Checkpoints

- ✓ How well am I taking advantage of educational or vocational training opportunities?
- ✓ What am I doing to develop the independence and maturity I will need for the next phase of my life?
- ✓ How am I preparing to fulfill the covenant I have made to stand as a witness of God?
- ✓ What steps am I taking to keep from selling myself short when it comes to dating and marriage?

✓ How well am I counseling with the Lord in planning my life? Do I truly submit my will to His?

✓ What am I doing to prepare to enter the house of the Lord to make further covenants?

✓ Does the way I clothe my body show that I view it as a temple of God?

✓ How well do I understand the sacred nature of being a wife and a mother?

✓ What am I doing to prepare to be the best wife and mother I can be?

And Samuel grew, and the Lord was with him,
and did let none of his words fall to the ground.

1 SAMUEL 3:19

CHAPTER TWELVE

LACING UP YOUR BOOTS

A FTER YEARS OF FLIGHT training, I was assigned
a trainer by the name of Wayne Dossier, a West Point
graduate. He taught me how to wear my flight suit, how to
wear my oxygen mask, and how to wear my gravity suit. (In a jet airplane, the more tightly a pilot makes a turn, the more gravity he experiences. He can experience gravity several times greater than his natural
body weight. The gravity suit, called a G-suit, expands with air in an
effort to prevent the blood in the pilot's body from leaving the brain.)

Before I met Wayne Dossier, I had sometimes not even worn my
flight boots. I'd worn street shoes. And when I did wear my flight
boots, I did not lace them properly. I couldn't see how flight boots
had much to do with flying. But one day when I was suiting up
in the locker room to fly as Wayne Dossier's wing man, this West
Point graduate saw me putting my boots on and said, "No, this is
how you lace them up." I couldn't see why the way you laced your
boots was so important, but this instructor seemed to know what he
was talking about, so I followed his instructions. "You don't know
when you're going to come out of that airplane," he said, "and when

you do, you don't want to ruin your career because you can't walk anymore."

He was right. That day as I sat on the tarmac in my F-100 single-seater fighter, a fire-warning light came on, indicating that the plane was on fire. I had ten seconds to get out of the airplane. Following the emergency procedures I knew from my training, I managed to vault out of the cockpit to the runway about fifteen feet below. To this day the swelling in my ankles from that jump hasn't gone down completely, but the doctor said my ankles would have been absolutely shattered without the boots. Lacing up those boots tightly gave me the support I needed to save me from fracturing my ankles.

In life, how we respond to wise counsel—even if we may not understand the importance of the counsel at the time—can prepare us for life's tests and save more than just our ankles. The prophet Samuel was still a child when he first heard the voice of the Lord. But it wasn't just the fact that he heard the Lord's voice that made him a prophet; it was how he reacted to it. "And Samuel grew, and the Lord was with him, and *did let none of his words fall to the ground*" (1 Samuel 3:19; emphasis added). Samuel paid attention to all of the words of the Lord. Samuel as a prophet was now speaking for God. The surrounding verses indicate that the Lord does not let Samuel's words fall to the ground, because they are His words. Soon all Israel knows that God has established Samuel as His prophet (1 Samuel 3:20).

As youth of Zion, you have been given wise counsel by prophets, parents, and local priesthood leaders. Do you pay careful attention to that counsel, or do you let it fall to the ground because you don't understand it or think it isn't important or doesn't apply to you? What the Lord said in 1831 applies to the youth today when it comes to *For the Strength of Youth* and other prophetic counsel you have been given: "These words are given unto you, and they are pure before me; wherefore, beware how you hold them" (D&C 41:12).

Lacing up our boots, or following the counsel and standards given by those who know, is especially important for those who have entered into covenants. Why? Because Lucifer knows we are valuable to the Lord, and he wants us to fail. Isn't it interesting that those who are faithful are always sought by the adversary? That is our challenge—to ensure that we don't yield to him and his diabolical plans. We must never forget that the adversary wants to negatively influence every Church member, perhaps more than anyone else in the world.

Why do we sometimes lose our eternal perspective and ignore the standards we've been given, deciding not to lace up our spiritual boots? A survey by Embry-Riddle Aeronautical University (called "the Harvard of the air") was submitted to the Federal Aviation Administration in 1980 and published in the *Stars and Stripes* so that servicemen everywhere could learn from the results. The Embry-Riddle staff did studies on seven hundred airplane accidents involving small, private airplanes as well as large, commercial jetliners. In 95 percent of the cases, the accidents involving these aircraft had nothing to do with equipment failure or with lack of proper training and skills.

The accidents were caused by pilot error and were divided into five categories. It is useful to consider these categories as a lens for what may be happening in our own lives: invulnerability, machoism, antiauthority, impulsivity, and being out of control.

INVULNERABILITY

In the accidents that were evaluated, the pilot often thought or even said out loud, "I can do that, even though it is dangerous, and still not jeopardize the flight." Youth's way of saying that is simply, "I can do that and still not get hurt or punished." It's the equivalent of running down the football field to see how close to the sideline you can get without going out of bounds—and kicking up just a little chalk dust. Invulnerability says, "I can go to the club; I can associate with certain kinds of people; I can listen to certain kinds of music; I can read certain kinds of literature; I can go to certain kinds of movies; I can handle that."

But we can't, really. Far too many good youth have been lost because they overestimated their ability to resist sin. They say they plan to get married in the temple, but they don't think they need to follow the Church's dating standards. They say they will go on missions, but they don't think they need to follow the rules about what they should watch or read or listen to. We should all be very careful about feeling invulnerable.

Several years ago I was watching television one evening and saw a commercial for a child's cosmetics kit. There are a lot of mothers in this country and a lot of older sisters who might buy a little cosmetics kit for a six- or eight- or nine-year-old. But having a little girl put on eye makeup and lipstick and start to attract those around her, while still at an age when she literally does not know what she is doing, is asking for trouble. It's the same thing with any young lady who starts dating before the age of sixteen—she, too, is asking for trouble. There is a high correlation between early dating and immoral conduct. Dating only after age sixteen is the advice of all the prophets in my lifetime. Listen to them. They give their counsel because they care for us. They want to protect us in the same way that my trainer cared about me enough to help me—to tell me to lace up my boots. How grateful I am for good counsel!

On one occasion J. Reuben Clark Jr., who later served in the First Presidency, was giving his teenage daughter counsel about when to come home from a date. "Daddy, what is the matter? Don't you trust me?" she complained. "No, my darling, I don't trust you. I don't even trust myself," he replied.[1] When we believe we are invulnerable to the temptations of the adversary, we are actually at greatest risk.

Once one of my teenaged grandsons was telling me about a movie that he thought I would really enjoy, although he said there were some parts that I might have to block out. "I'd love to see that movie," I replied, "but I don't think I'm old enough." He was puzzled until his grandmother explained to him what I meant. "I get it now, Grandpa," he said. "You are never going to be old enough to see that movie, are you?" If the content isn't appropriate for teen-agers, it isn't appropriate for adults.

MACHOISM

Sometimes pilots who get into accidents say such things as, "This is going to make a bigger guy of me; this will help me establish my-self as better than others." The Embry-Riddle researchers told about a pilot who buzzed a pickup truck. The second time, he hit the truck and wiped out both his airplane and the truck. Fortunately, no lives were lost in this particular accident, but the question was asked, "What would make a guy do something like this?" Machoism leads pilots and youth to take foolish risks because they think that doing so will make a bigger person out of them in the eyes of their peers or themselves. That's not too smart, Embry-Riddle says, because macho pilots end up losing their lives. We had a saying when I flew: "There are old pilots and bold pilots, but not old, bold pilots."

Macho pilots may lose their physical lives, but if we are macho, we may end up losing our spiritual lives. The street gangs that are so prevalent today are based on machoism. In the mentality of the gang, one has to be tough to be accepted or to impress a significant other. The gang becomes family to each member. In a gang-type

---

1. Quoted in Harold B. Lee, *The Teachings of Harold B. Lee,* ed. Clyde J. Williams (Salt Lake City: Bookcraft, 1996), 629–30.

crowd, group psychology perpetuates itself, and gang members end up doing things they later regret and never would have done alone. Because of the gang culture, gang members think that doing negative things rather than positive things will make them feel "big" and important. But these momentary feelings of self-importance are quickly replaced by regret and feelings of self-doubt and poor self-esteem. Often underneath the macho exterior is fear and immaturity. We must be careful of the macho image—that which makes us feel like a bigger person because we are able to challenge authority.

ANTIAUTHORITY

The third reason many pilots crashed is that they rebelled against authority—they didn't follow the proper flight plans, they didn't learn the proper procedures, and they didn't follow orders. This is a trait, Embry-Riddle said, found in people who hate being told what to do.

I submit that it is a trait found in people who haven't grown up. Some youth may think, Wouldn't it be nice not to be told what to do? Wouldn't it be nice to be the President of the Church and not be told what to do? Think about that one for a minute. The prophet is not free to do whatever he wants because it is not his church. It is the Savior's church; He is the one who directs the prophet. Even the prophet obeys a higher authority.

In this regard, I learned a great lesson as a young man. My father was from Idaho and was brought up on a sugar beet farm. He told me I could never learn how to work if I grew up in New York. So he sent me out to Utah to work on a ranch in Skull Valley. I worked with my uncle and cousin, and I also learned a great deal about the gospel. I found that there were thousands and thousands of acres for the cattle to graze in, but all the cattle would come up to the fence and put their heads through it.

Why on earth did they go up to the fence and stick their heads through, I wondered? As a boy from New York I could not understand it. I asked, "Uncle Frank, these cows have got all those acres out there. Why do they push against the fence?"

That is often the way it is with us and the gospel of Jesus Christ. By living the principles of the gospel we have so much opportunity for learning, growth, and joy. We can laugh and enjoy life. Yet some of us push against the fence. We try to find the hole in the south forty. Then, when we find it, we romp out into the unfenced open and say, "Look at us! We're free! No restrictions!" But soon we're out on Highway 90, get hit by a semi-truck, and wonder what happened. We likely blame someone else, as those poor cattle would blame the farmer for not keeping the fence mended.

While this example may seem humorous to some and harsh to others, we should acknowledge that most of the time it is not total disobedience—it is not completely breaking through the fence and leaving the pasture—that gets us into trouble. It is, rather, selective obedience. We may recognize what we must do to be obedient, yet we selectively do only part of what we are commanded to do. We pick and choose the commandments we'll obey.

The Bible gives us a marvelous lesson in the story of Samuel and Saul. Under the direction of the Lord, Saul had been set apart by the prophet Samuel to become king of the Israelites. Saul had been a choice young man. The scriptures say, "There was not among the children of Israel a goodlier person than he" (1 Samuel 9:2). But eventually he decided to practice selective obedience by obeying only some of the commandments.

Before one battle, Samuel told Saul that the Lord commanded him to utterly destroy the Amalekites—animals and all. Saul's army was made up of more than two hundred thousand "footmen" (1 Samuel 15:4). After their victory, Saul and his army brought back the best of the animals for themselves. Saul reported to Samuel, "I have performed the commandment of the Lord" (1 Samuel 15:13).

Samuel replied, "What meaneth then this bleating of the sheep in mine ears, and the lowing of the oxen which I hear?" (1 Samuel 15:14).

Saul claimed that he had obeyed and blamed the disobedience on the people: "Yea, I have obeyed the voice of the Lord. . . . But the people took of the spoil, sheep and oxen, the chief of the things which should have been utterly destroyed, to sacrifice unto the Lord thy God in Gilgal" (1 Samuel 15:20–21). Saul had practiced selective obedience and blamed his disobedience—as we too often do—on others.

"And Samuel said, Hath the Lord as great delight in burnt offerings and sacrifices, as in obeying the voice of the Lord? Behold, to obey is better than sacrifice. . . .

" . . . Because thou hast rejected the word of the Lord, he hath also rejected thee from being king.

"And Saul said unto Samuel, I have sinned: for I have transgressed the commandment of the Lord, and thy words: because I feared the people, and obeyed their voice" (1 Samuel 15:22–24).

This, then, is the key to the story of Samuel and Saul and the principle of obedience to divinely directed authority: Our allegiance to the Lord and His prophets must be greater than our desire to be accepted of men.

In 2 Nephi we are taught: "Yea, and there shall be many which shall say: Eat, drink, and be merry, for tomorrow we die; and it shall be well with us.

"And there shall also be many which shall say: Eat, drink, and be merry; nevertheless, fear God—he will justify in committing a little sin; yea, lie a little, take the advantage of one because of his words, dig a pit for thy neighbor; there is no harm in this; and do all these things, for tomorrow we die; and if it so be that we are guilty,

God will beat us with a few stripes, and at last we shall be saved in the kingdom of God" (2 Nephi 28:7–8).

The adversary would like us to think that no matter what our conduct, we will return to heaven. He promotes the lie taught by the anti-Christ Nehor: "All mankind should be saved at the last day, and . . . they need not fear nor tremble, . . . for the Lord had created all men, and had also redeemed all men; and, in the end, all men should have eternal life" (Alma 1:4). This is the deception of the world. As the Lord has taught us, wickedness—even a little wickedness—never was happiness (see Alma 41:10). And it never will be. Wickedness prevents us from returning with honor to our Father in Heaven.

IMPULSIVITY

In the Embry-Riddle study of pilots, the fourth reason for accidents had to do with acting without self-control or careful thinking. Think of someone who, upon impulse, decides to go swimming and, in the middle of his beautiful swan dive, realizes there is not enough water in the pool.

When we make serious mistakes, it is often because we act impulsively, without thinking our actions through. Shoplifting is usually done on impulse. So are lying, cheating, stealing, and many other sins. I wonder if some of our youth dress impulsively, without considering why they are dressing as they do.

After finding ourselves in trouble from our impulsive actions, we can easily compound the error by trying to cover them up. A mark of maturity is knowing when to ask for help and then doing so, using the advice to humbly correct our mistake.

My best advice for avoiding impulsivity is to ask ourselves the question, What could happen if I take this action? For example, if I wear this low-cut blouse, who will be attracted to me? What are their standards? How will they treat me? Or if I cheat on this test, what will happen when my teachers and parents find out? When we consider the possible consequences of our conduct before acting, we generally avoid the kind of mistakes that bring pain, grief, and sorrow to our lives.

Being Out of Control

The final cause of airplane crashes in the study was being out of control. In jet fighter pilot training, when the pilot could no longer control the airplane's maneuvering in terms of speed, turning radius, and landing, we said he was out of control. When we fail to be able or willing to curb or manage our physical appetites, we too get out of control.

Many times our lives get ahead of us in other ways, too. In our youth, especially, our lives move very fast, which tends to blur our judgment. We see this most clearly when members of the Church succumb to addictions, such as to drugs, alcohol, tobacco, pornography, computer games, and so forth. Standards help us avoid addictions, retain our agency, and keep things in control, just as the procedures of an aircraft and the rules of navigation help a pilot keep control of his or her plane.

Vertigo

As a fighter pilot, I learned about another danger not on the Embry-Riddle list: vertigo, in which a pilot becomes positionally disoriented in relation to the horizon because the equalizing fluid in his or her ears has been disrupted. While I was a jet fighter pilot, my instructor took me up in a simulation of weather conditions in which we had no reference to the horizon and would therefore have to rely totally on our instruments. Underneath a cloth covering inside the canopy, I was forced to fly solely by instruments, for I could not see outside the plane and had no outside frame of reference. As we flew, the trainer then turned us over very gradually until we were upside down. Then he gave me control of the airplane. Of course, I did what every other student did: I pulled backwards because I was losing altitude and I started diving toward the earth because I was upside down. Then I glanced at my attitude indicator—isn't that a marvelous name for a tool that tells you if you are on the straight and level, much like the Holy Ghost? As I started to pull back on the stick, I could see the little marks of the landing gear were upside down. The instructor was letting me learn an important principle of flying and a fundamental principle of life. It is, simply, if you turn over two or three degrees at a time, it's hard to tell you've changed position. If you keep turning slowly, in time you will be completely upside down and never know it.

If we are not careful, we can also experience spiritual vertigo. If we stray off course by only two or three degrees at a time, we can become disoriented and lose sight of our eternal destination, never realizing how far off course we are. In the Book of Mormon, we read that "Amalickiah caused that one of his servants should administer poison by degrees to Lehonti, that he died" (Alma 47:18). Similarly, the adversary often tries to lead us off the strait and narrow path by degrees. Often when young people come into my office, they say, "I can't really believe that I did what I did. I just was in darkness and didn't understand." But they usually didn't get there in a single step. Instead, it was one degree at a time.

There is a beautiful story about a melodious little bird that sang from the high branches and flew gracefully among the trees. This captured the heart of a man who sold worms for a living. One day, the melodious bird wanted some worms for herself, so she took a few inconspicuous feathers from under her wing to purchase them. As time went on, the bird ran out of inconspicuous feathers and had to remove a key pinfeather to support her habit for worms. Without her pinfeather, however, she could no longer fly and therefore had no desire to sing. Disappointed that the once melodious bird had lost her voice, the man left and took his worms away.

Do we give away our morality one inconspicuous feather at a time and thus lose that which once made us useful and appealing to others? If so, it is helpful to remember the high cost of sinning by degrees. What we suffer, as a result, inevitably consumes us unless we are willing to humbly and sincerely repent.

Spiritual vertigo, brought about by degrees, is not just a problem for individuals. It is also a problem for entire societies. Fifty years ago, there seemed to be a very short distance between where the world was and where Church standards were. In those days we may have had a tendency to compare ourselves with the world and take satisfaction that our standards were just a little higher. Many did not fully realize how fast the world's standards were actually changing. Today, we know it is not enough to be just a little better than the world, for the world has become measurably less sensitive to the things of God. As members of The Church of Jesus Christ of Latter-day Saints, our principles must remain constant, for God is the same "yesterday, today, and forever" (D&C 20:12).

All or Nothing

When I was in pilot training, all the members of my squadron were given the simple and clear instruction: "Don't fly acrobatic patterns at night. You are beginning pilots without instrument flight training." Some time later, an otherwise good pilot and a great friend chose to disobey that command. As he flew loops and barrel rolls through the night sky over Texas, he looked through the cockpit canopy and thought he saw stars above him, but really he was seeing the lights of oil rigs below. As he pulled up on the stick to climb higher into the night sky, he dived toward the earth and crashed into the twinkling lights of the oil field below.

So it is when we practice selective obedience. As we change our position relative to the Lord, the deceptive forces of the adversary work on us, and we begin to experience spiritual vertigo. While it may *seem* like we are going in a safe direction, we are in fact headed for disaster.

In our premortal life, our decision to follow the Lord was all or nothing. We "let none of his words"—none of His plan for the salvation of our souls—"fall to the ground" (1 Samuel 3:19). There was no thought of selective obedience or resistance to authority. Rather, we shouted for joy at the prospect of coming to earth and laced up our boots for the glorious opportunity to receive a body, learn the lessons of mortality, and become like our Heavenly Father. I testify that giving our whole heart to following the Savior now, just as we did before our birth, is the way to complete our mortal journey home and return to Him with honor.

CHECKPOINTS

✓ How carefully do I follow prophetic counsel? Do I let God's words fall to the ground?

✓ How well do I lace up my boots when it comes to living the gospel?

✓ Do I ignore standards because I feel invulnerable?

✓ Do I take foolish risks to look macho?

✓ Am I pushing against the fences?

✓ Do I act impulsively, without considering the consequences?

✓ Am I getting spiritual vertigo? Where am I on my attitude indicator?

✓ Am I true to my standards without flaunting them?

Ye must watch and pray always lest ye
enter into temptation; for Satan desireth to have you,
that he may sift you as wheat.

3 Nephi 18:18

CHAPTER THIRTEEN

OVERCOMING THE ADVERSARY

AS A YOUNG MAN, I HAD the opportunity to work summers on a ranch with my wise Uncle Frank Hatch, who taught me an important lesson about shepherding. He described to me how lambs are enticed and led away from the safety of their mothers' sides and from the flock that loves and cares for them.

Some cunning coyotes appear to play near the flock—running, frolicking, tumbling. Their playfulness looks inviting to the lambs. Soon the lambs find themselves enticed to wander from the protective environment of the flock and their mothers' nurturing sides. In their innocence, they don't realize that the coyotes are actually hunting, looking for a weak lamb or one that has strayed. When the time is right, they swiftly attack, cutting the wayward lamb off from the flock, ultimately killing and devouring it.

This is also Satan's way. In the book of Job the Lord asked the devil where he had been. Satan answered, "Going to and fro in the earth" (Job 1:7).

We should never forget that. Like a coyote tracking the lambs' every move, the adversary follows us each day. As the scriptures say, he lies at our door (see Genesis 4:7; Moses 5:23), waiting for the right moment to snatch us. "Be sober, be vigilant; because your adversary the devil, as a roaring lion, walketh about, seeking whom he may devour" (1 Peter 5:8). He entices us with what seem to be "good times." If we heed his enticements, we become entrapped. And if we are not rescued and brought back to the flock, we find ourselves cut off—not able to go to the temple, to make and keep our covenants, and to receive the ordinances that are necessary for us to come back into the presence of God the Father and His Son, Jesus Christ.

The Adversary Is Real

I do not wish to dwell on the adversary more than necessary, but it is important that we understand our enemy. Lucifer was one of Heavenly Father's most brilliant spirit sons. Lehi taught that "an angel of God . . . had fallen from heaven; wherefore, he became a devil, having sought that which was evil before God.

"And because he had fallen from heaven, and had become miserable forever, he sought also the misery of all mankind" (2 Nephi 2:17–18).

When Lucifer rejected Heavenly Father's plan, he wanted to deny us our agency. He claimed he would "redeem all mankind," but he wanted to do so in a way that "sought to destroy the agency of man" (Moses 4:1, 3). He was vain and selfish. He wanted for himself all the honor and glory of Heavenly Father's plan. The Savior was willing to execute the Father's plan with exactness; Lucifer rebelled. Because of his rebellion, he and the one-third of Heavenly Father's spirit children who chose to follow him were cast out of heaven. Lucifer, whose name means the "Shining One," or

"Son of the Morning," was told that he would now be known as Satan, or the devil.[1]

Since then, Satan and his followers have been permitted to come to earth to tempt and try us—to make every effort to influence us to do wrong. None of them has a mortal body, and they are jealous of ours. Just as Heavenly Father and Jesus Christ will do everything in Their power to help us return to Their presence, Satan and his followers will do everything in their power to keep us from returning home and achieving eternal life.

Satan Targets Us

As the adversary targeted the Savior and Peter, so he also targets us. What the Savior taught Peter applies to each one of us: "Satan hath desired to have you, that he may sift you as wheat" (Luke 22:31). More than anyone else, the adversary wants to "have" the faithful. He accomplishes this by luring us away from all that is good—by sifting us as the kernel of wheat is sifted from the stalk on which it has grown. When he lures us away, he deprives our family, friends, and acquaintances of any positive influence we may have on them. He also deprives our posterity that will come after us, whose lives would have been better if we had remained faithful. By "having" us, Satan is able to achieve his greatest desire—to thwart the work of God.

Can you see how great the scope of our adversary's rebellion is and how terrible the consequences? He has more than a passing interest in tempting us; he is committed to our destruction and that of our families, generation upon generation. This is why he works so hard to get us to fail at keeping the covenants we have made to

1. LDS Bible Dictionary, s.v. "Lucifer," 726.

our Heavenly Father at baptism and in the temple. Our failure to be faithful is his great success.

Battling for Our Souls

Young people today live in a world full of choices that older generations did not have. Some of these choices are inspired by the Light of Christ and lead us closer to Him, and others plunge us into the darkness of the adversary. Every time we go out into the world, with every private and public decision we make, we either move closer to the Savior or closer to the adversary.

This is because Satan and his followers are in competition with Heavenly Father and Jesus Christ for us. They are literally battling for our souls. In this battle, winning the loyalty of our spirits and bodies is worth everything to them. Evil spirits do not have bodies, and they desire to influence and possess our bodies. Only by choosing the light and drawing closer to Heavenly Father do we become His, and only when we are His can we return to His presence. I hope we understand that. There is nothing, literally nothing, that is worth failing in our mission to live the gospel and return to the presence of our Father. A few moments or hours of pleasure, the fleeting satisfaction of feeding a carnal obsession with the vain things of this world—none of these things are worth losing our eternal reward.

Satan Laughs

Heavenly Father commanded his children "that they should choose me, their Father," but "Cain loved Satan more than God" (Moses 7:33; 5:18). When we love Satan more than God, it pleases Satan and grieves God (see Moses 5:21; 7:31–33).

I once had an opportunity to accompany President Spencer W.

Kimball to a distant land. We were given a tour of the various sites in the area, including underground catacombs—burial grounds for people who had been persecuted by so-called Christian zealots. As we walked up the dark, narrow stairs of that place, President Kimball taught me an unforgettable lesson. He pulled my coattail and said, "It has always troubled me what the adversary does using the name of our Savior." He then said, "Robert, the adversary can never have joy unless you and I sin."

As I contemplated this comment and studied the scriptures, I began to understand what President Kimball may have meant. I can almost hear the anguish in the voice of the Lord as He cries out to all the inhabitants of the earth as recorded in the Book of Mormon: "Wo, wo, wo unto this people; wo unto the inhabitants of the whole earth except they shall repent; for the devil laugheth, and his angels rejoice, because of the slain of the fair sons and daughters of my people" (3 Nephi 9:2).

When we sin, we may foolishly agree with Cain, who gloried in his sin and declared, "I am free" (Moses 5:33). In reality, when we sin we become captive to the devil, whom Enoch saw in vision: "And he beheld Satan; and he had a great chain in his hand, and it veiled the whole face of the earth with darkness; and he looked up and laughed, and his angels rejoiced" (Moses 7:26). It is our sins that make the devil laugh, our sorrow that pleases him and gives him counterfeit joy.

This is the false and fleeting joy of the coyotes cavorting in the distance and the mirage of happiness that lures the vulnerable lamb. When we look at those who are living in sin and imagine that their laughter means they are truly happy and free, we should remember that the devil also laughs, and all that follow him rejoice in our destruction.

A Frenzied Attack

Some think that Satan is passively waiting for us to seek him out and find him, but the scriptures teach otherwise. Satan is described by the prophets as one who "goeth up and down, to and fro in the earth, *seeking* to destroy the souls of men" (D&C 10:27; emphasis added). They also teach that Satan's evil designs upon the peoples of the earth will intensify as the Second Coming of our Lord and Savior Jesus Christ draws near at hand (see 2 Thessalonians 2:1–10; D&C 10:33; 52:14; 86:3–10).

How does the adversary make this attack? We are bombarded with messages from the media that evil is good—that immorality, drinking alcohol, and doing drugs are normal and relatively harmless. The message is, Everybody does it; the implied message is, If you want to be included by everybody and be happy, you'd better do it too. Using such tools as television and the Internet (tools that might otherwise be helpful), he can draw even the faithful into gambling or pornography. In fact, enticing messages sometimes unexpectedly pop up on our computer monitors. With an explosion of these messages in virtually every dimension of our lives, the adversary is able to make a truly frenzied attack. "And thus [Satan] . . . leadeth them along until he draggeth their souls down to hell" (D&C 10:26).

This attack is infinitely more successful when the adversary gets us to believe, as the old commercial said, "You only go around once in life, so grab for all the gusto you can." That worldly philosophy is stated more clearly in the scriptures: "Eat, drink, and be merry, for tomorrow we die" (2 Nephi 28:7). If the adversary can persuade us that there is nothing after this life to live for, he succeeds in getting us to live his way—for the moment, without regard for our eternal blessings. With this in mind, we can see why the message of the

First Presidency and the Quorum of the Twelve Apostles has been to remind us who we are and what we can become. Heavenly Father and His chosen servants want every parent, bishop, and priesthood and auxiliary leader—every shepherd of the Lord's flock—to teach that what happens in this life matters not only now but in the eternities to come.

KNOWING OUR WEAKNESSES

Because the battle for our souls is real, we must anticipate how the adversary will test us. None of us is immune to his clever, perfectly tailored temptations. The hero of Homer's *Iliad*, Achilles, had a mother, Thetis, who dipped Achilles in the waters of the River Styx so that he became invulnerable. Thetis was successful, as the story goes, except for that part of her son's heel by which she had held him. That was his *Achilles' heel.* There he was unprotected.

We are all vulnerable. We all have a proverbial Achilles' heel, and the adversary knows what it is. He also knows the Achilles' heels of our loved ones, our friends, our roommates, our brothers and sisters, and our parents. He tries to use all of our weaknesses to his own advantage.

Do we know what our Achilles' heel is and what we have to protect ourselves from? Do we know what our weaknesses are and the situations we must avoid? Captain Moroni wisely shored up his weakest cities first (see Alma 49:14–15). We, too, can better defend ourselves against the adversary when we recognize our greatest weaknesses and shore ourselves up where we are most vulnerable.

PROTECTING OURSELVES

If we are prepared, the fury of the adversary will not be fatal. In fact, the Lord has told us that "if [we] are prepared [we] shall not fear" (D&C 38:30). How can we prepare ourselves so that we have no need to fear? Every mother would love to dip her children into the waters of the River Styx and give them protection. What can we do to protect ourselves?

While we know we will be tested by the adversary, we don't have to make his job easier by willingly inviting him into our presence. The closer we place ourselves to evil, the more likely we are to participate in it. After Jesus went into the wilderness and fasted for forty days, Satan came to tempt Him with the same things he uses to tempt us: wealth, power, and worldly passions. Jesus told him to get behind Him and tempt Him no more (see Matthew 4:1–11). By our actions, we either invite Satan to stand squarely in front of us or to get behind us.

For example, at times in our lives we may believe we can go into a bar and not drink at all, because we feel so strong. Or perhaps we think we can handle "just one" drink. But how do we know that by taking that one first drink we won't become an alcoholic? How can we know that when we take drugs, tobacco, and so on, or look at a first pornographic image, we won't become addicted to these terrible vices? How can we think we can be promiscuous and not pay the price of alienation from the Spirit, loss of self-esteem, sexually transmitted diseases, or out-of-wedlock pregnancy?

The same care we would exercise in avoiding substance abuse and sexual misconduct applies generally in our relationships with the opposite gender. How we conduct ourselves in dating relationships is a good indication of how we will conduct ourselves in a marriage relationship. To avoid tragedy, we must treat those we date with honor and respect. The thirteenth Article of Faith states: "We believe in being honest, true, chaste, benevolent, virtuous, and in doing good to all men. . . . If there is anything virtuous, lovely, or of good report or praiseworthy, we seek after these things." Is our music lovely and praiseworthy? Are our friends, our speech, our books and magazines, our television and Internet habits of good report? Or are we using our agency to place ourselves within the adversary's sphere of influence?

In all our life's activities, we need the fortification of the Holy Ghost. Through Him we are able to put on the whole armor of God and overcome the influence of the world in our individual lives and our families. Mothers and fathers should prayerfully invite the Holy Spirit to dwell in their dedicated homes. Having the gift of the Holy Ghost helps family members make wise choices—choices that will help them return to their Father in Heaven and His Son, Jesus Christ, to live with Them eternally.

Our temple covenants are also a source of protection and strength. There is no way for the adversary to reside in the temple. He does not have a temple recommend! The Light of the World resides there, making it impossible for the prince of darkness to enter. When we are in the temple, we can truly be in the world and not of the world. There we can be protected from all that is worldly.

Joseph Smith knew that the Saints needed to have the strength of the temple—to be endowed with power from on high in their great trek west. As he rode out of Nauvoo for the last time, on his way to Carthage, he taught a marvelous truth. He knew he was going to his death, "like a lamb to the slaughter" (D&C 135:4). But he was not thinking about death as much as about eternal life. At that time, the walls of the Nauvoo Temple were built up only about four feet from the ground. As Joseph crested the hill where the temple was being constructed, he paused. Perhaps he could see in vision the completed edifice, its walls rising high into the air. What he did see on that beautiful morning was the "City Beautiful," filled with Latter-day Saints striving to live the gospel. With that sight before him, he declared, "This is the loveliest place, and the best people under the heavens." Then he added these important words: "Little do they know the trials that await them!"[2]

It is significant that such great people as those who lived in Nauvoo would also be greatly tried. Though Joseph Smith was a prophet, he was not given to tell them exactly what was ahead of them; however, he knew what they needed in order to make their journey successfully, as recounted by Sarah Rich:

"Many were the blessings we had received in the House of the Lord, which has caused joy and comfort in the midst of all of our sorrows, and enabled us to have faith in God, knowing He would guide us and sustain us in the unknown journey that lay before us. For if it had not been for the faith and knowledge that was bestowed upon us in that temple by the influence and help of the Spirit of the Lord, our journey would have been like one taking a leap in the dark, to start out on such a journey in the winter as it were, and in our state of poverty, it would seem like walking into the jaws of death. But we had faith in our Heavenly Father, and we put our trust in Him, feeling that we were His chosen people and had embraced His Gospel; and instead of sorrow we felt to rejoice that the day of our deliverance had come."[3] The journals of my own great-grandparents who received the endowment about that same time record similar feelings.

The strength that Sarah Rich and others received was a fulfillment of the dedicatory prayer Joseph Smith gave for the Kirtland Temple: "We ask thee, Holy Father, that thy servants may go forth from this house armed with thy power, and that thy name may be

2. B. H. Roberts, *A Comprehensive History of the Church of Jesus Christ of Latter-day Saints, Century One* (Salt Lake City: The Church of Jesus Christ of Latter-day Saints, 1930), 2:248; spelling modernized.

3. Sarah De Armon Pea Rich, "Journal of Sarah De Armon Pea Rich," typescript, 1960, Provo, Utah, Brigham Young University Library, Americana Collection, 42–43; spelling and grammar modernized.

upon them, and thy glory be round about them, and thine angels have charge over them" (D&C 109:22). Being endowed with power meant that the early Saints had the ability to call upon the power of heaven in those circumstances where spiritual guidance and strength would be needed.

Today, as we go through our trek in life, we need that same endowment of power. Just as the early Saints faced hardships, angry mobs, being driven from their comfortable homes in Nauvoo, and an arduous journey, we face genuinely challenging circumstances ourselves. We also know of the dramatic changes in our culture as the Second Coming approaches and of the difficulties of being faithful in a world where the adversary reigns. In our journey back to our Heavenly Father, we need the power of temple covenants and worship—not only for ourselves but for our families.

CALLING UPON GOD

With our temple blessings, we are prepared to face the inevitable temptations of the adversary. How do we do this? We learn an important lesson from Moses' encounter with Satan. Shortly after Moses saw God in a vision, "Satan came tempting him, saying: Moses, son of man, worship me" (Moses 1:12).

Moses remembered who he was and knew how to discern between light and dark, which helped give him the strength and wisdom to resist Satan's temptations. "Who art thou? For behold, I am a son of God, in the similitude of his Only Begotten; and where is thy glory, that I should worship thee . . . , for it is darkness unto me?" (Moses 1:13–15).

Declaring his total allegiance to God, Moses commanded, "Get thee hence, Satan; deceive me not." Apparently Satan did not immediately obey, because Moses had to repeat his charge: "Depart hence, Satan" (Moses 1:16, 18).

Even then, Satan did not go away easily. He never does. Because he is persistent in tempting us, we must be persistent in resisting him.

Satan then "cried with a loud voice, and ranted upon the earth, and commanded, saying: I am the Only Begotten, worship me" (Moses 1:19).

It should tell us something about what a formidable foe Satan is when we read that "Moses began to fear exceedingly; and as he began to fear, he saw the bitterness of hell." But Moses did not give in to his fears. Instead, "*calling upon God,* he received strength" (Moses 1:20; emphasis added).

Only with God's help can we truly conquer the adversary. We need the power of prayer to protect us from Satan's temptations. The Savior taught those gathered in the land of Bountiful:

"Behold, verily, verily, I say unto you, ye must watch and pray always lest ye enter into temptation. . . .

"Therefore ye must always pray unto the Father in my name. . . .

"Pray in your families unto the Father, always in my name, that your wives and your children may be blessed" (3 Nephi 18:18–21).

In our day, the Lord has again emphasized the need for constant prayer if we are to prevail in our battles against the adversary: "Pray always, that you may come off conqueror; yea, that you may conquer Satan, and that you may escape the hands of the servants of Satan that do uphold his work" (D&C 10:5). By calling on the Lord daily, we develop confidence in the Lord to help us resist the temptations of the adversary and "come off conqueror."

IN THE NAME OF JESUS CHRIST

Moses took one more critical step in casting the devil out of his life. After calling on God and receiving strength, he commanded Satan to depart for the fourth and final time but with one important addition: "In the name of the Only Begotten, depart hence, Satan" (Moses 1:21). Only when Moses invoked the name of the Savior did Satan finally depart from his presence.

We invoke the name of the Savior in our lives when we take His name upon us and live so that we always have His Spirit to be with us. Only when we rely "wholly upon the merits of him who is mighty to save" (2 Nephi 31:19) can we ever completely conquer Satan. Only with faith in Christ—with the shield of faith—can we avoid the fiery darts of the adversary.

The Power Is in Us

We read that Satan came among the posterity of Adam and Eve, saying, "I am also a son of God; and he commanded them, saying: Believe it not; and they believed it not, and they loved Satan more than God. And men began from that time forth to be carnal, sensual, and devilish" (Moses 5:13). We must remember that this scripture recounts a lie that Satan wants us all to believe: "And [Satan] commanded them." We must teach our children that Satan cannot command us to do anything. When we follow the Savior's example and command Satan to depart, he must leave us: "Then saith Jesus unto him, Get thee hence, Satan: for it is written, Thou shalt worship the Lord thy God, and him only shalt thou serve. Then the devil leaveth him, and, behold, angels came and ministered unto him" (Matthew 4:10–11). Whenever we choose the Lord over Satan, God strengthens us so that we can conquer Satan.

As a second witness of this principle, Paul taught, "There hath no temptation taken you but such as is common to man: but God is faithful, who will not suffer you to be tempted above that ye are able; but will with the temptation also make a way to escape, that ye may be able to bear it" (1 Corinthians 10:13). Some may remember the old adage: "The devil made me do it." Again, the adversary cannot make us do anything. He cannot influence us unless we allow him to do so, and he knows that! The only time he can affect our minds and bodies—our very spirits—is when we *allow* him to do so. And we make this allowance whenever we turn off the light of God through our disobedience and sin. Without that light, the darkness of the adversary inevitably comes in.

How then do we turn the light back on when darkness approaches? The next two verses in Moses 5 are a key:

"And the Lord God called upon men by the Holy Ghost everywhere and commanded them that they should repent;

"And as many as believed in the Son, and repented of their sins, should be saved; and as many as believed not and repented not, should be damned; and the words went forth out of the mouth of God in a firm decree; wherefore they must be fulfilled" (Moses 5:14–15).

We have been given agency, we have been given the blessings of the priesthood, and we have been given the Light of Christ and the Holy Ghost for a reason. We have the power to choose whether to love God more than Satan and the pleasures of this world. As Lehi taught, we are "free to choose liberty and eternal life, through the great Mediator of all men, or to choose captivity and death, according to the captivity and power of the devil; for he seeketh that all men might be miserable like unto himself" (2 Nephi 2:27). We choose the light and welcome it in by repenting and returning to the path of obedience.

NEVER GIVE UP

Staying on the path means being watchful—being on guard for situations in which we may become weak and vulnerable. For example, when something disappointing, difficult, or even tragic happens in our lives, do we lose confidence in the Lord and try to console ourselves by turning (or returning) to sin? If so, we learn by sad experience that after we have transgressed, the light of Christ leaves us. We lose the influence of the Holy Ghost. We are cast into darkness, becoming utterly lonely and depressed. We don't recognize that Satan is influencing us. We can't see the truth of God's love. We are right where the adversary wants us—off the strait and narrow path, "wandering in strange roads" (1 Nephi 8:32), and without any hope of finding happiness and peace again if we do not turn around, repent, and return to Him.

At such times, Satan deliberately tempts us to retreat to the sanctuary of our private thoughts and chambers. Such retreat ultimately puts us further under his darkening influence, leading us to despondency, frustration, and feelings of worthlessness. When this happens, we are susceptible to people who further weaken us. Their influence is like corrosion on a radio's delicate contact points, rendering our spiritual receiving antennas and transmitters nearly useless.

Soon we are living as a spiritual hermit. A hermit is one who suffers from extreme selfishness: All of the gifts and talents he has been given to help others are neutralized, for he is following the adversary's way of living entirely for self. Satan wants us to follow him into this kind of withdrawal, where we truly believe we cannot come back into the circle of the Lord's love. To everyone, everywhere, I testify that we can. With the Savior's help, we can always come back.

OUT OF SATAN'S GRASP AND BACK ON THE PATH

By calling upon the Lord for strength, and invoking the name of the Savior in our lives by obedience to His commandments, we get on the Lord's path. Then we are "free to choose" again (2 Nephi 2:27)—to choose to reject feelings of shame for sins for which we have already repented, to refuse to be discouraged about the past, and to rejoice in hope for the future. As Alma taught his son

Corianton, "Only let your sins trouble you, with that trouble which shall bring you down unto repentance" (Alma 42:29). Remember, it is Satan who desires that we be "miserable like unto himself" (2 Nephi 2:27). Our desires for good and for happiness must be stronger than his desires for evil and misery. Choose to be happy and confident about life and about the opportunities and blessings that await us here and throughout eternity.

As we make that choice, we will find ourselves filled with God's love for us. We will also discover that our hearts are drawn out in mercy and forbearance toward others. Our joy will increase as we resist the temptation to judge those who have strayed and unceasingly love them and reach out to them. When we bring others back to the fold of God, we also find ourselves in the safety of His flock and the comfort of His arms. There we experience the reality that Jesus truly can heal us all as none other can.

Now and Always

As Latter-day Saints living in the last days before the Second Coming, we know that Lucifer is going to "rage in the hearts of the children of men" (2 Nephi 28:20). Just as John prophesied, in this last dispensation of the fulness of times, "the devil is come down unto you, having great wrath, because he knoweth that he hath but a short time" (Revelation 12:12). He is working with a sense of urgency. With our own sense of urgency, we must protect ourselves now and always if we are to win the war against the adversary.

As difficult as it may be for us to stay pure and worthy in the first two decades of our lives, it can be even more challenging for us and our families to defend ourselves against the buffetings of Satan as the years go on. I pray that the youth of the Church will hearken and hold fast to the word of God and not be overpowered by the fiery darts of the adversary and led away to destruction (see 1 Nephi

15:24). I pray, especially, that their parents and leaders—the shepherds God has provided them—will watch over them and help them avoid the coyotes who seem to play, even as they cunningly entice us to destruction. May all of us heed the call of prophets, ancient and modern, to come to the Lord's house, make and keep sacred covenants, and receive a fulness of joy, happiness, safety, and peace. It was the true and faithful in 3 Nephi who greeted the Savior when he came to the temple. May we be ready to greet Him when He comes again in these latter days.

CHECKPOINTS

✓ How vigilant am I in recognizing that the adversary has targeted me?

✓ What is my Achilles' heel? Do I take steps to shore up my weaknesses?

✓ Do I really believe that I have the power to command Satan to depart from my life?

✓ What do I do to continually fortify myself with the help of the Holy Ghost?

✓ Do I seek refuge in the temple from the adversary's influence?

✓ Do I call upon God and exercise faith in the Savior to conquer the adversary?

✓ How well do I learn from my mistakes?

✓ When I slip up, do I wallow in loneliness and despair, or do I return to the strait and narrow path and leave my sins behind?

PART 2

DECADE OF DECISION

Multitudes, multitudes in the valley of decision:
for the day of the Lord is near in the valley of decision.

JOEL 3:14

DECADE OF DECISION

Preparation for our decade of decision began in our premortal life when we exercised our agency to come to earth and experience mortality. Our first decade in mortality was a great learning experience. We were cared for and nurtured. We learned to walk and talk and control our mortal bodies. We learned, once again, that agency allows us to experience the blessings and consequences of our choices. The second decade of our lives was a preparatory period—the time in which we prepared to make the momentous decisions ahead.

Now that we have two decades of mortal preparation behind us, we enter perhaps the most influential decade ever: the *Decade of Decision.* In the coming ten years, we will lay the foundation for the rest of our lives, including decisions about whether to enter the Lord's house and make sacred covenants; whether to serve Him as a full-time missionary; whom to marry, where to marry, and the nature of the family we will raise; what gifts and talents to cultivate; where and what kind of education to obtain; and what occupation to prepare for and pursue.

The adversary will seek to distract us from making these decisions well, and sometimes he will attain his goal simply by persuading us to put off making important decisions entirely. Yet these decisions will determine who we are and what we will become, and now is the time to make them. "To every thing there is a season, and a time to every purpose under the heaven" (Ecclesiastes 3:1).

*This life is the time for men to prepare
to meet God; yea, behold the day of this life is the day for
men to perform their labors. . . . This day of life . . . is
given us to prepare for eternity.*

ALMA 34:32–33

CHAPTER FOURTEEN

MAKING LIFE'S MOST IMPORTANT DECISIONS

W HEN I WAS FORTY-TWO years old, I was in a board meeting when the chairman's secretary, who usually did not interrupt such meetings, brought me a note: "Marion T. Romney wants to speak to you. His secretary says that you will come if you know that. I would like to tell her that you will call back later."

"I think that's Marion G. Romney," I said, and I took his call. My secretary was very surprised. She too had fully expected I would stay in the meeting.

President Romney asked me five questions. He asked me if I would go on a mission; he asked me if I was worthy; he asked about my seventeen-year-old son, my finances, and my health. I called my wife immediately afterward and then went home. We agreed to go.

A few weeks later President Spencer W. Kimball called. "Brother Hales, do you mind if we change your mission?" he asked. I had thought I was going to the London England Mission. But I figured someone else would have that call, and I said, "I will be glad to go wherever you send me."

He said, "Do you mind if we change it to Salt Lake City?"

And I said, "No, that will be fine, President."

"Do you mind if it is a little bit longer than three years?"

"However long you want it, President."

"We would like a lifetime of service."

The preceding twenty years swept before me, not to mention the coming twenty. I had been blessed with extraordinary professional opportunities at a young age. I would be leaving all of that behind, but the call was clear. I would let go of everything that I had known to become an Assistant to the Twelve.

But let me tell you when the real decision was made to accept that calling. It was not when President Kimball phoned but when I was a student at Harvard University. I was working very hard. I was working as hard as I could when a mission president came to me and asked me to be an elders quorum president. I had served as the branch president and Sunday School superintendent while I was in college and in the Air Force. But now the great decision came. I knew the demands of being an elders quorum president, and I knew that if I accepted that call, I might fail in school.

While I was weighing the decision, my wife said to me, "I would rather have an active priesthood holder than someone with a master's degree from Harvard." Then she put her arms around me and said, "Together, we will do both."

We put ourselves in the Lord's hands when we made that decision. That was when we committed ourselves to follow the Lord, whatever the sacrifice. That level of commitment doesn't come with a call from a prophet; it comes with a call from a mission president, a stake president, a bishop. It comes when an elders quorum president asks us to be a home teacher or to fellowship a family living next to us and bring them to church.

Robert as a young man

Throughout our lives—especially in the decade of decision—we all face decisions that can affect our eternal destiny. How do we make the right choices when there are so many temptations and so many people telling us what to do with our lives? There are five important elements that allow us to make good decisions:

1. Have an eternal plan with objectives that we are committed to achieve.
2. Study and pray about our decisions, continually seeking spiritual guidance, courage, and commitment, as well as wise counsel from mortals we trust.
3. In every major decision, examine and understand our motives.
4. Make decisions in a timely way, yet without rushing them.

5. As much as is reasonable, take responsibility for our destiny rather than letting events and circumstances determine where we will go and what we will do.

Let's consider each of these basic elements and what they mean for each of us.

An Eternal Plan

Each of us already has a plan to guide us in our lives—the eternal plan that was given to us in the premortal world and that will take us back into the presence of our Heavenly Father. During our mortal probation on earth, we are tested with enticements and opposition in all things. But if we use our agency wisely and are obedient and faithful to the laws, ordinances, and covenants provided us, we can attain eternal life. Every time we make a choice in our lives, we should weigh the ultimate effect of our decision against our goal of attaining eternal life.

I hope that every time we make an important decision, we will say to ourselves, What is the effect of this decision on my eternal progression? What are the eternal consequences? What should the eternal perspective be? With every decision we make, we can say to ourselves, Does it move me closer to that goal or away from it? Then many of the decisions will be easy and clear-cut, because we then can say, I know who I am: I'm a child of God. I know where I'm going, and I know what I must do to achieve that eternal goal.

Study and Prayer

I was once brought in to help turn around a company that was losing thirty million to forty million dollars a year. I sat down with the individual who had been running the company, and he actually told me what his IQ was. "Everyone around me has an incredible

IQ," he explained before we met with the company's top leaders. "You're going into a room with four people, and you're talking 800 IQ in there."

"Whew, that's pretty impressive," I said. "Can they make a good decision?"

Intelligence alone does not always result in wisdom.

We will not make the right eternal choices based solely on our analysis of facts and pure intellectual skill. Nor can we simply go to the Lord and ask Him to give us answers if we have not done our homework. Earnest study and pondering, together with fasting and prayer, are the way to build reliable knowledge and deep wisdom.

Oliver Cowdery learned this truth when he sought to translate the Book of Mormon, apparently without putting forth much effort of his own:

"Behold, you have not understood; you have supposed that I would give it unto you, when you took no thought save it was to ask me.

"But, behold, I say unto you, that you must study it out in your mind; then you must ask me if it be right, and if it is right I will cause that your bosom shall burn within you; therefore, you shall feel that it is right.

"But if it be not right you shall have no such feelings, but you shall have a stupor of thought that shall cause you to forget the thing which is wrong" (D&C 9:7–9). We must do all we can to honestly assess what is reasonable and possible in our situation and then go to the Lord to get the confirming feeling of peace that tells us the plan is right.

SEEK COUNSEL FROM OTHERS

Along with study and prayer, seek guidance and counsel from trusted advisors—your parents, your priesthood leaders, your teachers, your educational administrators, and, if you are married, your companion. Advice and counsel are vital because the people who love you and bear responsibility with you (and for you) know you best. "A wise man will hear, and will increase learning; and a man of understanding shall attain unto wise counsels" (Proverbs 1:5). This is a time when we make an assessment of our gifts and talents—what has been given us so that we can make a contribution and share it with others during our sojourn on earth. When seeking wise counsel, we can turn to those who have exhibited obedience to the commandments and willingness to follow the promptings of the Spirit in their lives.

As a young man, I was blessed to be able to counsel with President Harold B. Lee about several important decisions in life. On one occasion I was visiting Salt Lake, and he asked me to come by his office. He knew something I didn't know—that someone would be asking me to represent a certain organization. He put both his hands on my shoulders, looked me directly in the eye, and said, "Be careful who you give your name to." I have always been grateful for the counsel of wise mentors.

We must learn how to receive counsel and advice from others. Talking to people does not count unless we listen. If we listen, our advisor will become a trusted friend who can provide referrals and help to open doors for us.

When I was at Harvard Business School, I took a course from a renowned teacher, Georges Doriot (credited with being one of the first American venture capitalists). One day I went to him to seek advice about what to do with my life when I graduated. He said he would be happy to help me but that I first needed to agree to do two things. "Mr. Hales, first you must interview yourself and be honest with yourself about your talents, your strengths, and your weaknesses." He then told me I had to take him a plan for my life, and I had to promise to do what we agreed I would do when he counseled me.

Seeking wise counsel is part of doing our homework before taking important decisions to the Lord.

MOTIVES MATTER

A good check and balance in decision making is to look carefully at our motives. We should ask ourselves, Are my motives selfish, or is there charity in the decision I am about to make? Do I fear God more than man? Be aware of your true motives.

Beware of greed. We make poor and irrational decisions if our decisions are motivated by greediness of any kind—for money, possessions, power, titles, or the recognition of men. Too often we see fine men and women of integrity become temporally successful and then abandon their standards. This is the common consequence of insatiable greed. The larger home, the boat, the summer cabin, the airplane—when the appetite to accumulate these becomes too strong, the desire for what really matters grows weak. Too often those who crave temporal riches lose their spiritual treasures, including marriage, family, and even themselves—who they really are.

Don't spend your life focused on or obsessing over the things of this world. We cannot take them with us when we die. This is true not only of wealth but of fame and worldly honors.

When I was about a junior in high school, my parents went on an extended trip to Europe to pick up my brother from his mission. While they were gone, I was invited to try out for a semiprofessional baseball team. Being invited was a real honor, extended to only a select few. I showed up at the tryouts with my favorite black ash bat—to me it was a thing of beauty. I was there to try out as a pitcher, but during batting practice I suddenly got in a groove and began stroking ball after ball over the fence. Soon I signed a contract that obligated me to play in a double header every Sunday.

I still attended church in the morning, and I'd had it written into my contract that I had to play only through the seventh inning of the second game so that I could get back in time to prepare the sacrament in the afternoon. (In those days we had Sunday School in the morning and sacrament meeting in the evening.) I thought I had it all figured out. But then one Sunday, as I was warming up in the outfield and the centerfield doors were open, I saw my uncle and cousins drive by. My cousins had insisted they'd seen me playing baseball, but my uncle—who observed the Sabbath very strictly— did not believe that was possible. He brushed off what my cousins said, but after a couple of Sundays, he showed up at the ballpark to check it out for himself.

When I saw him standing on the sidelines, I knew I was in trouble. Soon I received a call from my stake president, William F. Edwards, a wonderful man who was a well-respected figure on Wall Street. "Robert, we'd love to have you over for lunch on Sunday."

"I'm sorry, President," I replied, "but I don't think I can make it."

"How about the next Sunday?" he suggested.

"I can't make it then either," I admitted.

"How about the Sunday after that?" he persisted. He had me, and I knew it.

"President, I think we need to talk," I finally confessed.

When we talked, he never told me what to do. Instead, he had me read some articles about athletes from Brigham Young University who had chosen not to play on Sunday, and he spoke with me about the importance of the Sabbath. He was a wonderfully wise priesthood leader. On my own I finally went to the manager of my team and told him that I'd made a big mistake. He took me to the owners

Robert at age fifteen

of the team, and I explained my situation to them. They were impressed and very gracious, and they let me out of my contract. I had learned an important lesson about placing the things of God first in my life. This was an important decision that helped me better understand who I was and what I should become.

We also make poor and irrational decisions if we are motivated by fear: fear of man, fear of not being popular, fear of failure, fear of public opinion. When we stand at the crossroads of life, we may want to be accepted by others, but ultimately we must decide whether we fear man more than we fear God.

In my own experience, I have never understood why we wouldn't put God's opinion first. There is no reason to fear man. The choices we make today with God's help will directly influence the number and kinds of opportunities we will have in the future. Such decisions will gradually broaden the opportunities available to us.

If we fear others and seek only to please them, however, we will gradually lose our own standards and limit the opportunities available to us. This typically happens cumulatively, over time. We say to ourselves, I'll have just one social drink. But taking one drink makes it easier to take the second, and rationalizing that our choices help us get ahead, our behavior slides. Eventually we lose who we are and what is most valuable to us: the influence of the Holy Ghost, the priesthood, and the values of the gospel—everything.

Few people think their first drink can lead them to alcoholism. No one believes that the first pornographic image a person sees can create a compulsive obsession, robbing him of his family, his work, and his body, mind, and spirit. Some may think, I can take one extra pill, right? That isn't going to hurt anything. Many begin innocently by taking prescribed medication for acute pain but then self-medicate beyond what has been prescribed. Suddenly they're hooked, and life begins to unravel.

In examining the motives behind our decisions, maintaining our agency should always be uppermost in our minds. If we are making decisions that limit our agency and future opportunities, we should return, undo the gate, go back down the path, and start over again. Then somewhere along the line we should be ready to ask ourselves, This time am I going to allow the Spirit of the Lord to be with me, to help me? Am I going to change my life?

MAKING TIMELY DECISIONS

There is a time and a season for all of our decisions. Making right decisions at the right time brings happiness and peace. Some decisions must wait until circumstances change and our understanding develops, but many of the most important decisions can and should be made now. For example, we can decide the principles, or axioms, that will influence our decision making in the future. Remember that making no decision at all can be just as deadly as making the wrong decision. Ultimately, many of our decisions will have eternal consequences.

That doesn't mean we should rush them, however. As we study a matter out in our minds, patience and pondering should have an important place in our decision-making process. Reflecting on our eternal goals does take time, and hasty decisions are often unwise decisions.

President Joseph F. Smith gave these sobering words of advice to leaders and members in his day to help them make decisions. It is a statement I had displayed in my office while I was Presiding Bishop. "In leaders undue impatience and a gloomy mind are almost unpardonable, and it sometimes takes almost as much courage to wait as to act. It is to be hoped, then, that the leaders of God's people, and the people themselves, will not feel that they must have at once a solution of every question that arises to disturb the even tenor of their way."[1]

Taking Control of Our Destiny

Many people approach life as if they were a twig floating down a river rather than kayakers who direct the course they take. Too many of our youth are like the twig, simply floating through life and into the critical moments of their destiny. When we do that, we are subject to the whims of the world and the currents of life. Many of us are going through life saying to ourselves, If I just keep going long enough, I'm going to get somewhere. But we don't define exactly where that somewhere should be.

---

1. Joseph F. Smith, *Gospel Doctrine* (Salt Lake City: Deseret Book, 1939), 156.

How tragic it is when we fall into believing that all is predestined and cease to believe in a loving God of miracles who wants to help us succeed. The idea that we are predestined to go down a certain road and that wherever we go and wherever we end up is where we should have been all along—no, I am not a believer in that. I hope you aren't. There are too many of us who go through life, regard some action of our own doing, and say with conviction, Well, that must have been what was supposed to happen to me. It isn't true. What we do to ourselves is not necessarily our destiny.

Don't let life just happen. Our goals, motives, and diligent efforts determine where we go in life. Life is not predestined. What we want and what we set out to do on a daily and weekly basis shapes what we accomplish in our lives. If we have no goals, then we are like Alice in Wonderland. We are traveling somewhere but nowhere in particular. Of course we are going to end up somewhere if we keep going, but is that where we want to be? Is that where Heavenly Father wants us to be?

As we embark on the decade of decision, we should first decide to know more about ourselves, who we are, what our capabilities are, and what we want to accomplish. Each of us has a talent that is unique. Our job is to find out what that talent is and what our contribution should be. We can decide where we are going to be six months from now, one year from now, five years from now. If our goal is self-sufficiency, we can begin now to identify the steps to achieve that goal.

We then pursue our goals with all our heart, might, mind, and strength. We are doomed to failure if we pursue them in a vacillating manner. Acting with conviction and determination is vital: if our course is wrong, we will quickly recognize it and make the necessary adjustments. But if we pursue a course tentatively and indecisively, it is difficult to know whether the course is wrong or whether our effort is simply insufficient. As we act with boldness, we will know what to do and correct our course accordingly.

WE ARE HERE TO ACT

I testify that as we make righteous decisions during this decade of decision, we will be ready to make righteous decisions in the future. If we will remember who we are and act with our eternal goals in mind, we will always have the light of the Holy Ghost to guide us. As we study and pray, seeking direction from the Lord, He will provide it, as long as our motives are pure and we are patient. Above all, we must remember that we are on this earth to act, not just to be acted upon (see 2 Nephi 2:14–16). By planning and making conscious choices, we choose our eternal destination.

CHECKPOINTS

✓ How well do I weigh decisions against an eternal plan?

✓ Do I seek to make wise decisions through study, prayer, and wise counsel?

✓ When choosing an eternal companion, how thoroughly do I do my homework before deciding whom to marry?

✓ What kinds of motives drive my decisions?

✓ Do I fear God more than man?

✓ How are my decisions affecting my agency?

✓ Am I making timely decisions without rushing them?

✓ What am I doing to make sure I choose my course consciously rather than just letting life happen?

And Jesus said unto them, Come ye after me,
and I will make you to become fishers of men.

MARK 1:17

CHAPTER FIFTEEN

BECOMING FISHERS OF MEN

W HEN I WAS A YOUNG General Authority, I had the opportunity to accompany President Spencer W. Kimball to many area conferences. During the planning and preparation for the Mexico and Central and South America area conferences in February 1977, we were scheduled to hold meetings in La Paz, Bolivia, which is twelve thousand feet above sea level. Dr. Ernest L. Wilkinson and Dr. Russell M. Nelson advised us that President Kimball should have four to six hours' rest to acclimate his heart and blood pressure to the high altitude. President Kimball was very tightly scheduled during area conferences, and this allowed him little time for rest. (In reality, the doctors accompanied the General Authorities so that we could keep up with President Kimball!)

I talked with President N. Eldon Tanner and President Marion G. Romney, President Kimball's counselors, to seek their assistance in getting President Kimball to rest in La Paz before the start of the area conference. They only smiled and said, "You can try."

Detailed plans were presented to the First Presidency for these area conferences. I saw President Kimball make two small red check marks next to La Paz, Bolivia, where there were two meetings that he was not scheduled to attend. "What are these meetings? Why am I not attending?" he asked.

There was a pause, and then I replied, "That's a rest period, President Kimball."

"Are you tired, Elder Hales?" he asked.

We arrived in La Paz, and the first meeting was a cultural event. President Kimball would not rest. My head ached; it felt as though it would explode in adjusting to the altitude. We breathed oxygen to attempt to speed up our becoming acclimated to the twelve-thousand-foot altitude; but President Kimball took no oxygen. He greeted, embraced, and shook hands with two thousand Saints.

After the last meeting, he invited a thousand more of his beloved Lamanite brothers and sisters, who had come down from the Altiplano, to shake his hand. They came and embraced him and shook his hand vigorously. He wanted to show his love for the Lamanite people.

Dr. Wilkinson was concerned with the President's vigorous activity and approached him. He asked President Kimball if it would be possible for him to stop soon. President Kimball said, "If you knew what I know, you wouldn't ask me that question." President Kimball was driven by the knowledge that we are preparing for the Second Coming of Jesus Christ. He knew that it was his responsibility, along with those who were chosen to work with him, to take the message to all nations in their own tongue.

President Kimball told the General Authorities, "I am not afraid of death. What I am afraid of is that I will meet the Savior and he will say, 'You could have done better.'" That is a prophet's way of teaching us that we should be striving to do better than our best each day.

Can you feel the dedication and urgency of a prophet's voice to move the kingdom forward?

"Are you tired, Elder Hales?" has a way of ringing in my ears when I rest for a moment. If we knew what President Kimball knew, then we, too, would work with all our heart, might, mind, and strength. I can only wonder how many more young men would serve missions and how much better prepared they would be if we all had President Kimball's sense of urgency. Young women would also work harder to prepare for future opportunities, whether to serve missions or to share the gospel in other ways.

Choose to Serve

I hope that all physically and emotionally able young men will feel President Kimball's sense of urgency. If that sense has not come, seeking an understanding and a witness of the Atonement will plant it in our hearts. I do not know when or where this witness will come. What I do know from my own experience and my experience with missionaries is this: When we have a burning desire to know for ourselves, a witness is given. Through the power of God's Spirit we learn and we know that Jesus is indeed the Son of God, our Savior and Redeemer, and that there is a God in heaven, who is our Father.

The scriptures teach, "And ye shall seek me, and find me, when ye shall search for me with all your heart" (Jeremiah 29:13). Once you have received that precious knowledge, you will spend the rest of your days on earth expressing gratitude in prayer to our Heavenly Father and living each day to be worthy of the blessings of the Atonement. This is the preeminent blessing of serving a mission:

to know our Heavenly Father and His Son, Jesus Christ, as only a called and set apart servant of the Lord can know Them.

Going on a mission also teaches us to live the law of consecration. It may be the only time in our lives when we can give to the Lord all our time, talents, and resources. In return, the Lord will bless us with His Spirit. He will be close to us and strengthen us.

When we serve as missionaries and the focus is off ourselves and on doing the Lord's work and helping others, an opportunity for great growth and maturity occurs. When a young elder leaves the comfort of family and friends and masters the skills of functioning in the real world, he becomes a man and develops more faith in the Lord to guide him.

Young men and young women, prepare to share your testimonies throughout your lives. Young men, prepare also to serve as full-time missionaries. In doing so, both young men and young women will be preparing for a lifetime of faith-filled service.

PREPARE FAITHFULLY

"Seek not to declare my word, but first seek to obtain my word, and then shall your tongue be loosed; then, if you desire, you shall have my Spirit and my word, yea, the power of God unto the convincing of men. . . . Study my word which shall come forth among the children of men" (D&C 11:21–22).

Great Olympians do not suddenly start preparing for the Olympics a week or even a year before the competition. They faithfully prepare for that day from the time they are young. It is the same for great missionaries. They do not suddenly start preparing for their missions a day or even a year before their call. They faithfully prepare for missionary service from the time they are young boys.

Now is the time to prepare for your mission. Develop your gifts and talents. Pray, study, be obedient, be humble, and be diligent now so you will be able to teach with the Spirit, testifying of the truthfulness of the gospel with power when the time comes to serve a full-time mission.

Serve with All Your Heart

When Joseph Smith's father asked him in 1829 what the qualifications were for the ministry, Joseph took the question to the Lord. This is what the Lord told him:

"Now behold, a marvelous work is about to come forth among the children of men.

"Therefore, O ye that embark in the service of God, see that ye serve him with all your heart, might, mind and strength, that ye may stand blameless before God at the last day" (D&C 4:1–2).

That, in one word, is diligence. There is no way you can stand blameless before the Lord on your mission without each day giving all of your heart, might, mind and strength. Then and only then can you expect to have the Spirit to be with you to guide you and direct your actions to do good, endure to the end, and attain eternal life. Halfway commitment is never enough.

One Sunday when I wanted to play ball, my father said something I'll never forget: "Don't be a mugwump." He was an Idaho farm boy, and a mugwump is someone who sits on a fence with his mug on one side and his wump on the other—in other words, someone who can't make up his mind. My father often reminded me that the very fact I'm here on earth shows I made a good decision. Otherwise, I never would have come to earth and received a body.

Years later, as a young man attending college, I was surprised to find myself lying in bed some Sunday mornings, trying to decide whether or not to get up and attend church. I was working sixty hours a week and taking a full load at the university and dating, so I was exhausted. Finally, I said to myself, Why are you having to make this decision again every week? Didn't you make that decision as a deacon already? From then on, I never struggled with the decision of whether to attend church.

Once we make up our minds to attend church and keep the Sabbath day holy, the indecision is gone. Every Sunday from then on, we do not have to decide what to do on the Sabbath day. The same is true of all other commandments we decide to live faithfully.

If you decide to serve a mission, once you're there, don't be a mugwump. Many young men enter the mission field having made great sacrifices. They may have had to postpone athletic, artistic, scholarship, and career plans. There may be great financial sacrifice on the part of the family. They may have even left a young lady whom they love dearly and whom they may lose to some other young man who comes home from the mission field first. In fact, when I was a mission president, some of our missionaries would get depressed when they focused on the sacrifices they had made. So my wife would tell them, "I don't know how or why you came on a mission, but you're a success for being here. Now that you're here, make the most of it."

No matter how much an individual or family may sacrifice for a mission or anything else, unless missionaries choose obedience, consecrating all their time, talents, and resources in the service of the Lord while they are in the mission field, they cannot fully realize all the great blessings the Lord has in store for them. Work with all your heart, might, mind, and strength so that you can receive all the blessings the Lord has reserved for you (see D&C 4:2). For

*Area conference in Paris, 1976: (left to right) President N. Eldon Tanner,
President Spencer W. Kimball, Elder Thomas S. Monson,
Elder Robert D. Hales, and Elder Charles Didier*

missionaries who work halfheartedly—who just go through the motions—missions are actually more difficult. Worst of all, they have little to show for their labor when they are through. What's more, a mission is a microcosm of life. What we put into it is what we get out of it.

President Spencer W. Kimball had a meeting at six o'clock one morning. When the meeting concluded and President Kimball left, someone jokingly made the comment, "Just because he can't sleep, why can't he let us get some rest?"

President Kimball worked very hard, and so does President Thomas S. Monson. When he was a bishop in his early twenties, President Monson's ward had eighty-seven widows. He decided to give them a gift each year at Christmas, but he didn't just buy something at the store. Instead, he took a week of vacation to personally deliver dressed chickens raised in his own coops to each of the eighty-seven widows. Even after he was released as bishop, President Monson continued to deliver Christmas chickens (although he no longer raised and dressed them himself) to each of the widows until they had all passed away.[1]

It is the obligation of all of us who are members of this great Church to serve God with all our "heart, might, mind and strength" (D&C 4:2) so that when each of us stands before the judgment seat, we may stand blameless before our God. How marvelous it would be to hear the Lord say to us, "Well done, thou good and faithful servant" (Matthew 25:21).

PLAY THROUGH THE SMALL HURTS

Serving diligently requires us, as an athlete might say, to play through some pain. There may be times when you need medical attention for illness or injuries, but too many missionaries use minor physical aches and emotional pains as an excuse for not giving their all. In the book *Run to Daylight!* NFL coaching legend Vince Lombardi describes a scene in which he enters a locker room as the brand-new coach of the Green Bay Packers. He has men who are 6'6", 6'7", 6'8", weighing 250 to 280 pounds, 300 pounds—giants. And they are all whimpering around in the training room. One is in the whirlpool bath, another is getting a rubdown, another is being taped up for the kind of bruises that would be considered minor injuries compared to some injuries that these men can receive in their athletic endeavors. Vince Lombardi walked in on this scene. He told them they had the finest physicians and physical therapists known to man when they needed them, but he wanted them to forget their

1. Thomas S. Monson, "Our Brothers' Keepers," *Ensign*, June 1998, 34.

small hurts. Coach Lombardi exclaimed, "If you want to be champions, you're going to have to learn to live with small hurts and play with small hurts. Now I don't want to see anything like this again."[2] Too many of us dwell on our "small hurts." In our lives, to endure to the end faithfully we have to learn to endure the "small hurts" in life and keep going until the end has come.

DESIRE TO SERVE

No missionary should be called to full-time service unless he truly wants to serve. As the Lord explained in response to Joseph's question about qualifications for the ministry, "Therefore, if ye have desires to serve God ye are called to the work" (D&C 4:3).

None of us would serve missions if we didn't have a desire to serve God. I want you to know that. A missionary may feel it is because his parents expect him to go, or because a young lady he knows would really appreciate his going, or because his brothers, sisters, cousins went—but the real reason we serve is that in our heart we want to serve the Lord. It may take some a few more months than others to really find that out with a surety; but that is why they chose to serve, or they would never have been called.

LABOR WITH AN ETERNAL PERSPECTIVE

"For behold the field is white already to harvest; and lo, he that thrusteth in his sickle with his might, the same layeth up in store that he perisheth not, but bringeth salvation to his soul" (D&C 4:4).

What a beautiful gospel plan. When we devote our lives to thrusting the sickle into the field with all our might—*all* our

2. See Vince Lombardi, *Run to Daylight!* (New York: Grosset & Dunlap, 1963), 12.

might—we are laying up treasures in a storehouse that will not perish. The blessing given to those who have the desire to serve the Lord by loving and helping their fellowmen is very clear. As we thrust in our sickles with all our might and help others, we bring salvation to our own souls. That is the Lord's plan.

KEEP MOTIVES PURE

"And faith, hope, charity and love, with an eye single to the glory of God, qualify him for the work" (D&C 4:5).

Missionaries have plenty of opportunities to develop faith and to overcome fear. They may end up in a strange land where, despite studying the language in the Missionary Training Center, they can't understand a word when the first few people talk to them. They'll want to panic, but it's faith that takes them to a higher level.

People will also ask them questions about doctrine that they can't answer. This may rattle their confidence, but we should never let somebody else determine how we are going to feel about ourselves. When missionaries experience rejection at the door, I hope they won't turn against their companion and against the Church or against themselves and who they are and what they are and what they know. We should never let someone else determine who we are. Rejection by a stranger is most often fear of the unknown. Oftentimes our challenge will be to discern through the Spirit those who recognize who we are—representatives of the Lord Jesus Christ sent to them to bear testimony of Him.

With faith, we can overcome our fears and doubts. We know where we came from, why we're here, and where we're going. We understand our purpose in life is to be able to return to the presence of our Heavenly Father with honor. All of the philosophers and great thinkers through all the ages have searched for the truth we have. That knowledge should make us confident but not cocky. Missionaries filled with faith are not troubled by the questions they cannot answer because they know they have the answers to the questions that matter most. As we testify of the truths we know, our fears will flee.

Each one of us should be mindful that as we serve the Lord, in addition to faith we need an eye single to the glory of God. This helps to qualify us for the work. What does this mean? It means, for example, that if a missionary is called as a district leader, he should not feel that he is better than another missionary because of his title. If we seek after positions, we will fail. We must have "an eye single to the glory of God" (D&C 4:5). When a person starts looking for an office or starts building himself up in his own mind, he no longer has an eye single to the glory of God. Ultimately, either he will destroy himself or he will have to repent.

Become a Lighthouse

The Lord concludes his list of qualifications with this charge: "Remember faith, virtue, knowledge, temperance, patience, brotherly kindness, godliness, charity, humility, diligence" (D&C 4:6). Each one of us must have these qualities if we want to qualify for the labors of the ministry. Missionaries should live so that their lives are testimonies of service to those who live around them.

When I was first called as a General Authority, my seventeen-year-old son said, "Dad, do you really think you will be like them someday?"

That says it all to me. "Do you really think you will be like them someday?"

The only thing I could think to say was, "With the help of the Lord, I can start."

Some may feel the same way when they are called to be full-time missionaries. They may think of the best missionaries they have known and wonder, Can I really be like them someday? Heavenly Father places a mantle on those He calls to do His work. He has us do things we are completely incapable of doing without His help and guidance; we will find that out every day.

As a missionary for The Church of Jesus Christ of Latter-day Saints, you will be a representative of our Lord and Savior, Jesus Christ, teaching the truths of the restoration of the gospel and the plan of eternal salvation to the inhabitants of the earth in this last dispensation of the fulness of times. You will be set apart and commissioned to accomplish the Lord's purposes to bring His children to the waters of baptism, to confirm them as members of His Church, and to confer the gift of the Holy Ghost. Those you teach, as well as your younger brothers and sisters and your friends, will all look to you as a lighthouse, a beacon.

There are few things so dangerous as a fallen lighthouse. If we do things unworthy of our calling, those who love and respect us could be negatively influenced by our poor example. When the fog comes into their lives, they naturally listen for the clarion sound of our testimony and search for the light of hope and optimism that once shone in us. Without that sound, without that light, they are helpless—worse than helpless. They were depending on us, and we have let them down.

Once while I was flying a jet aircraft, all the electricity in the plane went out unexpectedly. I was at about thirty-five thousand or forty thousand feet in the clouds, and there was nothing to guide me—no radio for ground control approach and none of my electrical instruments. I had to keep flying and flying and flying until I could find a hole in the cloudy sky where I could see lights below on land and then roll the plane over on its back and fly through that opening using my own sight rather than instruments—all while I still had fuel. That is what happens when we have no instruments to guide us.

Contrast that with having all of your instruments, all of your indicators, and a clear voice guiding you. With that kind of help you can come in for a safe landing even though there is only about five hundred feet of land as you break through the clouds. You touch down safely right on the end of the runway, all because you have guidance.

Once again, it is well to remember the warning that there are few things so dangerous as a fallen lighthouse. When we realize what we mean to our family and friends, we may be surprised. As we mature and we return from our missions, we may hear our younger brothers or sisters say, "I can do what I want. It is my life. It doesn't hurt anybody else." I hope you will understand when I say that they are seriously mistaken. I would recommend that when you are on your mission, you write some letters to your younger brothers and sisters and tell them you love them. Tell them what this mission means to you. When my older son was on his mission, his letters meant far more to my younger son than anything I could have said as his father.

It is a humbling responsibility to think that when you return to your own ward one day and give a talk, all those young people will look up at you and ask themselves, Can I really be like him someday? You will be an example to those young Aaronic Priesthood boys. What you do with your life and how you act is going to affect them all. Don't ever think you can do one thing on your own without affecting a number of other people. It is impossible.

PRAY

"Ask, and ye shall receive; knock, and it shall be opened unto you" (D&C 4:7). Please don't forget to pray. Remember that Alma taught us to pray every night and morning for the rest of our lives: "Counsel with the Lord in all thy doings, and he will direct thee for good; yea, when thou liest down at night lie down unto the Lord, that he may watch over you in your sleep; and when thou risest in the morning let thy heart be full of thanks unto God; and if ye do these things, ye shall be lifted up at the last day" (Alma 37:37).

KNOW AND TESTIFY OF THE SAVIOR

You will be called and set apart to go forth and serve throughout the world, teaching and testifying of our Savior Jesus Christ. For you, as missionaries, your finest teaching will be of our Savior and His atoning sacrifice, that He loved us enough to suffer for us to fulfill the Atonement. To accomplish the purpose of your mission you must teach and testify of the divine nature of our Lord and Savior Jesus Christ. You will teach this great truth: "For God so loved the world, that he gave his only begotten Son, that whosoever believeth in him should not perish, but have everlasting life" (John 3:16).

The fruits of the Atonement will be central to all your personal missionary labors and all that you will teach and testify of during your mission. In fact, it will be the center of your whole life. The very purpose of your mission, the very purpose of being here in mortality, in fact, is to gain a testimony of the Atonement for yourself and help your investigators do the same. In the book of Acts we are instructed to "seek the Lord, if they are willing to find him, for he is not far from every one of us; for in him we live, and move, and have our being; . . . For we are also his offspring" (JST Acts 17:27–28).

TEACH WITH THE SPIRIT

"And the Spirit shall be given unto you by the prayer of faith; and if ye receive not the Spirit ye shall not teach" (D&C 42:14). The Holy Ghost is vital to our missionary labors and throughout our lives. We must teach our investigators the importance of the Holy Ghost in their lives, too.

When you are feeling the Spirit and your investigators are feeling the Spirit, you need to stop and call it to their attention. They don't know what it is. They just know that it's nice to be with the missionaries. They will keep inviting you back for dinner because they just want that feeling in their home, because of your countenance and the spirit they feel in your presence. But you need to help them understand that what they are feeling is the Holy Ghost.

Both you and your investigators also need to understand that "the Spirit of the Lord doth not dwell in unholy temples" (Helaman 4:24). Even though you and I and new converts have received the gift of the Holy Ghost, the Spirit will dwell with us only on the condition of our obedience to keeping the laws, ordinances, and covenants we have taken upon ourselves.

If we are rebellious, immoral, unclean in mind or body, profane, slothful in priesthood callings and duties, or if we have other sins that we have not confessed and forsaken, the Spirit will withdraw. Therefore, we must keep ourselves clean and work with all of our heart, mind, and strength in the service of the Lord to preserve the greatest gift we have been given in mortality—the gift of the Holy Ghost!

HOLD NOTHING BACK

I learned of a missionary in Germany who served while I was a General Authority presiding over Western Europe. The night before flying home, the elders slept in bunk beds in the basement of the mission home. When the lights were turned out, one missionary called out the usual German bedtime wish, "Schlafen Sie wohl," meaning, "Sleep well." In the darkness, one elder, who apparently harbored regrets about how he had served, replied, "At least you can."

I ask the Lord's blessing upon every young man in the Church that he will prepare faithfully for a mission, and I pray that those young men and women who serve will feel the urgency of this great work. May you serve with all your hearts, holding nothing back, so that you will be able to sleep well the last night of your mission, knowing that you are returning with honor. Such a mission can set your life on a course that will then, if you live worthily, lead you to attain eternal life, be exalted, and return with honor to the presence of God the Father and Jesus Christ to dwell with Them throughout eternity.

CHECKPOINTS

✓ Why am I choosing to serve a mission?

✓ What commitments have I made that will help me be a faithful, diligent missionary?

✓ How can I gain a greater sense of urgency about sharing the gospel?

✓ How am I preparing myself to be the best missionary I can be?

✓ Will I work halfheartedly or with complete diligence?

✓ How well do I play through the small hurts?

✓ What are my motives in sharing the gospel? How pure are they?

✓ What kind of lighthouse am I for others?

✓ How well do I know and love the Savior and His Atonement?

✓ Will I serve so that I can sleep well the last night of my mission?

Behold, he who has repented of his sins, the same is forgiven,
and I, the Lord, remember them no more.

DOCTRINE & COVENANTS 58:42

CHAPTER SIXTEEN

MOVING ON

WE HAVE DISCUSSED why young men serve full-time missions and how they are blessed for doing so. Now I'd like to address those who may not have an opportunity to go on a mission.

DON'T GIVE UP THE FIGHT

As the Brethren have raised the requirements for young men serving as full-time missionaries, many find themselves unable to serve. I worry that some who do not complete full-time missions will feel that they don't quite belong in the Church or that they will be second-class citizens for the rest of their lives. I fear they will give up the fight.

As someone who has often felt awkward when asked the question, "Where did you serve your mission?" I hope this chapter will help all of us.

The Lord Will Have You Serve

I want to share my own story in hopes of helping others who have been unable to serve full-time missions. I hope that they will be inspired to be worthy to serve the Lord in whatever capacity they are called. But in doing so, I want to be very, very clear: the counsel from prophets for young men in the Church today is to prepare and become worthy so that you can serve a mission, as long as you are physically able. Some will be excused from full-time service because of health or other circumstances, and some will not be allowed to serve full-time missions because of lack of worthiness. But those decisions are to be made by your bishop and the Brethren. No young man in the Church today can excuse himself from the obligation to serve a mission.

The situation was very different in my day. That is why I would be terribly disappointed if any young man ever used my example as an excuse to avoid becoming a full-time missionary himself.

When I was of missionary age, the Korean War was in full swing, and the Mission Home was closed for a time. Unlike today, when prophets have clearly called for all able, worthy young men to serve missions, only a limited number of young men were allowed to serve full-time missions.

I did not serve a full-time mission as a young man. When I was deciding how to proceed with my life as a college student during the Korean War, I had the privilege of meeting with an apostle, Elder Harold B. Lee. He told me, "The Lord will have you serve your mission in the military."

I had enrolled in the Reserve Officer Training Corps during college, so when I graduated, I was stationed in Albany, Georgia, with the Air Force. I was married by that time, and we had been there only a few weeks when we went to a Church dance at Valdosta,

Georgia. When Mary and I walked into the room, we were standing alone because we were new and didn't know anybody.

Then I saw a distinguished-looking man walk across the floor, right through all the dancers, and he came directly up to us. He asked me why the Spirit was telling him that he should get to know me better. He was Berkeley L. Bunker, the mission president.

I said, "I have no idea, President Bunker."

He said, "Well, that's what it's telling me. Tell me about yourself."

Then he asked Mary to tell him about herself.

Unbeknownst to me, we were having an informal interview, because about two or three weeks later, I was called to be the branch president. I had a marvelous experience as president of the Albany Branch.

When I was first called, we met in a little room with about fifteen to twenty people on the base. We were almost all military; two or three families came onto the base to attend sacrament meeting. I began looking through the records and discovered many members who had been less active for years. They had joined the Church, but when the missionaries were actually tarred and feathered and sent out of town, these members were told as children by their parents, "You are a member of the Church but never tell anyone."

As branch president, I became responsible for the missionaries. We had a couple of full-time missionaries and other members serving as missionaries locally who had not been able to serve full-time missions because of the Korean War. There were two of these local missionaries in our area, so we divided up and began by visiting the members who hadn't come to church in years.

Many of them had never been to a Church meeting and said, "Yes, I'm a member of the Church. Can I come out now?"

Our branch soon began to grow.

*The home in Albany, Georgia, remodeled to use
as a meetinghouse, 1956*

We found a beautiful old southern colonial home owned by three elderly women. It was in disrepair. They didn't know what to do with it but thought they might rent it to someone. It was ideal for what we wanted to do. We were meeting on Turner Air Force Base, and we wanted a place in the community to hold Sunday meetings for our growing branch.

By taking out one wall, we would have an area large enough to seat ninety to one hundred people, although we didn't have anything close to that many members attending at the time. Some of the branch members questioned why we needed to be able to seat so many, but I knew that someday we would fill those seats and need more.

I told the owners that we would really like to have our branch meet there. I told them that our priesthood holders would remodel the inside of the house, and they said they would take care of the outside, including the landscaping and the painting of the outside of the house.

There was a lot of painting and wallpapering to be done, so I knew it was going to be difficult. The branch members wanted to put a sign in front of the building, but I told them we needed to finish the renovation first. I needed to motivate the branch, so I said, "Look, district conference is coming. Let's have the meetinghouse in dedication order by then so we can dedicate it at the conference. One day an Apostle will come and visit this home that you've made into a house of the Lord."

So we worked diligently inside this home as the time for district conference was approaching, and we were able to get some help taking the wall out. About midnight on the Friday before district conference, I got a call from the branch members. They had painted over some wallpaper, and it was bubbling. We really had a mess on our hands, but we worked through the night and steamed all the wallpaper off, cleaned the wall, and painted it so that it was ready for the conference.

The next day we had the district conference meeting. In those days it was the custom to have two sessions with a beautiful southern buffet between meetings. As we began the second session, I saw a very distinguished-looking man walking around on the front porch. Then he came inside, where he walked to the back and then to the front porch again before going upstairs and back down. I leaned over to the district president and said, "I wonder who that is."

He replied, "I don't know, but he acts as if he owns the place."

Then, as the visitor entered the room where we were meeting and came toward the front, I recognized his face: He was President

Henry D. Moyle of the First Presidency. I said to myself, "Oh, my heavens."

I was overcome by the Spirit as I witnessed what happened to me and the other priesthood holders who had worked through the night. When I had told them that an Apostle would visit this building someday, I had no knowledge that anyone from Church headquarters would ever be in Albany. Apparently President Moyle had been to the Church ranch in Florida, and the Church was going to put a cattle-feeding station in Albany.

When President Moyle came in, I told him, "You may wonder what's going on here"—because there was a lot of weeping—"but there was a promise given, and you've just fulfilled the promise to those who worked on remodeling this house."

He asked if there was time for him to give a talk. He got up and gave a masterful discourse on the Lord's blessings. He talked about what the building would mean to the town and prophesied that one day there would be a stake in Albany.

We all had been diligently working to build the Church, and I had told the branch members, "Once we start developing this branch, the Lord isn't going to forget us." And all of a sudden, President Moyle came to town. Soon there were more missionaries, and we grew to approximately 120 members.

President Moyle's prophecy came to fruition. Forty years later, in August 1996, the Brethren were kind enough to assign me, as a member of the Quorum of the Twelve Apostles, to organize the Albany Georgia Stake—one of the great experiences of my life.

Although I was not able to serve a full-time mission, I did serve as a missionary while in the military, as President Lee had foretold. I understand there are situations in which young men and young women may not be able to serve a full-time mission, but the

Lord will provide them the opportunity to serve and to do many things.

Prepare Yourself Now

Prepare yourself and live your life so that you will be worthy to enter the temple and receive the eternal blessings that await you there. Serving a mission is a wonderful and important experience, but if you are unable to serve, you can still return to the presence of Heavenly Father. You can still help build His kingdom on earth, if you make and keep temple covenants. But you must set your sights on getting to the temple. Ideally, you will go with your eternal companion, who is worthy to be sealed to you for time and all eternity. And then you must honor the covenants you make there. But don't compromise or feel like you're never going to be worthy to go to the temple or that you're never going to be able to be with somebody who's worthy to go to the temple. If we make mistakes and we fully repent, the Lord doesn't remember them (see D&C 58:42). While we should learn from them and not repeat them, we should forgive ourselves and move on with our lives.

Checkpoints

✓ How well have I forgiven myself for past mistakes and moved on with my life?

✓ Do I punish myself for missed opportunities—sometimes beyond my control—or make the most of the opportunities I have?

✓ How well do I allow others to leave past mistakes behind and progress?

Teach me thy way, O Lord, and lead me in a plain path.

PSALM 27:11

CHAPTER SEVENTEEN

Avoiding Spiritual Shortcuts

I LEARNED MANY LESSONS from the experience of remodeling a house for the branch in Albany, Georgia. One of the most important lessons was that we shouldn't paint over the wallpaper in life. It may look good for a moment, but it never lasts. And while we may think we've saved a bit of time in the short run, it will always take more time and effort in the long run to fix the problems we create in our haste. Whether we are building the kingdom of God or building our character, when we are seeking to accomplish great things—things of lasting value—it never pays to take spiritual shortcuts.

When my wife and I were on our honeymoon, we were heading to Salt Lake City from southern Utah, and I saw a road that looked like a shortcut. The farther we got up the mountain, the narrower the road got. By the time we reached the top of the mountain, we were in an open field with a sawmill; the road had ended. There was a little Indian boy sitting bareback on a paint horse, so I rolled down the window and asked, "Is this the way to Salt Lake City?"

He replied innocently, "Where's that?"

Knowing that I was in deep trouble, I asked my sweetheart, "Haven't you always wanted to tour a sawmill?" She is a lifelong learner—and a good sport—so she agreed, and we actually took a tour of the sawmill as part of our honeymoon. But as a result of this experience, we have an expression in our family that we use to this day: The shortest way to where we're going is the way we know.

Avoid the Shortcut Mentality

We live in a world in which numerous books promise to show readers shortcuts to success in everything from songwriting to business to romance. We are constantly bombarded with the message that we can have what we want now and pay the price later—or somehow never pay a real price at all. Our recent national and global financial troubles have resulted, in part, from far too many individuals and companies taking shortcuts. Our society has developed a shortcut mentality. In a day of instant oatmeal, instant messaging, and instant credit, far too many have come to expect instant gratification in everything. For those who struggle to wait the sixty seconds it takes for the microwave oven to heat their food, waiting until after we die to receive a fulness of the blessings we've been promised may seem impossible. In our home, I always want to reheat food in the microwave, but my wife gently insists that I let her put it in the toaster oven. "It will take a little longer, but it will taste better," she reminds me.

The truth is that we cannot receive the greatest blessings Heavenly Father has in store for us without developing the patience and faith to wait. Yes, the blessings of the gospel begin to flow in this life as soon as we exercise faith and begin keeping the

Lord's commandments. But there is usually a delay between our obedience and the realization of the promised blessings. Of people who have the faith to keep the commandments despite such delays, Paul wrote, "These all died in faith, not having received the promises, but . . . were persuaded of them, and embraced them, and confessed that they were strangers and pilgrims on the earth" (Hebrews 11:13). Like Abraham, Sarah, and the Saints of old, we will all have to make short-term sacrifices to obtain eternal rewards, being persuaded of promises whose ultimate realization is still afar off. Saints who live with an eye to eternity seek not the instant pleasures of this world but the everlasting blessing of a heavenly home (see Hebrews 11:14–16). To live in this way, Paul taught, requires the kind of patience that comes from faith: "For ye have need of patience, that, after ye have done the will of God, ye might receive the promise" (Hebrews 10:36).

I find it interesting that in several places in the scriptures we read of *waiting* for the Lord: "For they shall not be ashamed that wait for me" (Isaiah 49:23). In fact, at one point the Lord even defines his people in terms of their willingness to wait: "For the people of the Lord are they who wait for him; for they still wait for the coming of the Messiah" (2 Nephi 6:13). The Lord asks us to wait patiently on Him (see D&C 98:2) and promises marvelous things to those who do: "For since the beginning of the world have not men heard nor perceived by the ear, neither hath any eye seen, O God, besides thee, how great things thou hast prepared for *him that waiteth for thee*" (D&C 133:45; emphasis added). We wait upon the Lord when we walk in faith with a humble expectation that His promises are sure. We also wait upon the Lord when we obey a commandment before completely understanding the rationale behind it. As Adam answered when the angel asked why he was offering sacrifice, we may say, "I know not, save the Lord commanded me" (Moses 5:6).

In the scriptures we find some interesting examples of people seeking to take spiritual shortcuts. Those who built the tower of Babel planned to erect a structure "whose top may reach unto heaven." The builders also said to themselves, "Let us make us a name" (Genesis 11:4). In other words, these builders were constructing what some have called a "counterfeit temple," apparently trying to gain access to heaven and its blessings by taking a shortcut of their own creation.[1] Of course, it didn't work; man-made shortcuts to eternal treasures never do. God confounded their language and "scattered them abroad" (Genesis 11:8).

In the New Testament we read an interesting account of a sorcerer named Simon who joined the Church. Simon watched with interest as Peter and John laid their hands on the heads of new members and bestowed upon them the gift of the Holy Ghost. Desiring such remarkable power for himself, Simon made a simple proposition to the apostles: "He offered them money, saying, Give me also this power, that on whomsoever I lay hands, he may receive the Holy Ghost" (Acts 8:18–19). In essence, Simon sought to take a worldly shortcut to obtaining priesthood power. Perhaps in Simon's experience, he had always been able to get the things he wanted with money, leading him to assume he could do the same with this divine power. Peter's response was bold and clear: "Thy money perish with thee, because thou hast thought that the gift of God may be purchased with money" (Acts 8:20). Peter knew there are no shortcuts to obtaining priesthood power.

---

1. Lee Donaldson, V. Dan Rogers, and David Rolph Seely, "I Have a Question," *Ensign*, February 1994, 60.

Paying the Price

It can be difficult to walk the Lord's path when so many shortcuts beckon us. Many of us have heard about the enormous amount of food that the Olympic swimmer Michael Phelps eats each day when he trains. Some of us wish we could perform athletically like Michael Phelps, but we want to copy only his diet, not his rigorous training schedule. We want to eat the pancakes, the pasta, and the pizza without spending hours pushing ourselves in the pool.

Phelps showed great promise even as a child, but his coach knew he would need to work very hard if he was to realize his full potential. One day he pulled the young swimmer aside and said, "You've got a stroke that is going to set a world record someday, and you are going to do it in practice."[2] Phelps became a world-record holder by spending hours in the pool each day working on endurance, speed, and technique. The world records may have been set officially in the Olympics, but the coach was right: it was the endless hours of practice that made those records possible.

So often we want the world records without the practice. Remember the story of the ancient king who struggled to learn geometry from Euclid? In his frustration, he demanded a shortcut to knowledge, a simpler way of learning than the grinding process others had to use to master the subject. Euclid's reply was unforgettable: "There is no royal road to geometry."[3] Nor are there any easy shortcuts to returning home to our Heavenly Father and becoming who and what He wants us to become.

There are many ways the adversary tempts us to take shortcuts.

---

2. Bob Bauman with Michael J. Stott, "Training Michael Phelps," *Swimming World Magazine*, January–February 2003, http://www.swimmingworldmagazine.com/articles/swimtechnique/articles/200301–01st_art.asp; accessed 25 February 2010.

3. See Florian Cajori, *A History of Mathematics*, 2d ed. (New York: Macmillan, 1919), 30.

Financially, so many in the rising generation want to own the kinds of cars, televisions, and even houses that their parents have—without going through the years of education and provident living necessary to be able to truly afford such things. When I was in college, two of the most popular students on campus married each other. They were wonderful and seemed to have everything. They had well-to-do parents, who wanted to help out their newlywed children. One set of parents bought a beautiful home for the couple, and the other bought the furnishings and cars—one for each of them. Sadly, the marriage didn't last long. I do not know all the factors that led to the unraveling of their marriage, but I wonder if things might have turned out differently if together they had needed to scrape and save to provide for their own needs. There are few satisfactions greater than a couple's knowing that together they have made the sacrifices necessary to provide for their own needs.

MAKING FINANCIAL DECISIONS FOR THE LONG RUN

Focusing on the rewards of the moment, some young people may be tempted to take decent-paying but dead-end jobs now instead of getting the kind of additional training and education that will enable them to provide for their families well in the long run. Too often young people will take a short-term job that pays more per hour, not realizing that it lacks the growth potential over the long run. When I left Harvard Business School, I turned down some jobs that paid twice as much as the one I took with the Gillette Company because I knew I would have a much better foundation and greater opportunities there. My decision paid off well in the form of some wonderful executive opportunities at a young age because of what I learned at that company.

I also fear that far too many of us are vulnerable to get-rich-quick schemes because we have succumbed to a shortcut mentality. We want the wealth without doing the work. We should never forget the law of the harvest: We can't get something for nothing, and we reap what we sow. We should be extremely cautious about any financial scheme that promises great riches without the effort and training necessary to create great value. If it sounds too good to be true, it probably is.

TAKING SHORTCUTS WHEN REPENTING

Another way in which the adversary tempts us to paint over the wallpaper of our lives is when it comes to resolving sin. When my wife was the ward Relief Society president, she left me with the boys for the evening on occasion when she had a meeting. Sometimes we would do a wonderful job of cleaning the house to surprise her, but other times we had so much fun playing that we forgot to clean up. On one occasion we knew we were in trouble when we heard the car pull into the driveway. I quickly put the dirty dishes in the oven and dragged the unplugged vacuum cleaner across the carpet so it would look like it had been vacuumed. I told the boys to jump into bed with their clothes on and pretend to be asleep.

That worked only once. The second time we did it, my wife knew instantly what had happened. "All right, you guys, the party's over," she declared. The boys jumped out of bed, and we all helped clean up our mess.

We can't just hide our sins in the oven.

True repentance—complete with confession and a broken heart and contrite spirit—may seem like far too much trouble to some. Every year we end up sending home far too many missionaries who believed that they could, as it were, paint over the wallpaper of sin or go through only the motions of repentance without anyone knowing any better. Confession and genuine repentance look too painful and time-consuming, so they simply move on, hoping that forsaking the sin will be good enough. But just as painted wallpaper bubbles up in the end and creates far more trouble than if we'd just done the job right in the first place, these missionaries discover they cannot ignore their consciences forever. They can still walk the path that leads to forgiveness, but that path is now longer, harder, and more embarrassing than it would have been had they simply done things right in the first place.

Taking Shortcuts in Becoming

Finally, we may also be tempted to take shortcuts in becoming who Heavenly Father wants us to become. Sometimes we hear individuals in the Church who touch our lives with the words they speak from the pulpit. We may even long for their speaking or teaching gifts. Perhaps you have seen missionaries who have had a great impact on the lives of others. What we must realize is that they did not become such powerful gospel teachers by focusing simply on speaking techniques or by trying to look the part. They did it, in reality, in the practice of their lives.

Alma's dear friends, the sons of Mosiah, became the kind of men who "taught with power and authority of God" (Alma 17:3). Alma's record also tells us what the sons of Mosiah did to arrive at this result: "They had waxed strong in the knowledge of the truth; for they were men of a sound understanding and they had searched the scriptures diligently, that they might know the word of God. But this is not all; they had given themselves to much prayer, and fasting; *therefore* they had the spirit of prophecy, and the spirit of revelation, and when they taught, they taught with power and authority of God" (Alma 17:2–3; emphasis added).

There are no shortcuts to becoming powerful servants of the Lord. We must do it, with the Lord's help, in the practice of prayer and fasting, of scripture study and gospel living.

The Savior wants us to live up to our full potential to become perfect, even as He and His Father are perfect (see 3 Nephi 12:48). We cannot do this alone, but when we come to Christ, He gives us the power to become His sons and daughters (see John 1:12). Through His grace, we can be perfected in Him (see Moroni 10:32). But we cannot become what He wants us to become by taking shortcuts. To become like the Savior, we must emulate His *entire* example, including the most challenging parts. For example, we cannot enjoy the peace the Savior enjoys without learning to forgive as the Savior forgave. We cannot receive a fulness of joy in life unless we learn to serve others as the Savior served them. We cannot receive all that the Father has without giving our whole souls, as Jesus did, as an offering to Him (see Omni 1:26).

When we understand that our journey in mortality is a lifelong process designed to prepare us to return home to our Heavenly Father, we view life's challenges with greater faith and patience. If we are simply looking for instant pleasure or even shortcuts to eternal happiness, we sometimes become demanding and bitter in our attitude towards God. When we encounter trials and tribulations along the way, we may ask with an edge in our voice, Why me? Why do I have to suffer like this?

But when we realize there are no shortcuts to the things that matter most, we can better see how even life's most difficult experiences can help us become who the Lord would have us become. Instead of accusing the Lord or making demands of Him, when life gets hard, we ask humbly, Why this experience? How can I grow from this trial? It is no coincidence that Paul's powerful chapter on faith concludes with a note about the role of affliction in attaining eternal rewards. Joseph Smith translated the apostle's remarks this way: "And these all, having obtained a good report through faith, received not the promise: God having provided some better things for them through their sufferings, for without sufferings they could not be made perfect" (JST Hebrews 11:39–40). Paul understood this truth personally, viewing "our light affliction, which is but for a moment," as working "for us a far more exceeding and eternal weight of glory" (2 Corinthians 4:17).

When we have patience and faith, God truly provides better things for us, line upon line, through the suffering and experiences of life. As we submit to God's will, each experience will prepare us for the next step in our journey, and our journey will eventually help us realize our full potential as sons and daughters of God.

I testify that there are no shortcuts to eternal joy and happiness. There is no other way back to Heavenly Father but by Jesus Christ and obedience to the commandments He has given us. The Lord will surely remember those who forgo the instant pleasures of this world because they wait on His promises. Together with the Psalmist's, my prayer is this: "Wait on the Lord: be of good courage, and he shall strengthen thine heart: wait, I say, on the Lord" (Psalm 27:14).

CHECKPOINTS

✓ To what degree do I suffer from a shortcut mentality?

✓ Do I have the faith to wait on the Lord and His promises?

✓ How diligently am I willing to "practice" to obtain things of eternal value?

✓ When making financial decisions, how long-term is my thinking?

✓ How thoroughly do I repent?

✓ How willing am I to undergo the necessary spiritual changes to truly become who the Lord wants me to become, rather than just taking a few steps to appear more spiritual?

Wisdom is the principal thing; therefore get wisdom:
and with all thy getting get understanding.

PROVERBS 4:7

CHAPTER EIGHTEEN

EDUCATION FOR LIFE

W HEN I WAS A student at Harvard Business School, one of the courses my last year involved doing a project for a corporation, and our assignment was Gillette. At the time, Gillette sold men's razor blades. They asked the students a simple question: "What shall we do in the future?"

They chose six teams of six and gave each team a sum of money. We went to work and prepared our presentation. We proposed that they sell a lady's razor, something they had never done. We also talked about manufacturing and marketing deodorant, because Gillette was just getting into toiletries.

We threw everything we had into that project. My brother, who was a commercial artist in an advertising agency, even came up from New York City and did artwork for us. Our team and another finished in a virtual tie. Gillette decided to hire the two team leaders, even though Gillette had never before hired anyone from Harvard Business School. In subsequent years they started selling a lady's razor and created a toiletries division, which I helped to start up.

That is how I got my start with Gillette, which led to many

opportunities that helped me discover and develop certain gifts I had been given. Like all gifts we receive from God, I came to realize that those gifts and my education weren't given to me just so that I might earn more money, gain status, and have the physical things of this life or the titles of men. The things I learned during my formal education opened the door to career opportunities that, in turn, prepared me to serve in the kingdom of God. I have no doubt that the lessons I learned as an executive at Gillette and other companies helped prepare me for my service as Presiding Bishop of the Church. I felt that what the Lord said to Joseph Smith in different circumstances applied to me: "All these things shall give thee experience, and shall be for thy good" (D&C 122:7). Our opportunities and experiences in life are to enable us to lift, bless, teach, and help others to come to the Savior, partake of His Atonement, live His gospel, and inherit eternal life.

We will all have educational and other opportunities that can prepare us to contribute to the Lord's kingdom in unique and important ways. We have to understand that sometimes we will find ourselves in the right place at the right time. We have to take advantage of those opportunities; they come only once.

Discovering Your Gifts

We are clearly instructed that each of us is given a gift or gifts. Each one of us has different talents and different gifts. Not all of us understand what all of our gifts and talents are, but we have many. Do we know what gifts we have been given? Are we seeking to find our gifts? Through effort, experiment, and practice, our gifts are revealed to us.

Before a meeting of General Authorities years ago, Elder Jacob de Jager was asked if he could play the piano. His response was classic: "I don't know. I haven't tried to play the piano." Do we ever

Robert practicing the piano

stop to ponder how many gifts we have been given but have not yet discovered or developed?

When we were at an area conference years ago, there was a young lady who was studying opera. Her story of how she discovered her gift is interesting. She was a convert to the Church. When she joined the Church, she had never sung or played a note. There was a Church program for which some talent was needed, and she and two other girls sang in it. The person who taught the three girls their part of the program said to this young woman, "You have a beautiful voice."

She said, "No one ever told me that before."

The teacher said, "I would like to work with you a little bit."

They had a musical about a year later, and this girl had the lead in the musical. She went on to study opera—but she would never have realized she had this talent if she had not participated in that one program.

It is a remarkable blessing when we can help identify and develop gifts in others. It is especially satisfying when we help them recognize and cultivate gifts they did not know they had.

Several years ago I heard a young woman sing at a Christmas program. Her voice was a gift from heaven. Afterwards, I approached her and told her what a beautiful voice she had. She was overcome by the compliment. I asked if she had ever taken voice lessons.

"No," replied the girl's mother. "We can't afford them."

"If money were not an issue, would you want your daughter to have voice lessons?" I pressed.

The young woman and her mother said they would love to have that happen.

After they left, I talked with the bishop of the ward, which had several affluent members who had heard this gifted young woman sing. Soon she was taking voice lessons. The next year she sang a solo, and it was absolutely inspiring; the Spirit penetrated my heart as she sang.

How many hidden gifts and talents do we have? The decade of decision is the time for us to discover what our gifts and talents are and to decide which talents to develop further. In the process of doing that, we will have to take some chances. There's a risk/reward process in all of this. We will have to take some risks and be willing to fail and to learn from our failures and our mistakes.

The key that will unlock the door to many of those opportunities to develop our gifts is our education. During this time of learning, we should absorb like a sponge the knowledge that will prepare us for the choices we will make.

Education Is Essential

We are commanded to "study and learn, and become acquainted with all good books" (D&C 90:15), "obtain a knowledge of history, and of countries" (D&C 93:53), to "seek learning, even by study and also by faith" (D&C 88:118). Young men and women should work hard to obtain an education and to learn technical skills that will allow them to be self-sufficient and support their families.

How many of our social ills today originate in feelings of helplessness and frustration because youth are uncertain about the future and unprepared to be self-reliant? Without education of some kind, there is virtually no way to move forward in personal development. In many ways, the rising generation is stepping back and giving up.

As a society, should we do more to help provide technical training to those who qualify and desire to achieve technical competence and develop self-reliance? Indeed, whether we make it possible for our youth to become self-sufficient or not will be a test of whether we really demonstrate moral citizenship—whether we really do believe in the right of each individual to become self-reliant. While serving as a regent of higher education in Utah, I became aware that in today's world, kindergarten through twelfth grade may no longer be enough. Will the day come when "12 plus 2"—that is, high school plus two years of technical or advanced training in technology proficiency—is thought to be the minimum educational goal for each child?

Many of us have been raised in families that emphasize education and have helped provide opportunities for us to obtain a higher level of education. In many parts of the world, education is available after high school in universities, colleges, junior colleges, and technical and trade schools near home. Youth in the Church are extremely blessed because of the enormous investment the Church makes in subsidizing the cost of education at Brigham Young University, BYU–Idaho, BYU–Hawaii, and LDS Business College. And with the Perpetual Education Fund, the Church is now able to extend such opportunities to many more members throughout the world. Many other grants and scholarships are also available because of the generosity of those who are willing to help students with a desire to gain an education. What a shame it would be not to fully take advantage of such opportunities for higher learning.

I have watched as the prophets and educators of the Church have been sensitive to the fact that not all worthy young men and women have been able to take advantage of the Church schools in the past. Few things are more painful than to have to turn away deserving, qualified students from these schools. The Church has made significant progress in the last few years to enable the universities the Church sponsors to handle greater enrollment. And I have also been comforted by studies showing that when LDS students attend institute while attending other colleges and universities, they are just as likely to remain steadfast in the gospel as those enrolled at Church schools.

Taking advantage of educational opportunities can be a challenge in a world full of so many distracting choices. One thing is sure: As we go through life, there are always more things to do each day, week, month, and year than we have time and energy to accomplish. The secret is to choose wisely those activities that will help us achieve our divinely inspired goals and then have the strength of character and conviction to disregard what would distract or detain us from our eternal destination.

Hopefully, we are going to spend our lives developing the gifts and talents that were given to us. We must study Doctrine and Covenants 46, which teaches us about the gifts and talents we are all given. And we are all familiar with the parable of the talents.

Those who had two and five talents doubled them; the person who had one did nothing with it, so it was given to someone who would develop it (see Matthew 25:14–30). Every one of us is given gifts and talents. We need to discover what our talents are and develop them so that we can enjoy them and share them with others. We are stewards of these gifts and talents, and we will be held accountable for how we develop them. "For of him unto whom much is given much is required" (D&C 82:3).

Gaining an education is a way to discover and develop our talents. Obtaining all the education we can while we are on earth is important, as both a practical and a spiritual matter. While improving our ability to provide for our families is one important reason to obtain an education, we also know that "it is impossible for a man to be saved in ignorance" (D&C 131:6). As Joseph Smith reminds us, "Whatever principle of intelligence we attain unto in this life, it will rise with us in the resurrection. And if a person gains more knowledge and intelligence in this life through his diligence and obedience than another, he will have so much the advantage in the world to come" (D&C 130:18–19).

That is why we should never stop learning, even after completing our formal education. Learning means growing mentally and spiritually in this mortal probation. Learning from the challenges, opposition, and tragedies of life and enduring to the end are the purposes for which we came to live on this earth.

In Proverbs we are given a number of elements to guide our lives. For example, Solomon taught that we need to "know wisdom and instruction; to perceive the words of understanding" (Proverbs 1:2). There is a difference between our intelligence, which is God-given, and knowledge, which is what we gain through study and through life's experiences.

Dr. Edwin A. Lee once told the story of a perpetual student at

Columbia University who had been left a trust fund of some kind that was to continue as long as he remained in school. He remained a student at Columbia until he died, obtaining every degree it had to offer. Yet while he became widely read, he did not become wise:

"He was a man who was the epitome of erudition. No field of knowledge was foreign to him. He was probably more widely read than the best of his professors. He was a cultured gentleman. But he was not a truly intelligent man. Certainly such intelligence as he possessed was not that which is the glory of God. Inherently he was selfish. He never married. He was without ambition or influence. He was a joke to the students and a freak to the faculty. He knew a prodigious lot, but his real index of intelligence was low, no matter what his IQ."[1]

Proverbs also helps us to understand that the real purpose of mortality is to be a learning experience to gain wisdom and understanding in our hearts. "Incline thine ear unto wisdom, and apply thine heart to understanding" (Proverbs 2:2). It is important to understand that the knowledge we gain because of our intellect must be developed, through our actions and obedience, into wisdom. That wisdom, then, will bring understanding to our hearts so that we will know truth with a surety, and it will guide our choices. "Happy is the man that findeth wisdom, and the man that getteth understanding" (Proverbs 3:13).

Trusting the Lord

In the advanced curriculum of life, sometimes the more knowledge we gain, the easier it is to forget our Heavenly Father and the need for His guiding hand. "Trust in the Lord with all thine heart;

---

1. Edwin A. Lee, "The Glory of God Is Intelligence," inauguration services of Howard S. McDonald, 14 November 1945, in Brigham Young University multimedia records, 1941–2000, University Archives, L. Tom Perry Special Collections, Harold B. Lee Library, Brigham Young University, Provo, Utah.

and lean not unto thine own understanding. In all thy ways acknowledge him, and he shall direct thy paths. Be not wise in thine own eyes: fear the Lord, and depart from evil" (Proverbs 3:5–7).

Our greatest strengths can become weaknesses to us whenever we forget that our gifts, talents, and intellect are given to us by God—whenever we rely on the "natural man" (Mosiah 3:19) and forget that God is the giver of all the gifts of life. If we would keep our strength from turning to weakness, we must confess His hand in all things, and obey His commandments (see D&C 59:21). I would hope that we will also take the opportunity to express thanks to all those who have helped us develop our talents—our parents, our friends, our teachers—who have given to us so that we might be prepared. A sincere recognition of our teachers' contribution to our lives is small payment for their sacrifice to share their gifts and talents with many who pass through without acknowledgment of their service.

It is important that we don't get too puffed up with the intelligence we have been given or the unusual gifts which we may recognize that we possess, because all of these gifts, whether they be physical, mental, or spiritual, are given to us by our Heavenly Father. We are wise when we "remember how merciful the Lord hath been" (Moroni 10:3) in giving us capable bodies, able minds, supportive families, and many other blessings. It has always amazed me when I observe in others (I include myself) pride or conceit in a gift or talent that was genetically given to the individual at birth as a gift from God. For example, one's degree of intellect or basic intelligence, known as an IQ (Intelligence Quotient), is in fact God-given. When this gift is coupled with the blessing of having excellent memory, many facts can be learned and recited in a classroom or test, yielding a superior grade in a difficult subject or discipline.

In fact, the education process is quite competitive and can cause us to become self-absorbed. It can even be an ego trip that can become quite selfish, centering on "me" and "my" objectives. In the process, if we are not careful, we will lose sight of the fact that the real purpose of an education is to provide for our needs, such as living expenses for ourselves and our family, uplifting society, and building the community and the Church, but most of all, to lift, strengthen, and provide welfare to those who are less fortunate and in need.

The same could apply to our appearance and even our personality, characteristics that are passed on through genes from our parents and other ancestors. In like manner, our aptitudes for so many gifts, such as music, art, athletics, hand-eye coordination, mechanical ability, etc., are products of genetics and our environment. As I observe life, it becomes more apparent to me that the dominant, heavenly, genetic gifts we bring into life at birth far exceed the environmental influences of the world around us. We must seek to discover who we are and what incredible gifts have been given to us for our journey in mortality.

We must remember to give thanks to our Heavenly Father for the blessings and gifts that He has given to us.

SWITCHING GEARS

During our formal education, we are primarily focused on our *own* learning, our *own* growth, our *own* development. As we move into the working world and service in the Church, we have the opportunity to lift our sights beyond ourselves. Some philosophers believe that human beings can be interested only in themselves. But true disciples of the Savior know otherwise. He gave His life for all mankind, and we who follow Him have the opportunity to lose our lives in service to others.

In college and graduate school, we use our intelligence to succeed as individuals. We measure ourselves against a standard set by the performance of our peers. We feel as if we have been competing with them and that our grades reflect how well we have fared in that contest. Some continue this approach in the working world, using what they know to look good and to impress others. I've seen this with many MBA students who accept their first job thinking that what they know and say is more important than who they are and how they relate to others. They fail miserably in their jobs because they are still trying to be at the top of their class.

To help others succeed, we must achieve a different standard. In the world we will discover many people who seem to be average in their intelligence and yet are very, very successful. Why? Because they know that it is impossible to succeed alone. The only way to truly succeed is to help others succeed as well. We must use our education not to distinguish ourselves from others but to devote ourselves to them—to helping them grow and flourish, even if it seems to be at the expense of our own prominence and glory.

After graduating from business school as a young man, I learned an essential lesson. A competitor company was taking away our loyal customers, and I was assigned the responsibility of developing a new product to safeguard our market share. This responsibility humbled me, to say the least. In preparing me for this assignment, the chairman of the board said to me in a private conversation, "Bob, I have confidence in the abilities you have learned thus far. Now I want you to expand your vision and understanding. I want you to learn to think like a leader and see the 'whole picture'!"

What was the "whole picture"? I soon realized it included not only my own gifts and talents but also the gifts and talents of others. I had come from a marketing background and had fallen into the myopic mentality that my area of expertise was most important. Although marketing is necessary, I began learning the importance of all the other elements in the process: research, finance, sales, development, testing, manufacturing, and so forth. Needless to say, that learning experience changed my life. I understood more deeply the doctrine of the Lord: "To every [one] is given a gift. . . . And all these gifts come from God, for the benefit of the children of God" (D&C 46:11–26).

LEARNING TO SERVE

Education, from a worldly perspective, is often focused on the "getting" of the things of this world, as opposed to the "giving" that is taught within the kingdom of heaven. As we grow in understanding in the gospel, we learn that education is important to help us serve with our time, talents, and means in the family, Church, and community with greater effectiveness. The reason we obtain an education is not solely to improve our value in the marketplace or for selfish reasons of intellectual gamesmanship.

During our decade of decision we need to decide what we are going to give back to the world for all that we have been given. The hymn "Because I Have Been Given Much" has great meaning because we must determine how we are going to spend our time and talents to help others.[2]

The motto of Brigham Young University is "Enter to learn; go forth to serve." It is important to gain an education to help us to be self-sufficient, but it is equally important to gain an education so we will be able to lift and strengthen others—family, friends, neighbors, members of our ward and stake, our community, and other acquaintances. The goodness that comes from education can provide sustenance for the poor and needy, education in universities for those who cannot afford it on their own, or, in addition to many

---

2. *Hymns of The Church of Jesus Christ of Latter-day Saints* (Salt Lake City: The Church of Jesus Christ of Latter-day Saints, 1985), no. 219.

other worthwhile causes, the rich rewards of temples with which we are blessed throughout the world.

In continuing our education or choosing our employment, we should be careful not to achieve things for how they appear to others. Comparing ourselves to others will bring only unhappiness and self-depreciation. We must not try to be something we are not, but we must strive to be the very best we can be.

The world expects us to become educated to compete for a prestigious occupation with a lofty title or position that will make us wealthy and give us an abundance of temporal possessions. The Lord expects us to become educated to collect the riches of eternity so that we will be better prepared to be a good companion and father or mother and able to provide for our family. He expects us to gain the knowledge and experience necessary to be a good wife and mother who is better prepared to teach and nurture her children. He expects that both husband and wife will have the wisdom to obey the commandments of God and to serve others.

Choosing a Career

In choosing an occupation, please be mindful of what you do best—not just what you like to do but where your aptitudes are and where the gifts and talents are that you have been given. Then ask yourself, Where can I get the best training experiences to develop my talents? Look for the college or company where you can make a contribution and continue your learning and training. Look for the best environment where you can develop your gifts and talents. Even if you are going to go into business for yourself or back into a family farm or dairy or whatever it might be, make sure you first work with somebody who is successfully doing that type of work. Take an opportunity to observe how someone else is doing it right. Then you will gain the experience and the confidence to be able to do it yourself. Whatever endeavor you want to explore, associate with people who have valuable experience. For example, if you want to be a writer, don't just start writing on your own—associate with very competent teachers and professional writers, whether they be publishers or advertisers or practitioners in any other field of writing. Associate with people who really know what they are doing.

IT'S YOUR RESPONSIBILITY

Don't let life determine for you what you are going to be. You will want to take that responsibility on yourself.

When I was a teenager, I helped my father varnish the floor in a downstairs room in our house. He watched me as I slowly painted myself into a corner and had no way to get out without stepping across the freshly shellacked floor. I asked, "What do I do?"

I'll never forget his answer: "Robert, don't ever do that in your life."

Don't drift through life and let random living decide for you what you are going to be or what you are going to do with your life. Now is the best time to get to know yourself, to know what your gifts and talents are, and to know who best can assist you to develop them, always bearing in mind that your objective is to someday help others develop their talents. I hope you understand the opportunity that is yours to learn during this season of life and prepare yourself for the rest of your sojourn in mortality.

CHECKPOINTS

✓ Do I recognize the gifts God has given me? Am I willing to take some risks to discover them?

✓ Do I take full advantage of the opportunities I have for education?

✓ Do I allow myself to get puffed up about my God-given gifts?

✓ As I become more educated, do I become more reluctant to seek the Lord's guidance in my life?

✓ In the workforce, am I still competing with others, or do I work with them to help them succeed?

✓ Do I use my education and gifts to lift others or only myself?

✓ Am I drifting through life, or am I making prayerful, conscious decisions about how best to use my education and gifts?

Nevertheless neither is the man without the woman,
neither the woman without the man, in the Lord

1 CORINTHIANS 11:11

CHAPTER NINETEEN

CHOOSING AN ETERNAL COMPANION

W HEN CHOOSING AN eternal companion—the most important decision we make in our decade of decision—we do not present a list of names to the Lord and ask Him to decide. Instead, we exercise our agency by participating in dating experiences. It is through these experiences that we learn about others and ourselves and are prepared to choose an eternal companion. Part of that preparation is to do our "due diligence."

DUE DILIGENCE

Acknowledging the limitations of any analogy and without wanting to diminish the seriousness of eternal marriage, consider this simple comparison from the world of business. Before one corporation acquires another, it thoroughly researches the other firm's strengths and weaknesses and its compatibility with the host company's strategic vision and way of doing business. Bundled together, these research activities are commonly referred to as "due diligence." Due diligence includes asking such questions as "What lawsuits or

Robert and Mary Elene Crandall Hales on their wedding day in 1953

other kinds of problems are lurking in the shadows?" "What are the company's assets?" "What are the company's greatest liabilities?" Only after conducting thorough due diligence can a company make a well-informed decision about whether another company should be acquired. The better the due diligence, or research "homework," the fewer postacquisition surprises and the more successful the two firms will be working together.

Obviously marriage is infinitely more meaningful than merging companies, and eternal marriage is in no way an acquisition of one individual by another; however, this comparison is still instructive. Individuals considering marriage would be wise to conduct their own prayerful due diligence—long before they set their hearts on marriage. There is nothing wrong with making a T-square diagram and on either side of the vertical line listing the relative strengths and weaknesses of a potential mate. I sometimes wonder whether doing more homework when it comes to this critical decision would spare some Church members needless heartache. I fear too many fall in love with each other or even with the idea of marriage before doing the background research necessary to make a good decision.

It is sad when a person who wants to be married never has the opportunity to marry. But it is much, much sadder to be married to the wrong person. If you do not believe me, talk with someone who has made that mistake. Think carefully about the person you are considering marrying, because marriage should last for time and for all eternity.

Before we get married, it is necessary to learn not only who a person *is* but who he or she wants to *become*, especially on the inside. As the Lord looks on the heart, so we should, too. Does this person *want* to be married in the temple? Does he or she *love* what being in the temple means and what it requires of both husband and wife? What kind of parent does this person want to be? What kind of commitment does he or she have to the gospel and the Church?

Far too often we see young men and young women go to the temple to be married but then never go back to the temple or continue to be fully engaged in Church service and activity. What this tells me is that such young men and women did not know each other as well as they thought they did and that they did not understand their temple covenants.

The Right Criteria

In choosing an eternal companion, sometimes we use the wrong criteria. Over the years I have occasionally asked my wife why she married me. Her response reflects criteria for marriage that look beneath the surface, beyond the public persona to the person within: "I watched you, and you were the same when you were with your parents and when you were with my parents, when you were at church and when you were with me—you were always the same. And when we went on dates, we talked about the important things of life. When we would talk, I knew that you had a plan for your life. I also watched the way you treated your mother and your sister, and I realized that's the way you treated my mother, my sister, and me."

When it comes to choosing a mate, our due diligence cannot merely be about how much money is in the bank account or what kind of car is in the garage but about how much goodness is in the heart and how much loyalty there is to the Lord. What are the qualities we should seek in an eternal marriage companion?

- Choose a best friend, someone you are able to trust.
- Notice how the person talks to and about his or her mother and father and brothers and sisters. Be sure it is with respect. After you marry, he or she will most likely talk to you and your family in the same way.
- Have some serious discussions about what the person wants to do in life. Measure how he or she looks at the future, not just the present.
- What kind of language does he or she use, especially when upset or angry?
- What are the person's other friends like? Do you feel comfortable with those friends and enjoy being around them?
- How does the person speak about his or her priesthood leaders?
- Does he or she desire to go to the temple?
- Is the person worthy to hold a temple recommend?

Asking these kinds of questions about those we are dating helps us apply the right criteria to choosing an eternal companion. Answers to these questions tell us more than just where the other person is today; they help us understand the kind of person he or she will be tomorrow, in the new circumstances of marriage.

PROPER EXPECTATIONS

While criteria for choosing an eternal companion should help us think about the future, those criteria should not raise expectations for perfection now or in the years to come. President Spencer W. Kimball taught us that we are not looking for soul mates—for a marriage that was made in heaven in our premortal state. The important thing is that we find someone the Lord approves of and with whom we feel we are compatible.

Shortly after I was called to be a General Authority, I gave a devotional address at Brigham Young University. Afterwards, my wife and I found ourselves in a crowded elevator as we departed from the Marriott Center. One young woman who had heard my address stepped in front of me, tapped me on the chest, and said, "I want someone just like you."

My dear wife quickly intervened and said in a playful way, "Go get your own." Then she taught this student a lesson I'll never forget. "You go find your own, and when you find him, he will not be a General Authority. But over time, you will grow together."

On another occasion, a young man approached me after a fireside. He was single, and he recited to my wife and me a long list of the qualities he expected to find in his mate. He was expecting a combination of a rocket scientist, Miss America, and an opera star. After listening patiently to his rather unrealistic expectations, my wife calmly said, "Yes, and when you meet her, would she have anything to do with you?" He was initially offended, but when she added, "You will eventually marry someone you know and love," he understood. He later wrote and thanked us because he returned to his hometown and married his childhood sweetheart. In dreaming about some glamorous, ideal mate, he had overlooked the woman who was the best match for him.

DATING

From our friendships, then, with high yet realistic expectations, we choose those whom we would like to date. At the same time we make sure we are becoming the type of person our future mate would want to marry. We ask ourselves, Do I have the same qualities I am seeking in my eternal companion?

The wise young man and young woman choose to date those who share their values. As we date, we assess the spiritual inclinations of the people we are getting to know. We take account of their spiritual maturity. Marriages are most likely to succeed when both partners share a vision, goals, and a strategic plan for the eternities. This is a marriage in which both partners have a deep and abiding desire for a temple marriage, for an eternal family, and to live in the presence of our Heavenly Father.

For these wise young men and women, it isn't enough merely to find the other person handsome or beautiful, for there are many handsome and beautiful people in the world who are not happy or happily married. It is true that early courtship is often based on physical attraction, but this attraction is only one part of the enduring marriage relationship. In time physical beauty fades. The decision to marry should be based primarily on inner beauty, and that beauty is evident in divine gifts and the shaping influence of righteousness. It is the beauty of a faithful soul.

SEEKING THE LORD'S APPROVAL

Having done our due diligence, we then make a decision and take it to the Lord. In this way, we become accountable for our decision and responsible to prayerfully resolve the challenges that may arise.

When we present our decision to the Lord, we pray sincerely, with real intent, being willing to accept whatever answer the Lord gives us. We have learned from Joseph Smith's experience with the lost Book of Mormon manuscript of 116 pages that if we persistently and impatiently demand approval from the Lord, He may eventually allow us to do what we want—possibly at the expense of learning valuable life lessons and to the detriment of our spiritual welfare.

Knowing that Heavenly Father wants us to study it out in our minds has everything to do with understanding His will for us (see D&C 9:8). In my own experience in counseling others, I have learned that there are times when a young person prays about two possible eternal companions and the Spirit seems to be silent. If we have done our due diligence and prayed with faith, patience, and real intent, Heavenly Father may be telling us that either of our choices would be a worthy and acceptable mate. We are then free to make our decision based on our own due diligence and the feelings of our hearts.

THE LIMITS OF REVELATION

Occasionally, in their enthusiasm to marry, some young men in the Church lose sight of the fact that they are entitled to receive revelation only for themselves about whom to marry, not for the young women they date. We have the right to obtain revelation about whom we should marry, but we do not have the right to receive revelation that the other person should marry us. No young woman should ever marry a young man based on revelation or inspiration he has received. She has the right to receive her own revelation regarding this matter of eternal consequence. When a young woman receives a marriage proposal, she has the privilege and responsibility to make her own decision about whether to accept it or not. Wise is the young woman who, when confronted by a suitor who says he has had a dream that she should be his wife, replies, "Thank you. I will let you know when I receive the same dream."

BE IN THE SEALING ROOM OF THE TEMPLE

When the one you have grown to love and cherish is married in the temple, *be there* as his or her eternal companion. *Be there* to be sealed for time and all eternity. *Be there* worthy of your companion and worthy of all the ordinances of the temple and of entering into the new and everlasting covenant of marriage. Besides deciding to accept the restored gospel and follow the Savior in baptism, this is the most important decision you will make in your life. I testify that if we fully involve our Heavenly Father in making that decision by exercising our agency through meaningful dating, doing our due diligence, using the right criteria, and receiving our Heavenly Father's approval, we will be blessed to succeed in choosing our eternal companion.

CHECKPOINTS

✓ How thoroughly do I research a potential eternal companion before falling in love?

✓ What are my criteria for choosing a mate? Are they more temporal or eternal?

✓ Do I set high yet realistic standards in seeking an eternal companion?

✓ How open am I to receiving direction from the Lord when I seek His approval of my marriage choice?

✓ Do I ever seek to impose inspiration I have received on others for whom I have no stewardship, including someone I am dating?

Establish a house, even a house of prayer,
a house of fasting, a house of faith, a house of learning,
a house of glory, a house of order, a house of God.

DOCTRINE & COVENANTS 88:119

CHAPTER TWENTY

THE HOUSE OF THE LORD

I CAN REMEMBER WHEN my grandfather took some of my cousins and me to the Salt Lake Temple grounds when I was about ten years old. As we stood outside the temple, he encouraged us to walk up to it and touch it. Grandfather said, "Live your life in such a way that you can go to the temple." I then promised him that when I was old enough, I would be able to go to the temple. I can still remember that day.

The holy temple is more than just another church building. It is the house of the Lord—a place where we may go to be in the world and not of the world, a place dedicated and consecrated to Him and to learning and living His ways. We know from the revelations and the experiences of prophets that when the Savior comes to the earth, He comes to His holy house. We also know from our personal experience that in His house we are able to make covenants with Him and to be endowed with His power from on high.

Sometimes we think of the temple as something that happens to us on the way to a mission and marriage. Not so. The temple is a destination in itself—a culminating goal of the decade of decision.

Elder and Sister Hales in front of the Salt Lake Temple

It is also the portal to future blessings and opportunities in God's kingdom. We enter into the physical world through the gate of our mother's womb, and we enter into God's kingdom through the gate of baptism. As adults, we enter through the gate of the temple to make covenants that allow us to obtain the highest degree of celestial glory. The temple also prepares us to endure to the end in righteousness before we pass through the gate of death and enter into the presence of our Heavenly Father and Jesus Christ to live with them eternally.

Just as the temple is a culmination of our decades of preparation and decision, so the temple is also a preparation for the future of our lives, here and hereafter. For this reason Latter-day Saints have always been instructed to build the Lord's house here on earth. It is a house of many dimensions and purposes, including "a house of prayer, a house of fasting, a house of faith, a house of learning, a house of glory" (D&C 88:119; 109:8). It is where we obtain the knowledge and experience we need to return to our Heavenly Father and His Son, Jesus Christ, with honor.

A House of Learning and Perspective

How does the temple help us prepare for our eternal lives? The temple is the greatest of all houses of learning, the greatest university. With the endowment as our eternal curriculum, we learn about the foundation of this world, the purpose of mankind in mortality, and how to achieve that purpose and receive the eternal blessings of God. The endowment teaches us how to become like Heavenly Father and Jesus Christ so that we can live in Their presence. It also helps us in our daily efforts to do so. The temple ordinances and covenants are the fruit of the Savior's Atonement, which allow us to return to His presence. As we learn, we are able to focus more clearly and completely on His role in our lives and on our commitment to endure to the end in following Him. In the endowment we are taught where we came from and why we are here on earth, and we are given the promise of achieving life eternal in the celestial kingdom if we obey the Savior's commandments and keep our covenants with Him.

In the temple, we also obtain a new and different perspective of our lives and of heaven and earth. We see ourselves as the literal spiritual offspring of God—as royal sons or daughters of God. The joys of eternity, which can seem so distant outside the temple, are within reach, even close at hand, within those holy walls.

A House for Pondering

In the context of temple learning and perspective, the tribulations of life also become more meaningful and understandable to us. The temple is a place where we can ponder on the challenges of life, seek our Heavenly Father's will, and find the strength to do it. It is a safe and secure place like none other where we can pour out our desires and concerns in prayer and know that we are heard and understood. When we are troubled or have crucial decisions that weigh heavily on our souls, we can take them to the temple and there, in prayer and pondering, receive guidance from the Spirit of God.

We are taught in the scriptures that temples are "a place of instruction for all those who are called to the work of the ministry . . . that they may be perfected in [their] understanding . . . in all things pertaining to the kingdom of God on the earth" (D&C 97:13–14). To be perfected in our understanding does not require the Savior's physical presence. Indeed, before His crucifixion, Jesus said He would send the Holy Ghost to provide the teaching, direction, comfort, and strength He had offered His disciples in mortality (see John 14:15–17, 26). Peaceful, prayerful pondering in the temple is the way we seek and receive the Holy Ghost to provide the same blessings for us.

Sometimes these blessings of the Spirit should be sought individually, but they can and should also be sought and received with our eternal companions. Through the years, I have taken the time to tarry, ponder, and communicate with my wife and with the Lord. Before going to the temple and while we are in the temple we deliberate on our family's needs and seek spiritual guidance in our own lives, our relationship, the needs of our children, matters of health, and the desires and gratitude we feel in our hearts. The opportunity of silently pondering and quietly conversing in the temple is an essential blessing for all eternal marriages and families.

A HOUSE OF COVENANTS

As we ponder on the circumstances of our lives, nothing brings us greater security, strength, and comfort than our covenants. A covenant is a sacred, solemn promise to God and a promise He makes to us. Heavenly Father provides the opportunity for us to make such covenants because He loves us, He wants us to live with Him, and He knows that making covenants will make that possible.

The making and keeping of covenants becomes a marker along the path of our spiritual progress. As we have discussed, baptism is the first of these covenants. As the years pass, each subsequent covenant is an opportunity to move farther along the path. Temple covenants, in particular, help us stay on course, for they endow us with direct, tangible, and practical blessings that keep us moving toward the Savior, keep our hand on the rod of iron—His holy word—and keep our gospel footing sure.

But for these covenants to be binding—for them to have their promised effect and bring their promised blessings—we must be faithful to them. What does this faithfulness require of us? In the holy temple we learn about obeying. Obedience to temple covenants includes willingly sharing with others what we have been given and building God's kingdom on earth. It means loving others and making sacrifices to serve and bless them. Faithfulness to our covenants also means being completely chaste before marriage and faithful to our spouse after marriage. And faithfulness to our covenants is always more likely when we regularly attend and serve in the temple.

Ultimately, deciding to make covenants with our Heavenly Father is a decision to prepare to receive immortality and eternal life—to submit ourselves to His work and glory. The temple is our culminating preparation in this life, and it takes a lifetime of temple attendance for that preparation to occur.

Consider the pattern of our gospel preparation up to this point. We are given the preparatory gospel of faith, repentance, baptism, and the gift of the Holy Ghost—the doctrine of Christ as outlined in the Fourth Article of Faith. Young men are given the preparatory Aaronic Priesthood to help them become ready to receive the Melchizedek Priesthood and someday enter the house of the Lord. Young women are prepared to make sacred covenants by focusing on cultivating sacred and divine attributes.

Through our youth and as we enter young adulthood, living the gospel prepares us to enter the temple by helping us be clean and worthy. No unclean thing should enter the temple (see D&C 109:20). The cleansing required of us must be both of our actions and of our intents—of what we do with our hands and how we feel in our hearts. "Who shall ascend into the hill of the Lord? or who shall stand in his holy place? He that hath clean hands, and a pure heart; who hath not lifted up his soul unto vanity, nor sworn deceitfully" (Psalm 24:3–4).

Then, when we enter the house of the Lord, the ordinances and the Spirit that attends us sanctify our souls. This sanctification begins with the initiatory ordinances of washing and anointing. These are preparatory ordinances. They provide the cleanliness and purification we need to receive the endowment. The instruction of the endowment also purifies us by giving us guidance about how to conduct our lives and by providing us with covenants that can lead us to eternal life.

All of what we experience in the temple helps us continue to be purified and sanctified. That is possible because everything in the temple is founded in the Atonement. The Atonement was itself a preparatory act, an act by which all of us can be prepared to return to the presence of God. Our covenants make that return possible—both because God has promised it, based on our faithfulness, and because through our covenants we are given the strength to faithfully keep our promises to Him.

A House for Sealing Eternal Families

Because of the temple, what is recorded on earth is recorded in heaven, and what is sealed on earth can be sealed in heaven for time and all eternity. The eternal covenants we make with the Lord in the temple can never be broken—except by our own disobedience. In the culminating temple ordinance—eternal marriage—husband and wife are promised that, if they are faithful, they will enjoy a family union with each other, with their children, and with the Lord throughout all eternity. This is eternal life.

Isn't it amazing to think that a man and a woman can enter a room in the temple as two beings who will be parted at death and emerge as one, sealed together across death to live for time and eternity? Isn't it amazing to consider that their unborn children will be born in the covenant Heavenly Father has made with their parents and that they too will be joined as a family forever? Isn't it amazing that parents who are sealed in the temple after their children are born are also able to kneel at the altar to be sealed to their children, as if those children had also been born in the covenant, with all of the attendant blessings poured without reservation upon them? Isn't it amazing that the sealing power links generations of a family forever and ever?

What an extraordinary thing it is that the Lord has said again to men in our day, "And verily, verily, I say unto you, that whatsoever you seal on earth shall be sealed in heaven; and whatsoever you bind on earth, in my name and by my word, saith the Lord, it shall be eternally bound in the heavens" (D&C 132:46). We are blessed with the sealing keys restored to the earth in this dispensation. A sealer in the temple is a representative of the Savior, and those who are kneeling at the altar before that sealer are very close to the veil and very close to heaven. When they make their covenants, it is so important for them to understand that they are virtually in the presence of the Lord.

Temple marriage provides these and many other eternal blessings. Children born in the covenant or sealed to their parents receive all the blessings of the covenant made with Abraham. They are adopted into the family of Abraham, Isaac, and Jacob, and receive the blessings promised to their posterity.

One summer day in 1953, my wife and I were sealed in the Salt Lake Temple. In that sealing room are large mirrors on opposite walls. The mirrors are placed at just the right angle to reflect each other so that you will see hundreds of images of yourself on both sides of the sealing room.

The officiator for our sealing was Elder Harold B. Lee. After the ceremony Elder Lee drew my wife and me to the middle of the room. He asked us to look into the mirror on one side of the sealing room. "Now, Brother Hales," he said, "the many images you see of yourself represent the eternities you came from." Then, pointing to the mirror on the opposite wall, he said, "Over here are the eternities of where you are going. And where you are standing in this sealing room by this altar is merely one image called mortality. It is a very short but important period of time of our eternal existence. How we live in mortality will determine what our lives will be in the eternities to come."

That was one of the great learning moments of my life. As I looked into those mirrors, I felt a sense of the eternities. I realized that an argument between my wife and me in this life would not be worth it, for it would affect my life in the world to come. To break the vows that we took in this life would not be worth it, for it would compromise that glorious vision of ourselves as eternal beings and of our eternal life together.

Because of our temple sealing, that life may include Heavenly Father's highest reward if we are faithful—exaltation in the highest degree of the celestial kingdom. In the Doctrine and Covenants we read: "In the celestial glory there are three heavens or degrees; and in order to obtain the highest, a man must enter into this order of the priesthood [meaning the new and everlasting covenant of marriage]; and if he does not, he cannot obtain it" (D&C 131:1–3).

As two young people on the beautiful summer day of their temple sealing, we had begun to obtain the greatest desire of our hearts: eternal life together. In the days that followed we learned that going back to the temple was a continual reminder that our desires would be fulfilled and gave us strength to do our part.

A House for Redeeming Our Kindred Dead

Temple patrons are blessed not only by receiving their personal endowment and making their own covenants but also by performing ordinances for those who have passed on—who have passed through the veil and await the opportunity to be redeemed and loosed from the bands of death. In Doctrine and Covenants 138, in what is called the vision of the redemption of the dead, we receive a glimpse of what happens in heaven when we receive our own ordinances here on earth and serve as representatives, or proxies, for those who have died.

In the spirit world, the faithful spirits of the just knew that after the Crucifixion and the Atonement were complete, the Savior would visit them and liberate them from death, and they anxiously awaited His coming:

"While this vast multitude waited and conversed, rejoicing in the hour of their deliverance from the chains of death, the Son of God appeared, declaring liberty to the captives who had been faithful;

"And there he preached to them the everlasting gospel, the doctrine of the resurrection and the redemption of mankind from the fall, and from individual sins on conditions of repentance. . . .

"And the saints rejoiced in their redemption, and bowed the knee and acknowledged the Son of God as their Redeemer and Deliverer from death and the chains of hell.

"Their countenances shone, and the radiance from the presence of the Lord rested upon them, and they sang praises unto his holy name" (D&C 138:18–19, 23–24).

Because of the Savior's example of service to all mankind through His atoning sacrifice, we know that resurrection and the opportunity for eternal progression were granted to all who have come to live on this earth, all who are now living, and all who will yet live on this earth. Each time we perform an endowment for a deceased person, we are reenacting this precious moment when Jesus appeared and taught the Saints in heaven. The effect of our service is the same: If deceased persons choose to accept the temple ordinances of baptism and the endowment performed in their names, they are freed from bondage and the "chains of hell" (D&C 138:23) and are allowed to continue on their eternal path. In that moment there is great joy in heaven, the same joy as was among those who "assembled awaiting the advent of the Son of God into the spirit world" (D&C 138:16). We can feel that joy in the temple, especially when we are performing ordinances for and in behalf of our kindred dead—our deceased family members. That joy fills our souls with meaning and purpose, and helps us to keep the covenants we ourselves have made to return to our Heavenly Father with honor.

A House of Power

When the Lord first commanded the Saints to gather in Ohio, where they would build the first temple of this dispensation, He was very clear about His purpose: "There you shall be endowed with power from on high" (D&C 38:32; see also 95:8). When he dedicated the Kirtland Temple, Joseph Smith prayed: "And we ask thee, Holy Father, that thy servants may go forth from this house armed with thy power, and that thy name may be upon them, and thy glory be round about them, and thine angels have charge over them" (D&C 109:22).

Joseph Smith once said, "Go to and finish the temple, and God will fill it with power, and you will then receive more knowledge concerning [the Lord's] priesthood."[1] In Doctrine and Covenants 84, the Lord revealed to Joseph Smith more about the nature of the power we find in temples:

"And this greater priesthood administereth the gospel and holdeth the key of the mysteries of the kingdom, even the key of the knowledge of God.

"Therefore, in the ordinances thereof, the power of godliness is manifest.

"And without the ordinances thereof, and the authority of the priesthood, the power of godliness is not manifest unto men in the flesh;

"For without this no man can see the face of God, even the Father, and live" (D&C 84:19–22).

For believing and faithful Latter-day Saints, the endowment means being endowed with power, the power of godliness, the power that prepares us to live in the very presence of God. That

---

1. Joseph Smith, *Teachings of the Prophet Joseph Smith,* sel. Joseph Fielding Smith (Salt Lake City: Deseret Book, 1938), 323.

same power prepares us and fortifies us for our journey through life. Just as the early pioneer Saints were protected by the endowments they received in the Nauvoo Temple before a long and difficult journey across the plains, we, through our endowments, are protected in our trials and tribulations on the long journey back into the presence of our Heavenly Father. In some ways, temples are the armory of the armor of God—they are an essential part of that whole armor of God meant to protect us in this last dispensation when we know that Satan has been loosed upon the earth.

A House for Preparing Our Children

Among our most urgent and sacred obligations on earth is to teach our children the gospel and guide them back to our Heavenly Father. Helping them to understand the temple—not just the building but why we have it and how it blesses us—will be essential to their spiritual well-being and ours.

I would encourage families to fulfill President Howard W. Hunter's desire to have a picture of the temple in every home.[2] Long before our children are eligible to do baptisms for the dead or to go on missions, it is important that they begin learning about the temple and the temple covenants. Our young people may believe the decade of preparation is focused on a mission or marriage—that is because it is easier to imagine these future experiences. In reality they are preparing first for the temple, for deciding to go to the temple is the decision that opens the way to everything else, including missionary service and temple marriage.

Having pictures of the temple in our homes is important. But there is even more we can do to help our children learn about the house of the Lord and its blessings. President Ezra Taft Benson

2. See Howard W. Hunter, "A Temple-Motivated People," *Ensign,* February 1995, 5.

frequently told the story of coming in from the farm to find his mother meticulously at work ironing beautiful white temple clothing in preparation for a long buggy ride to the Logan temple. Young Ezra pulled up a milking stool and sat upon it as he watched his mother at work. Sensing a teaching moment, his mother put the iron aside and taught a very important lesson that would stay with him throughout his life. "These are my temple clothes," she said. She then taught him about the temple, what it meant to her, and what it should mean to him. President Benson bore his testimony that his mother's teaching instilled in him the desire to go to the temple and partake of all the blessings available there.

My prayer is that our children will see us happily and willingly going to the temple often; witness our joy as we return; sense the learning, perspective, peace from pondering, and power that comes because we have been in the Lord's house; and understand the miracles that are ours because of the covenants we have made and the work we have performed for our kindred dead. Nothing will instill in our children and grandchildren a love for and commitment to the temple more than seeing its blessings in our lives. May that be our experience, and theirs.

Open the Door and Let the People In

Why do we want our posterity to attend the temple? We each need the temple in the governing of our own lives. Temples are so important to the governing of the Church that the First Presidency and the Quorum of the Twelve meet in the temple every Thursday morning, all of the General Authorities in Salt Lake City go to the temple the first Thursday of every month, and all of the General Authorities meet in the Salt Lake Temple before each general conference. It is in the temple that we discuss weighty matters of the

Church, we pray about them, we search the scriptures for answers, we ponder, and we receive revelation. This is a pattern we can use as individuals and as married couples in going before the Lord in the temple to seek guidance and comfort in our own lives.

For some, just thinking about this pattern brings feelings of yearning, regret, and pain. Some have not taken the opportunity to be endowed, even though they privately want to be. Some have been away from the temple for so long that they feel hesitant to return. Some brothers and sisters imagine that they are required to be perfect to enter the temple and have given up hope of ever being ready. Some are waiting for others to be worthy because they don't want to go alone. Still others imagine that going to the temple will be easier later. Whatever the reason we may not have gone to the temple, let me extend the invitation to prepare to go, beginning today. Heavenly Father wants us to.

Years before the Salt Lake City Temple was dedicated, President Wilford Woodruff had a dream. He saw many people milling around outside the temple, unhappy because they could not get in. Then in the dream President Brigham Young visited President Woodruff and gave him the keys to the temple. He told President Woodruff to open the door and let the people in.[3]

I testify that Heavenly Father is opening the door and inviting all to come in. We are prepared to enter the temple doors by keeping the basic commandments of the gospel. Our bishops can help us know what to do to be ready, and they can turn the priesthood key to let us in. So come, ascend the hill of the Lord, and claim the blessings of His holy temple.

---

3. See L. John Nuttall Papers, entry for 7 October 1891, cited in *Church News,* 6 February 1993, http://www.ldschurchnews.com/articles/23782/The-temple-is-the-heart-of-sacred -work.html; accessed 25 February 2010.

CHECKPOINTS

✓ How am I preparing myself to enter the temple worthily?

✓ How well am I keeping my temple covenants?

✓ How often do I return to the temple to be reminded of the covenants I have made?

✓ How fully do I realize the power available in the temple and in honoring my covenants?

✓ To what degree do I do everything within my power to obtain the sealing blessings for myself, my family, and my kindred dead?

✓ How well do I see life from the eternal perspective presented in the temple?

✓ Do I understand how eagerly many in spirit prison await the performance of their temple work?

✓ How fully do I take advantage of the temple as a place of instruction where I can ponder and receive answers to pressing questions in my life?

PART 3

DECADES OF
SERVING AND
PRESSING FORWARD

*Wherefore, ye must press forward with
a steadfastness in Christ, having a perfect brightness
of hope, and a love of God and of all men.*

2 NEPHI 31:20

DECADES OF SERVING AND PRESSING FORWARD

During our decade of decision, we have learned and embraced the actions and attitudes that will enable us to move forward with faith and optimism, making righteous choices and planting our feet firmly on the path to eternal life. As we have made and kept sacred covenants, sought the Holy Spirit's guidance in our decision making, and deepened our testimony of the Savior and His atoning sacrifice, we have consciously aligned ourselves with the forces of righteousness. This foundation of obedience and faithfulness will serve us well throughout the *Decades of Serving and Pressing Forward* that are to come.

None of us knows how much time is allotted to us in mortality—and the truth is, the breadth and depth of life are vastly more important than its length. Our season of serving and pressing forward allows us to build on the foundation of righteousness we have already put in place. It is now our privilege to take responsibility for our own happiness and to find ways to bring joy and fulfillment to the lives of others. When we have a sure understanding of what we were sent to earth to accomplish, nothing is beyond our reach.

From nurturing a celestial marriage and family, to living providently, to serving one another, to using the power of the Savior's love to repent and change, the *Decades of Serving and Pressing Forward* bring endless opportunities for us to press forward in our quest for eternal life. The Lord's plan is for us to have experiences that test, strengthen, and refine us, and these years will measure our commitment to Him and His divine purposes.

He inviteth them all to come unto him
and partake of his goodness; and he denieth none
that come unto him.

2 NEPHI 26:33

CHAPTER TWENTY-ONE

ONE CHURCH FITS ALL

T HE MESSAGE OF THE Church of Jesus Christ of Latter-day Saints to its single adult members is, in reality, no different from its message to all of our Heavenly Father's children. Just as He is no respecter of persons, so His gospel draws no boundaries based on marital status or any other circumstances. The glorious message is that Heavenly Father and Jesus live and that They love each one of us as individuals. The gospel of Jesus Christ has been restored so that each of us may have the knowledge and the ordinances necessary to return to the presence of God the Father and His Son, Jesus Christ. Some of our Father's children are married, some are single—but the gospel is the same for all; the doctrines are the same for all.

When called as a General Authority more than thirty years ago, I was asked to work with the single adult members of the Church. I learned much from the wonderful brothers and sisters with whom I served. I have had continuing opportunities to be taught by them about their particular circumstances, feelings, blessings, challenges, and opportunities. I have seen some brothers and sisters withdraw into their own cocoon to live with bitterness, loneliness, or despair. I have seen others soar as they lift and strengthen others, adding brightness to the spirits of everyone with whom they come in contact. I have shared their joys as they have related their successful experiences, and I have shed tears with some as they have opened their hearts in expressing their pain and frustration at not having all the desires of their hearts now.

One Gospel for All

Over the past thirty years, I have also learned a great deal about how the Lord cares for each of us. What I have begun to understand is that every one of us has challenges, pain, and opposition. None of us is exempt from the realities of mortality. "For it must needs be, that there is an opposition in all things" (2 Nephi 2:11).

Despite that opposition, all of us enjoy the eternal blessings of baptism, that is, membership in the kingdom of God. In His kingdom, as opposed to the temporal world, salvation is for everyone in whatever circumstances we may find ourselves: male, female, married, single, with children, childless, rich, poor, young, or old—the possibilities are endless. There are as many classifications as there are individuals. And yet there is only one classification that counts: We are all children of a loving Heavenly Father, who wants us to succeed and return to His presence. In that respect, we are all the same. We are not alone. We are all loved.

While we each struggle with certain challenges not shared by all members of the Church, the adversary would have us focus on our unique differences in an attempt to separate us from one another and from the love of our Savior. As members of the Church, we are obligated not to place a label on ourselves or others that implies a condition or category that would set us apart from or exclude us from the body of the Saints or the blessings promised to all.

For example, we sometimes hear single people describing the ward where they live as a *traditional family ward,* meaning a ward made up mostly of married men and women with children, as opposed to a singles ward. Wouldn't it be better if we all viewed ourselves as belonging to a *traditional ward family,* a ward family made up of adults, youth, and children—individual brothers and sisters—caring for and strengthening one another? God's love is infinite and is not restricted by conditions or categories.

We all belong to a community of Saints, we all need each other, and we are all working toward the same goal. Any of us could isolate ourselves from this ward family on the basis of our differences. But we must not shut ourselves out or isolate ourselves from opportunities because of differences we perceive in ourselves. Instead, we are enjoined, as baptized members of the Church, to share our gifts and talents with others, bringing brightness of hope and joy to them, and in so doing lift our own spirits.

Early one morning my wife and I were commenting that our parents had passed away—we were both orphans. We concluded that since we were both in our sixties, the deaths of our parents did not have the same effect on us as they would if we had been in our infancy or youth. We had outgrown our orphan status. It simply was no longer limiting to our growth.

Similarly, there comes a time in our lives when we realize that the fact that we are single simply does not limit our growth. Holding on for too long to membership in a ward for single members may separate us from the ward family. In essence, we can make orphans of ourselves and may feel alone. Loneliness in the kingdom of God is often a self-imposed exile.

A unique aspect of the Church is that its wards and branches are established on a geographic basis. They are created in such a way that members can be close to leaders who know and can nurture them. All members living within these geographical units have access to a meeting place and to priesthood and auxiliary leaders.

Some people may need a singles ward at a time of transition in their lives. We are grateful current policy provides for these circumstances and that people's lives are being blessed through their faithfulness and their membership in singles wards. A singles ward is an incubator to help and strengthen us to become spiritually self-reliant. We are in them for a time, but as we mature spiritually, we outgrow them. A singles ward is not to be considered a permanent ward. We encourage those who attend singles wards to understand that their stay is temporary—it is their opportunity to prepare to be a member of the traditional ward family. We hope the time comes when each single member feels the need and desire to join the traditional ward family and use his or her unique gifts and talents to touch the lives of all our brothers and sisters, not just the lives of other single members. The opportunities and responsibilities we all have for caring and fellowshipping in the ward family are boundless if we are willing to give of ourselves in love and service.

TAKING RESPONSIBILITY FOR OUR HAPPINESS

A few years ago we were at a farmhouse with our extended family. All of the family members were involved in activities except for one grandson. He sauntered into the kitchen and announced to his grandmother, "I'm bored." He had just expressed the condition in which he had placed himself.

Rather than trying to entertain him for the next several days, his grandmother showed great wisdom in taking this opportunity to teach him a very important lesson. First, she handed him a broom so he could help with some work; then she handed him a piece of paper and a pencil and asked him to sit down at the kitchen table. She pointed out a list of family activities that had been posted on the refrigerator door. She asked this young grandson to write down any of the activities from this list in which he would like to participate. His list was long. She then asked him to add to his list anything he would like to accomplish by himself. The list grew. He soon had more than enough interesting activities to keep him busy.

With his list in hand, he became happily involved and no longer dwelled on his earlier feelings of being bored. His grandmother had lovingly taught him to be responsible for his own happiness and not to be dependent upon others to bring joy and happiness into his life.

This experience applies to all of us, regardless of our individual circumstances. Like our grandson, we are responsible for our own happiness. Perhaps we should make our own list of ways to bring joy and happiness into our own lives and the lives of others. Our list may include—

- Praying: "Cast thy burden upon the Lord, and he shall sustain thee" (Psalm 55:22)
- Studying the scriptures
- Visiting with our bishop and our quorum leader or our Relief Society president
- Giving service to others
- Lifting and strengthening others
- Engaging in lifelong learning

And the list could go on.

Finding Joy in the Present

Because of His great love for each of us, Heavenly Father wants all of us to be happy. He has told us through the prophet Lehi, "Men are, that they might have joy" (2 Nephi 2:25). This joy we speak of is in the present. We do not have to wait for another day, another year, until our circumstances change, or until we pass through the veil and go to our eternal glory. We are to find joy in the present. If we love the gospel of Jesus Christ, we can find joy in Him and in whatever circumstance He allows us to be in.

Those who are alone and lonely should not dwell forever in the private chambers of their own hearts. Such retreat may ultimately lead to the darkening influence of the adversary, which leads to despondency, loneliness, frustration, and to thinking of ourselves as worthless. When we think of ourselves as worthless, we oft-times turn to associates who corrode our delicate spiritual contact points, rendering our spiritual receiving antennas and transmitters useless. What good is it to associate with and ask advice of others who are disoriented themselves and tell us only what we want to hear? Wouldn't it be better to turn to loving parents, priesthood and Relief Society leaders, and friends who can help us reach for and attain celestial goals?

Enjoying Eternal Blessings

In the Doctrine and Covenants we are told, "I, the Lord, will judge all men according to their works, according to the desire of their hearts" (D&C 137:9). Those who live faithful lives and who do not have the opportunity of marrying in this life will have every opportunity for blessings, exaltation, and glory that will come to those who enter into and honor the covenant of eternal marriage. The real question each of us must ask ourselves is, What are the desires and intents of our hearts today?

I testify that the leaders of The Church of Jesus Christ of Latter-day Saints respect and honor single adult members of the Church for their faithfulness, obedience, and dedication. All of the blessings of the Lord are in store for us if we will participate in the Church as it has been established, without placing ourselves in a special classification. We are all members of a ward family in the community of Saints, where we may all contribute with our individual gifts and talents. It would be good for all of us to follow the example of our Savior when, while suffering on the cross, he was concerned that his mother be cared for and that his tormentors be forgiven. We too should focus our concern on caring for the needs of others. Reaching out and helping somebody who is in need can dispel feelings of loneliness and imperfection—and replace them with feelings of hope, love, and encouragement.

I promise that you will be blessed as you give of your gifts, talents, and spirit. As you love and comfort another who is in need, the Spirit of the Lord will visit you, and you will find love and comfort in your life.

CHECKPOINTS

✓ How much do I focus on those things that unite me with other members of the Church?

✓ Do I isolate myself from the main body of the Church because of my differences?

✓ How well do I take advantage of opportunities for caring about and fellowshipping members of all ages and walks of life?

✓ Do I limit my friendships and service to those who share my particular circumstances?

✓ How well do I take responsibility for my own happiness?

✓ How much am I able to find joy in the present, whatever my circumstances?

✓ What are the desires and intents of my heart?

There is no fear in love; but perfect love casteth out fear.

1 JOHN 4:18

CHAPTER TWENTY-TWO

FEARLESS LOVE

I HAVE ALREADY TOLD THE story of Elder Harold B. Lee pointing out the eternal imagery in the mirrors of the sealing room when Sister Hales and I were married. After reminding us that what we do in this earth life would affect our opportunities in all of the eternities to come, he gave me some beautiful advice about marriage:

"Bring home flowers often enough that your wife doesn't say, 'What's the matter?' Court your dear wife in the same manner you did to bring her to the temple," Elder Lee counseled, "so that when you leave this life, she will want to be with you for time and all eternity." That was a great lesson for me.

To have that love throughout our married life on earth, we need to keep it alive by feeding it every day. This is the way our marriages progress from merely being performed in the temple to actually becoming celestial in nature.

Communication

Nothing aids this progress more than the communication of our love, which can be expressed any number of times during the day. Sometimes I will call my wife on the telephone just to tell her I love her. Sometimes I need the reassurance of her love. We express love for each other daily—more than once.

This kind of communication nourishes our marriage relationship. And because that relationship is a living thing, it has to be nourished to grow. For us to grow together rather than apart, we also need to communicate about what is happening in each other's lives—how we are feeling and thinking, challenges we are facing, desires we are having. Talking about our family members is also important, for their well-being has a deep effect upon ours. Without communicating about our lives as they are unfolding, we cannot grow together, and the blessings of being sealed in the temple will be lost.

Communicating about our lives is perhaps the most important work we do to establish our common commitment in marriage. Couples have come to my office who were sealed in the temple and have four or five children, and they say they have nothing in common. I usually suggest that they have their children in common and that they have the experience of bringing them into the world in common, but they do not immediately recognize this as truly a shared experience. As we talk, we reflect on their years together and consider why and how they have grown apart. The reason that emerges is almost always a lack of consistent and meaningful communication about what matters.

Meaningful communication begins with listening to each other. As our companions are talking, are we listening in order to have an open dialogue, or are we preparing an answer or a defense? Are we making an honest attempt to feel and understand the other's point of view?

Sometimes we become so preoccupied with life that we do not listen to each other well. I recall one occasion when I exchanged greetings at work with a colleague.

"How are you?" she asked.

"Fine," I replied automatically. "How are you?"

"I'm not so good," she replied. "My mother just died."

I'm embarrassed to admit that I was already thinking ahead to my busy day, so her reply just rolled over me, and I continued walking toward my office.

But my friend stopped me and asked, "Did you hear what I said? My mother died, and you were the one person here I thought I could talk to about it."

This woman was not a member of the Church, but she knew enough about me and my beliefs to know that I might be able to help her in her time of grief. Yet I had been so consumed with my own concerns that I had not listened. I would have missed the chance to comfort and lift this friend altogether if she had not persisted.

How often in our marriages, families, and friendships do we fail to listen or miss the unspoken cues from our loved ones that they desire our help? Listening to our spouses with genuine interest requires more of us than just hearing the words. It requires that we engage, care, understand, sympathize, and recognize the deeper meaning of what is being shared. Listening in this way is how we learn to appreciate each other's hopes and dreams and to understand how to help each other be happy.

KEEPING THE CHANNEL OF COMMUNICATION OPEN

Inevitably, despite our best efforts to communicate, we face challenges that lead to misunderstanding and sometimes miscommunication. When this happens, we are tempted to jump to conclusions, become closed, and stop communicating in an open, loving, and trusting way. An essential part of communication in marriage is keeping the channel of communication open. Perhaps the best way to do to this is to pray together daily. I counsel young adults who are about to be married to start praying together the first night of their marriage and then pray every morning and night thereafter.

Above all, I encourage them and all of us not to let frustrations fester. It is good to discuss our differences when they are small, when they first arise. Don't let little things become big things. Once, when I was traveling east and west for my corporate occupation and north and south for my Church calling, I returned home after a few weeks on the road expecting to be greeted like a long-lost warrior returning from the battlefield of life. Instead, my greeting was a plea from my lonely wife with two young boys as she pulled me face-to-face by my tie, looked at me eye-to-eye, and simply exclaimed, "Talk to me."

My wife's example shows us how we keep little things from becoming big things, because one or the other decides to avoid the "tea kettle effect," in which pressure builds until the whistle goes off. Resolving differences immediately is vital to preserving the harmony and trust on which open communication depends.

There have been times when the resolution of differences meant I needed to be softly corrected by my companion. For example, in trying to reach out and connect with members of the Church, I have occasionally told funny stories about our family life. Sometimes I have not been able to see that such a story might put my wife or my children in an awkward position. When this happens, Mary will take the opportunity to have a "companion council" and softly say to me, "Would you mind if you didn't tell that story again? It's a very tender experience for me, and I would appreciate it if we just kept it private."

In such companion councils, love and the Spirit of the Lord make the difference between hurt feelings and gratitude for the opportunity to learn and grow. Because I could tell that my wife loved me, I felt the Spirit of the Lord confirming her concern, and I desired to make a change. When we are filled with love in this way, we invite the Spirit of the Lord to teach and edify both of us. With that Spirit, we understand the innermost feelings and desires of our companions, and we anxiously look for opportunities to meet those needs, including companion scripture study, date nights, romantic interludes, and other activities that build trust and love between us.

Building Each Other Up

Love is especially important as a catalyst for positive growth. Sharing suggestions with our companion—both giving them and receiving them—is healthy and helpful, but without love such suggestions can easily be construed as tearing the other person down. Doctrine and Covenants 108 tells us to strengthen each other in *all* of our conversations, in *all* of our prayers, in *all* of our exhortations, and in *all* of our doings (see v. 7; emphasis added). Perhaps it would be easier if the scripture said *most*—that is, if the scriptures said to strengthen one another in *most* of our conversations and *most* of our prayers and *most* of our exhortations and *most* of our doings. But the Lord says *all*, which means He desires that we always build each other up, even when we are making suggestions for improvement. To strengthen one another in *all* we do is ultimately the way we grow together and become one—of one mind, one heart, one purpose, and one accord. Then our marriage truly becomes celestial, or Godlike, for the only way to be one with Him is to be one with each other: "If ye are not one ye are not mine" (D&C 38:27).

UNITY AND INDIVIDUALITY

As we seek to have unity in our marriages, we don't need to eliminate our individuality. In fact, sometimes unnecessary tension arises over matters on which there is no need for consensus.

Take toothpaste, for example. After you've left the wedding reception, stop at the first pharmacy and buy two tubes of toothpaste, because in just a few hours one of the tubes will be rolled very carefully from the bottom and the other tube will look as if someone jumped up and down on it to get the toothpaste out. To this day, my wife and I each have our own tube of toothpaste. It's a simple way to avoid needless arguments.

In many ways, we also have to just accept who our spouse is and learn to love him or her for it. I would enjoy having my wife golf with me, for example. But she told me early in our marriage that she didn't marry me for golf. She's played golf with me two or three times, and she's a good athlete. But that isn't where she wants to spend her time. So we sat down early and talked it over. She encourages me to golf for relaxation because I enjoy the game and the fresh air and exercise are good for my health. But she doesn't want me to try to make her feel guilty for not golfing with me. So I don't.

Every individual has to have his or her hobbies and entertainment. We may not do them all together. Couples should make reasonable allowances for appropriate individual interests. That doesn't mean that husbands and wives should always do everything they want without regard for how their hobbies and interests affect their spouse. There will be times when husbands will need to skip a round of golf so that their wives, who have been watching children all day, can pursue a hobby or interest of their own. Wise husbands will make sure that their wives have as many outlets and opportunities for recreation and relaxation as they themselves do. Both husbands and wives also need to be aware of the sacrifices their spouse makes to enable them to hold callings and pursue educational and professional opportunities.

Shortly after I was released as a bishop, my wife was called to be the Relief Society president. She went to her first meetings with the bishop—a welfare meeting and a priesthood correlation meeting—while I chased our two young sons up and down the hallways, through the parking lot, and around the cultural hall. At one point I lost track of one of them completely, and I frantically searched for fifteen or twenty minutes before I found him. Then we all waited, waited, waited. When she finally came out of the bishop's office, I was standing there, holding one boy in my arms and the other by the hand.

Evidently, the feelings in my heart were showing on my face. You can imagine the look. I didn't have the courage to say anything, but my countenance did: "Do you realize you have kept us waiting an hour and a half?"

All she did was raise five fingers on her hand and say, "Five years." That's how many years she had waited for me week in and week out. I began to realize it was going to be my job to support my wife in her calling just as she had supported me in mine.

Husbands, there will be times when your wife will say to herself that she can't get through another day. There will be two or three children around the house, your wife will be speaking on the level of a two- or three- or five-year-old, and at some point she will have to get out and have some entertainment or cultural refinement. She will want to have some opportunity to grow. Make sure you are there to take care of the children when she wants to go to a midweek

Robert, Mary, and their two sons, Steven and David, about 1962

Relief Society meeting or participate in a book club. And while she is gone, clean a few rooms, wash the dishes, vacuum the carpet, and have all the kids in bed when she comes home. That has got to be one of the most rewarding experiences you will ever have in your marriage—and it will be a great relief to your wife. At times, it is a much better way of expressing your feelings than just saying "I love you."

Just as husbands should be sensitive to their wives' needs, so wives should be sensitive to the demands placed on their husbands, who often carry a heavy burden as the primary financial provider for the family. Sometimes a young wife will have a "honey-do" list for her husband—a whole bunch of projects that have to be done, beginning the moment he walks in the door after a long day's work.

Sometimes such lists don't take into account how much energy was expended at work. And sometimes, when a husband doesn't jump right in to do the projects, she decides it means he doesn't love her. We should be careful not to base our love for our spouse on his or her willingness to do our projects. Never approach each other with the attitude of "love me, love my project."

Having said this, when a husband comes home, he needs to remember that his wife has been working just as hard all day as he has. He may be mentally and physically exhausted, but she's tired, too, and may be longing for some adult communication and some help in taking care of the children. He should not expect to be able to simply kick back and rest while she works alone all evening making dinner, taking care of the children, and cleaning the house.

Some of these things may seem minor, but it is almost always the small acts of inconsideration that lead marriages to unravel. Little things become big things over time and canker the soul of the relationship.

CLIMBING A MOUNTAIN

In all we do, our most important responsibility is to sincerely and deliberately consider each other's needs. A marriage partnership is not a crutch. We do not marry somebody we think is a little higher than the angels and then lean on our spouse and slow him or her down. We develop ourselves and our own gifts and talents to help and lift our companion. As our companion does the same, we develop and rise together.

Marriage is like climbing a mountain. We tie ourselves to a companion and start up the mountain of life. As a child comes along, we tie him to Mom and Dad and continue the journey. He will be totally dependent on us for a period. The ropes will hold all of the mountain climbers together, but there are many elements—the wind and the rain and the snow and the ice—that tear at us to pull us off the mountain. How do we reach the summit? If either Mom or Dad cuts the rope that binds them, the chances are that one or the other may fall off the mountain, pulling the rest of the family along. By staying together, however, they help each other reach the summit.

How do we stay together? We do what the other wants to do. I once met a man who said he had a date with his wife every Friday night—they went to *his* bowling league. I asked him if he'd ever asked her what she wanted to do for their date. I told him that a date is when you do something your companion wants to do. Do our companions go on dates and vacations simply because they are what we want to do? Whether it is a weekly date or a major move, wise couples and families sit down in family council and consider the plan from the point of view of each other. Then they make a plan together that meets everyone's needs. Of course there may be some trade-offs and compromises—two ballets might be worth one sporting event, or vice versa. But marriages succeed when both husbands and wives work to find solutions that meet both parties' reasonable wishes.

Disagree Amicably, Apologize Quickly

It has been suggested that if you really love someone, you never have to say you're sorry. I disagree with that. I think we need to be quick to say, "I'm sorry." And not only "I'm sorry" but to have the humility to say, "I'm sorry, and I will do better." When a husband and wife have had an argument, sometimes the best way to apologize is in prayer with your companion. Oftentimes a husband or wife can open up in prayer and say he or she is sorry while talking to Heavenly Father. Then they can talk with each other afterwards.

It helps children to see that good parents can have differing opinions and that these differences can be worked out without anger, striking, yelling, or throwing things. They need to see and feel calm communication with respect for others' perspectives so that they themselves will know how to work out their differences in their own lives, not only with their parents and their brothers and sisters but with those whom they meet in the world.

MANIPULATION AND ABUSE

I ache when I think of how we sometimes try to impose our desires on other human beings, especially one who loves us. Years ago, as a branch president, I interviewed a man and his wife. The wife was tearing down her husband—he was not the provider she had expected; he was not the companion she had dreamed about before her marriage; they could not communicate together without arguing and attacking each other.

Her husband loved her, and yet she hurt him. There were tears in his eyes as he absorbed the verbal abuse. I couldn't take any more and asked her, "Why do you hurt the person who loves you the most? Why do you hurt a husband who would do anything to help you?"

Her answer startled me. "Oh, I guess we argue and hurt those we love because we can hurt them the most."

I have never forgotten that incident. There is so much truth in the wife's words. We can't hurt a stranger as much as we can a loved one. We know just what to say or do to hurt our companions, parents, or brothers and sisters. We know where they are vulnerable. We know how they can be hurt the most by our actions.

It particularly pains me to learn of priesthood holders who hurt their wives or children either physically or verbally. Abuse is a mockery of sacred covenants we make in the house of the Lord. It is hypocritical to talk of compassion to others while we are rude or abusive within our own families. Let us put our own homes in order, seeing that the spiritual and emotional needs of our families are met.

I Will Show unto Them Their Weakness

Each marriage has its own Achilles' heel, and each spouse has opportunities for improvement. Do we understand our Achilles' heel and what we should guard against? Do we know the kinds of situations and misunderstandings we ourselves should take care to avoid and what our weaknesses are? The secret of a happy marriage is to protect the Achilles' heels of those we love and not take advantage of the weaknesses of those we know best, love most, and ultimately have the capacity to hurt most deeply. When we love our companions with all our hearts, we help them come unto the Savior. As they come to the Savior, He will show them their weaknesses and help them to overcome those weaknesses (see Ether 12:27).

Celestial couples think of each other before self. Selfishness suffocates spiritual senses. Remember that. Communicating with the Lord in prayer and with each other, we grow together and not apart. As we talk with each other, we keep the little things from becoming big things. We talk early about the "small hurts" without fear of offending. In this way, when the pressure in the tea kettle begins to build, there is no explosion of bitter feelings. We are willing to apologize and ask forgiveness. We express our love and grow closer. There is no fear in this kind of love (see 1 John 4:18). I pray that this love may be our aim and highest aspiration.

Checkpoints

✓ Do I treat my spouse in such a way that he or she will want to live with me for eternity?

✓ How well do I actively seek to keep love alive in my marriage? To what extent do I take my marriage for granted?

✓ How well do I listen when my spouse speaks? To what extent am I preoccupied or busy preparing a rebuttal?

✓ What do I do to keep little frustrations from simmering until they explode?

✓ How well do I encourage and enable my spouse to grow individually?

✓ How sensitive am I to my spouse's needs and desires?

✓ Do I use manipulative techniques to try to get my way in my marriage?

✓ How respectfully do my spouse and I disagree? How freely do we apologize?

✓ How focused am I on myself instead of on my spouse?

Seek not after riches nor the vain things of this world;
for behold, you cannot carry them with you.

ALMA 39:14

CHAPTER TWENTY-THREE

BUILDING A SOUND FINANCIAL FOUNDATION

ARLY IN OUR MARRIAGE, I received a promotion and was feeling particularly good about my professional situation. Mary and I were living in New York at the time, and I wanted to buy her an elegant new coat. But she knew better. She knew it wasn't practical for her or our family. She helped me see this when she said, "Oh, Robert, where would I wear it?" At the time she was a ward Relief Society president helping to minister to needy families.

Then she taught me an unforgettable lesson. She looked me in the eyes and gently asked, "Are you buying this for me or for you?" In other words, she was asking, "Is the purpose of this gift to show your love for me or to show that you are a good provider?"

I pondered her question and realized I was thinking less about her and our family and more about me.

On another occasion I wanted to buy her a beautiful navy blue polka-dot dress. I was in the Air Force, and we had missed Christmas together because I was on assignment overseas. When I got home, I saw the dress in a store window and suggested to my wife that if she liked it, we would buy it for a Christmas present.

After my prolonged pleading, Mary went to the store with me and went into the fitting room to try on the dress. The store clerk repeatedly told Mary that her husband would be disappointed if she did not accept his loving offer to buy the dress as a Christmas present.

Mary saw the price tag and did not know what to do. What could she say to stop the sales presentation? In desperation, she whispered jokingly to the sales clerk, "Don't listen to him—he drinks!"

It worked! Immediately the store clerk came out of the fitting room area with the dress and walked swiftly by me, not even looking at me, and replaced the dress in the store window.

As Mary and I left the store, I asked, "What happened?"

Mary replied, "It was a beautiful dress, but *we can't afford it.*" Those words went straight to my heart.

Just Say No

We live in an age of entitlement. Many believe they should have all that others have—right now. Unable to delay gratification, they go into debt to buy what they cannot afford, which always affects their temporal and spiritual welfare. For young people especially, the lesson is clear: We should not try to have now what it took our parents years of patient saving to acquire.

Over the years I have thought to myself, if more young couples could learn what my wife taught me, how blessed they would be! There would be less stress in their marriages, less contention, less divorce. When I talk with an engaged couple before they go to the temple to be married, I give them one phrase that, if remembered, will help them throughout their marriage to live joyfully within their means and avoid needless debt. It's the simple phrase my wife taught me in New York all those years ago: "We can't afford it."

When a mother and father are able to say that phrase to themselves, it becomes easier to say it to each other, and if they learn to say it to each other, they will be more comfortable saying it to their children and in their family councils. I have come to believe that in building a strong eternal marriage, the three most loving words a couple can say to each other are "I love you," and the four most caring words a couple can say to each other are "We can't afford it."

THE BLESSINGS OF PROVIDENT LIVING

Being able to say, "We can't afford it," requires us to develop a desire to live providently. Provident living includes a willingness to forgo luxuries, to avoid excess, and to use fully what we have. It includes learning to live joyfully within our means.

Sometimes we may feel embarrassed, ashamed, or less worthwhile if our family does not have everything the neighbors have. Provident living means not coveting the things of this world. It means using the resources of the earth wisely and not being wasteful even in times of plenty.

The living prophets have counseled us time and again to put our lives in order—to eliminate debt, to store food and other essential items, to pay our tithing, to obtain appropriate education, and to live the commandments. Doing so puts us in a position to do the Savior's work in our own homes, in the Church, and in the community. When we live providently it becomes possible to reach out to the poor and needy, the afflicted, the downtrodden, to "lift up the hands which hang down, and strengthen the feeble knees" (D&C 81:5). More important, provident living makes it possible for us, both in our youth and in our golden years, to answer the call of the Savior to "go ye into all the world, and preach the gospel to every creature" (Mormon 9:22). With these glorious opportunities and blessings before us, have we obeyed the simple but essential prophetic instructions to live providently?

To do so, we will need to focus more on what is eternal and less on what is temporal. We live in an age of greed—that insatiable, enslaving appetite for temporal things. Remember, *temporal* means "temporary," and temporary things cannot bring eternal happiness. So we remind ourselves: We don't want to spend our lives on the things of this world, for we cannot take them with us when we die.

"Lay not up for yourselves treasures upon earth, where moth and rust doth corrupt, and where thieves break through and steal:

"But lay up for yourselves treasures in heaven, where neither moth nor rust doth corrupt, and where thieves do not break through nor steal:

"For where your treasure is, there will your heart be also" (Matthew 6:19–21).

So look ahead. Take the long view. Be patient. Save your money. Remember that you don't get something for nothing in this life. The law of the harvest applies to all of us. It takes hard work to plant, grow, and reap the harvest.

Happy Are Those Who Live within Their Means

Some of the greatest times of our married life were when Mary and I had an apartment right across the street from what they called the Carousel on South Temple Street in Salt Lake City. It was a little hamburger place. We had an apartment on the ground floor that looked right out at this popular eatery. I can remember one time when we were home together on a Friday or Saturday evening and wanted to make it a special date night. Wouldn't it be fun to share a hamburger with my sweetheart?

I looked for money in my wallet, but there was nothing. I asked Mary if she had any money. Once again, there was nothing! So I began a search throughout the apartment for enough change to afford one hamburger. In desperation, I even searched underneath the cushions of chairs and the sofa and through all our pockets in the closets, trying to pull together enough money to walk across the street to get one hamburger.

In the end, we couldn't find enough money for one hamburger, so we didn't buy it. We didn't get it because we couldn't afford it. I was discouraged. My wife consoled me by reminding me that we had each other, and we were absolutely happy together.

Happy are those who learn to live within their means and are able to save a little for future needs. Having said that, our experience that weekend was a great motivator for me to get my education, work hard, and become a provident provider who could, on a special occasion, afford one hamburger!

USE FAMILY COUNCILS TO MAKE WISE DECISIONS

We can learn much from communicating with our companions and family members about temporal needs and finances. One of the best ways for a family to review spiritual and temporal needs is by holding effective family councils. In these councils we evaluate whether we are doing what is needed to ensure our spiritual well-being as we meet our essential temporal needs.

In a family council we review what the family expenses are and see if an adequate portion of our expenditures are going toward necessities. Along with the obvious necessities of shelter and food, we must not neglect the necessity of having adequate insurance—medical insurance, life insurance, and automobile insurance. We need to protect ourselves against possible catastrophic events that may come upon us, including accident, illness, loss of employment, and natural disaster.

We must also determine if an inordinate amount of our expenditure is going toward nonessential products or services. Some expenses that could be reviewed are cell phones, cable television, land line telephone, Internet services, credit card debt and service charges, recreational expenses, sports and hobby expenses, and so forth.

A family council becomes a safe and loving environment to discuss the difference between wants and needs. As we consider specific new expenditures or changes in family spending, questions we may want to ask are, Can we afford it? And even if we can, do we really want it? Will it detract from our spiritual well-being? Will it affect our devotion to the Lord and His Church or impede our ability to serve others? Will it help us meet our family goals? Will it allow us to save and invest for future needs and opportunities?

An effective way to address these questions is to establish a family savings and spending plan. This family plan or budget is a summary of the following key areas:

• Income after tithing and taxes
• Required or essential living expenses
• Optional or discretionary expenses
• Savings
• Vacation and retirement funds

Regularly reviewing these areas will help us teach our children to recognize the difference between wants and needs. This review is especially helpful in demonstrating how to plan ahead for goals and future opportunities and how to prepare for them financially.

When our children were young, we had a family council and set a goal to take our sons' dream vacation: a Colorado River trip. As I remember, we could probably have written out a check for the trip, but that would not have taught the lesson our sons needed to learn. We set a goal, and for more than a year, each time something came up we asked, "Do we want to do this now, or do we want the Colorado River trip?" This was a great learning experience for all of us. As a family, we all started to understand what we really needed and what we could do without.

The Slavery of Debt

A true understanding of the difference between needs and wants is increasingly rare in this world. As a result, personal, corporate, and national debt is on the rise, and more and more of our brothers and sisters are experiencing the slavery of debt.

In some cultures, debt can reasonably be incurred for education, a modest home, or a basic automobile—what may be necessary to provide for the basic needs of a family within that culture. When family members cannot control their wants and addictive impulses, however, families go into debt to buy things they cannot afford and do not really need. When that happens, they become poor temporally and spiritually.

How does debt produce this temporal and spiritual poverty? When we go into debt, we give away some of our precious, priceless agency by placing ourselves in self-imposed servitude. This servitude is an unyielding obligation of our time, energy, and means to repay what we have borrowed—resources that could have been used to help ourselves, our families, and others. In the grip of debt, we lose our agency to choose for ourselves and act according to our righteous desires and feelings. The choice to go into debt today determines the course of our lives tomorrow.

As our freedom is diminished by debt, increasing hopelessness depletes us physically, depresses us mentally, and burdens us spiritually. Living at the subsistence level, we become isolated, our self-worth is diminished, and our relationships with family, friends, neighbors, and the Lord are weakened. We do not have the time, energy, or interest to seek spiritual things.

After seeing the consequences of debt in the lives of young people, I suggest that during our decade of decision we make a hard and fast decision not to go into debt. That is, we do not finance on credit any item of any kind, except perhaps a house or a vehicle that is well within our means. If we have had to go into debt to obtain our education, we repay that debt as soon as possible and then go forward, refusing to buy anything we cannot pay for in full on the day it is purchased.

For many, this may require what is called "plastic surgery," which you may perform yourselves this very day (and without years of medical training!). All that is required is a pair of scissors. If you have a credit card that you cannot pay off completely every month, you are paying devastatingly destructive interest charges and need the surgery. If at this moment you have cards with a balance, I encourage you to put down this book and cut up the cards now.

Getting out of debt requires more than just some tactical changes. Overcoming addictive behaviors requires a change of heart—a mighty change of heart possible only with divine help. To pay our debts now and to avoid future debt requires us to exercise faith in the Savior not just to do better but to be better.

Our Deepest Hunger

When indebtedness has become a daily habit and a way of life, only the power of the Savior's love is strong enough to help us change. The spending behavior that leads to debt is very similar to addiction, and addiction is the craving of the natural man that can never be satisfied. If we set our hearts on the vain things of this world, our hearts can never be content. The hunger for worldly possessions cannot be satiated, and sooner or later it consumes *us*.

Why is this so? As children of God, our real and deepest hunger is for what the Lord alone can provide—His love, His sense of our worth, His security, His confidence, His hope in the future, and the assurance of His love. These are what bring us eternal joy, personal contentment, and the feeling that we have enough. Anything less than these gifts of God will always leave us empty and unfulfilled. To continue spending money when we are in debt is like reaching for the salt when our real hunger is for something sweet. Gulping down more and more salt will never satisfy the desire for sweet. We have to reach for what we really want if we're ever going to be truly filled.

So how do we overcome addiction? We must want, more than anything else, what we were born to want: to do our Heavenly Father's will and providently provide for ourselves and others. We must say, as did King Lamoni's father, "I will give away all my sins to know thee" (Alma 22:18). Then we can go to Him with steadfast determination and promise Him, "I will do whatever it takes to overcome this."

Through prayer, fasting, obedience to the commandments, and priesthood blessings, we then qualify ourselves for the strength, comfort, and hope that comes through the Savior's atoning sacrifice. Because of that sacrifice, we can begin to feel His love and power in our lives again. And we can feel and respond to the daily promptings of the Holy Ghost that will teach us to satisfy our deepest hunger.

We do not—indeed, we *cannot*—overcome alone. The Savior said, "Fear not, little children, for you are mine, and I have overcome the world" (D&C 50:41). We overcome our worldly habits and addictions because He Himself overcame the world, and we have chosen to be one with Him (see John 17). Through His Atonement we experience the mighty change of heart (see Mosiah 5:2; Alma 5:14) that changes everything else, including what we want and how we live.

FAITHFULLY PAY TITHES AND OFFERINGS

The foundation of provident living is the law of the tithe. The primary purpose of this law is to help us develop our faith in Heavenly Father and His Son, Jesus Christ. As we faithfully pay our tithing, we overcome our desires for the things of this world and focus on serving others. When this happens, we discover one of the greatest blessings of tithing: We are never possessed by the things of this world as long as we freely and willingly give one-tenth of our increase to the Lord.

In addition to faithfully paying tithes, making a generous fast offering helps us fulfill the Lord's charge to us to "remember the poor, and consecrate of thy properties for their support. . . . And inasmuch as ye impart of your substance unto the poor, ye will do it unto me" (D&C 42:30–31).

A fast offering is at least the cost of the two consecutive meals from which we abstain each month. By not eating these meals, we draw close to the Lord in humility and prayer and also participate in anonymous giving to bless our brothers and sisters all over the world. Paying fast offerings along with our tithes prepares us to live the higher law of consecration—to dedicate and give all our time, talents, and resources to the work of the Lord. By sacrificing to the Lord what we may think we need or want for ourselves, we also learn to rely on Him. We learn to trust that what we have been given, through the blessings of the Lord and our own diligent efforts, is sufficient for our needs.

The commitment to pay our tithes and offerings blesses us with discipline. Whenever we give to the Lord, we awaken a desire to be more careful with what He has given us. As a young married couple, Mary and I observed that our money seemed to go farther because we paid our tithing. That is the experience of millions of faithful tithepayers around the world.

Paying tithes and offerings also gives us a sense of purpose and meaning in life. As we pay our tithes and offerings, we recognize that their principal purpose is not to provide revenue for the Church or the poor. The commandment to pay tithes and offerings is to help us become like Heavenly Father by serving Him and His children.

New members of the Church quickly learn that the payment of tithes and offerings is essential to their growth in the gospel. It is one of the ways they demonstrate their desire to come unto the Lord and to leave the world behind. As all members obediently pay tithes and offerings, we see the hand of the Lord in our lives and our faith grows. That faith is necessary to be prepared to make and keep temple covenants and to obtain the power that comes of temple ordinances. It is also essential to sustain us through the trials, tribulations, and sorrows of life's journey.

Why Tithes and Offerings Matter Now

Clearly, we live in difficult times. We have seen financial storm clouds on the horizon for many years. As the days go by, that storm is coming over our lands and our homes. It is unsettling and stressful. At times it can place an individual and a family in deep anxiety, even fear and depression. Those who pay an honest tithe are in a position to invoke the Lord's help and, according to His will, receive His blessings.

As the circumstances in this world become less certain, having faith in His will becomes increasingly necessary. Too often I hear of couples who are otherwise faithful in keeping their covenants but who choose to forgo paying tithes and offerings for a season while they get into the home or car they desire. But paying tithes and offerings becomes more and more difficult when we put it off. We need to know and do the Lord's will now, and we need the blessings He wants to give us now. So we must decide to pay our tithing now.

Sometimes we think our personal circumstances justify an adjustment in the commandment to pay tithes and offerings. In truth, the more unusual or difficult our personal circumstances are, the more we need the blessings of exactness in our obedience. I can think of no more important piece of financial advice for children, for missionaries who have just returned, and for couples who have just been married than to pay their tithing faithfully, even when they are starting out—*especially* when they are starting out. Would they, or any of us, intentionally reject an outpouring of blessings from the Lord? Sadly, this is what we do when we fail to pay our tithing. We say *no* to the very blessings we specifically need and are seeking and praying to receive.

For this reason, no one is too rich or too poor to pay tithing. No one can afford *not* to pay tithing. For example, two missionaries visited a very poor family. The family's home was made of pressboard and sticks, with a dirt floor and no electricity or beds. Each evening the father, a farm laborer, spent his entire day's wages on groceries for dinner.

Departing from their humble home, the senior missionary companion thought to himself, "The law of tithing will surely be a stumbling block to this family. Perhaps we shouldn't bring it up for a while."

A few moments later, the junior companion, who had grown up in similar circumstances in his own country, voiced his own thoughts aloud: "I know the principle of tithing isn't taught for four more discussions, but can we please teach it the next time we visit? They need to know about tithing now because they need the help and the blessings of the Lord so much."

That young missionary understood that "there is a law, irrevocably decreed in heaven before the foundations of this world, upon which all blessings are predicated—and when we obtain any blessing from God, it is by obedience to that law upon which it is predicated" (D&C 130:20–21). He knew that the Lord wanted to bless this family and anxiously awaited their obedience so He could.

PROVE HIM NOW HEREWITH

If you are one who has doubted the blessings of tithing, I encourage you to accept the Lord's invitation to "prove [Him] now herewith" (Malachi 3:10). If you have gotten behind, start paying your tithing now and move forward. Begin today. Share with your bishop your commitment to pay a full tithe in the future, and work out a plan to be in the temple as soon as possible. Beyond the basic physical necessities of life, which are few, what the Lord has to offer us is infinitely more valuable than anything available in the world.

"Wherefore, do not spend money for that which is of no worth, nor your labor for that which cannot satisfy. Hearken diligently unto me, and remember the words which I have spoken; and come unto the Holy One of Israel, and feast upon that which perisheth not, neither can be corrupted" (2 Nephi 9:51).

I testify that the blessings of faithfully paying tithes and offerings will not perish but will nourish and sustain us in this life and prepare us for life in the presence of our Heavenly Father and His Son, Jesus Christ. May each of us unlock the windows of heaven and feast upon Their sustaining blessings now.

CHECKPOINTS

✓ What contention and stress in my marriage are due to money?

✓ How disciplined are we in financial matters? Can we and do we say *no* to buying things we cannot afford?

✓ How well are we following prophetic instruction to avoid and to get out of debt?

✓ Have we allowed our hearts to become set on the things of this world instead of on the blessings of eternity?

*And he also saw other multitudes feeling their way
towards that great and spacious building. And it came to pass
that many were drowned in the depths of the fountain; and many were
lost from his view, wandering in strange roads.*

1 Nephi 8:31–32

*And the mists of darkness are the temptations
of the devil, which blindeth the eyes, and hardeneth the hearts
of the children of men, and leadeth them away into
broad roads, that they perish and are lost.*

1 Nephi 12:17

CHAPTER TWENTY-FOUR

TRUE TO OURSELVES AND OUR MISSION

W HILE BEARING MY testimony in the presence of the First Presidency and the Twelve in my first meeting as a General Authority, I noticed something very interesting. Displayed on the walls of the meeting room in the Salt Lake Temple were paintings of all the Presidents of the Church of this dispensation, from Joseph Smith to Spencer W. Kimball. On the wall opposite Joseph's painting was a portrait of Hyrum Smith. I wondered, Why Hyrum? During my testimony I found myself thinking, Oliver, Oliver, where are you?

Afterwards I went to a dear friend, Elder Bruce R. McConkie, and asked, "Why would I have thought that?"

He held up his scriptures and said, "Your scriptures are the same as mine." He knew the answer was there. So I searched.

Later I went back to him and said, "It is true. The place of Oliver Cowdery was given to Hyrum Smith" (see D&C 124:94–95).

It is incredible that Oliver would fall away from the Church when you think of all he saw the Prophet Joseph Smith do and all he heard him say. He served as Joseph's scribe. He was a witness to the plates. He was with Joseph on that marvelous day, April 3, 1836, when Jesus, Moses, Elias, and Elijah appeared to them in the Kirtland Temple. He was with Joseph day in and day out, as companion, confidant, and friend. And while he was true to his witness of the Book of Mormon and eventually came back into the Church, he lost his place as the second elder of the Church because he was not always true to himself and to his mission.

Now every time I visit that room in the Salt Lake Temple, I am reminded of the importance of being faithful to the end. Like Oliver, if we are not careful and true to who we really are, we can lose our opportunity to participate in this work, and, if we do not come back, jeopardize our place in the kingdom.

Mists of Darkness

We don't know the end from the beginning. That is, we don't know what opportunities, adventures, and trials we have ahead of us. For example, we don't know whether our greatest test will be morality, an attitude about a doctrine, losing the Spirit because we refuse to forgive someone, or the illness, injury, or death of a loved one. But we do know that as we press forward each of us will be tested in some way. To recollect Nephi's vision of the pathway through life, all of us will find ourselves in the mists of darkness—forging ahead through experiences and circumstances that can deceive us, distort our perspective, and make it easy to wander off into broad and strange roads. Only when we hold on to the word of God, including the promptings of the Holy Ghost in our own hearts and minds, will we be able to stay on the path, take our rightful place, and receive our eternal reward.

The Lesson of Samuel Brannan

To stay on the path, we must heed more than just our own desires and feelings. In my office hangs a painting by Arnold Friberg of the ship *Brooklyn*. It serves as a sad reminder of the importance of being true to ourselves and our missions, and it clearly demonstrates the importance of following the prophets.

Samuel Brannan was a naturally gifted leader; he could have been a great leader. One historian called him "a man of more ability and zeal than high principle."[1] Interestingly enough, he once served as an apprentice to Oliver Cowdery in the Church's printing office.[2]

In 1846, as the Saints prepared to move west, Brigham Young called Orson Pratt, a member of the Quorum of the Twelve Apostles, to organize a group of Saints in the northeastern United States to gather to the West under the leadership of Samuel Brannan. They were to sail around Cape Horn at the tip of South America, land in California, and then travel overland to meet Brigham Young. The prophet wanted to explore all possible options for leading the Saints west, and Brother Brannan was entrusted by the Lord to lead this part of the effort.

On February 4, 1846, Brannan and 238 men, women, and children set sail on the ship *Brooklyn* from New York. If they thought their journey westward would be easier than that of the Saints who went by land, they were quickly disappointed. Terrible storms tried the patience and faith of all those aboard; the journey was horrendous. But the Saints remained faithful in their afflictions, surprising the crew as they sang the hymns of Zion during a life-threatening storm.

---

1. Hubert Howe Bancroft, *History of California, 1846–1848,* in *The Works of Hubert Howe Bancroft,* vol. 22 (San Francisco: The History Publishers, 1886), 5:545.

2. Stanley R. Gunn, *Oliver Cowdery: Second Elder and Scribe* (Salt Lake City: Bookcraft, 1962), 253.

The Brooklyn, *by Arnold Friberg*

The *Brooklyn* eventually sailed to the Sandwich (now Hawaiian) Islands to resupply before finally landing on July 31, 1846, in Yerba Buena (now San Francisco), California. They had sailed roughly twenty-four thousand miles in 177 days. Eleven passengers had died during the voyage.[3]

Once in California, Brannan found a spot of land that he thought would be ideal for establishing Zion in the West: "Along the headwaters of the majestic San Joaquin River, at the juncture of the Stanislaus, slept a land of breath-taking natural beauty, boundless level acres, and a climate which rivaled Italy. The soil was deep, wild game in plenteous abundance, and with a natural waterway to the Pacific seaports on the bay. A more perfect setting could hardly

---

3. See Joan S. Hamblin, "Voyage of the 'Brooklyn,'" *Ensign,* July 1997, 16–18.

be imagined," wrote one historian. Brannan "believed he'd marked the true site for Zion."[4]

Brannan must have been filled with desire and enthusiasm to succeed in his assignment. Certainly he had paid a dear price to find this new "Bountiful" in the West. He journeyed east to share his discovery with Brigham Young, meeting the prophet's party in Green River, Wyoming, on June 30, 1847. We can imagine the conviction with which he made his case to have the Saints settle in the fertile climes of California rather than the barren deserts of Utah. But the prophet would not budge from the vision that had been given him: The Saints were to settle in the Rocky Mountains.[5]

This was Brannan's moment of truth, the test that would determine whether he would complete the mission that had been given him. Brannan chose to go his own way rather than follow the prophet, and, as Robert Frost would say, that made all the difference.[6]

Brannan returned to California in August 1847, disappointed and defiant. Soon gold was discovered in California, making Brannan and some other Church members suddenly wealthy. Brannan collected tithes of the members, but he refused to send the tithing of the California Saints to Salt Lake. The Church even sent one of the Twelve to retrieve it, but Brannan refused to give it up, keeping the money for his own purposes. "You tell Brother Young . . . that I'll give up the Lord's money when he sends me a receipt signed by the Lord," Brannan is reported to have said.[7]

Brannan was excommunicated from the Church and left to

---

4. Paul Dayton Bailey, "Sam Brannan and the Mormons in Early California—Part III," *Improvement Era*, December 1942, 804.

5. See Hamblin, "Voyage of the 'Brooklyn,'" 18–19.

6. See Robert Frost, *The Road Not Taken and Other Poems* (New York: Dover, 1993), 1.

7. Ralph B. Jordan, "The Story of Sam Brannan," *Improvement Era*, July 1936, 406.

himself. He prospered for a season, engaging in everything from mining gold, to establishing a mill, to speculating in real estate, to operating a distillery. He became California's first millionaire and one of the wealthiest men in the West.[8]

But over time his fortunes changed. He lost his wife and his wealth. Known for his drunkenness, he died a penniless pauper in Mexico. His body lay unclaimed for sixteen months.[9]

Samuel Brannan had forgotten who he was and what he was about. First disappointed and then defiant, he failed to be true to himself and his mission and forfeited the opportunity to return to his heavenly home with honor.

Many of the Saints who arrived on the ship *Brooklyn* followed Brannan out of the Church, but some remained valiant. William and Jane Glover, for example, journeyed to Salt Lake City with their children and donated to the building of the Salt Lake Temple five thousand dollars in gold they had mined. Their donations, along with those of other Saints returning from California, "probably saved the Mormon money system and provided much of the liquid capital essential for continued economic growth."[10] They remembered who they were and what their mission was.

WISHES AND DREAMS UNFULFILLED

The knowledge of who we are and what our mission is may come to us gradually as we develop our talents and gifts and listen

8. PBS, "New Perspectives on the West: Samuel Brannan," http://www.pbs.org/weta/thewest/people/a_c/brannan.htm; accessed 26 February 2010.

9. See James E. Faust, "I Believe I Can, I Knew I Could," *Ensign,* November 2002, 50.

10. Kenneth J. Davies, *Mormon Gold: The Story of California's Mormon Argonauts* (Salt Lake City: Olympus, 1984), cited in Richard O. Cowan and William E. Homer, *California Saints: A 150-Year Legacy in the Golden State* (Provo: Religious Studies Center, Brigham Young University, 1996), 133.

to the promptings of the Spirit. Staying in tune with the Spirit will help us to choose wisely as we make our way in life.

Like millions of other young boys I had a dream of playing major league baseball. This was neither an idle dream nor a fleeting desire—it was a compelling drive occupying my youthful years. Hours of practicing and playing baseball competitively filled countless afternoons as I honed my athletic skills and followed advice from world-class players and coaches. The emotional ups and downs were punctuated with the elation of victory and the agony of defeat.

We have to understand that our hopes, dreams, and aspirations may not be fulfilled in our lives. Both our successes and our failures are the maturing moments of our life. What we learn from these experiences shapes our perspective. There are many reasons for our not achieving all of the goals we set for ourselves. Our goals may be unrealistic and beyond our mental, physical, or emotional capabilities. Or our goals may conflict with the natural evolution of circumstances around us, such as world events, social interactions, or the choices of others that are beyond our control.

My sister was one of the few people in the world to know of my dreams and disappointments. Many years ago, she gave me a card with a picture of a boy about ten years old, mitt in hand and bat slung over his shoulder, standing at the entrance to a stadium. My caring sister recognized her little brother's boyhood dream that had not been fulfilled. She wrote tender words of comfort on the back of the picture: "I could not resist this card. It is *so you!!!* . . . I love you and think of you often."

The picture was a poignant reminder of a dream not realized—to one day play for my favorite team, the New York Yankees, in Yankee Stadium. I have kept that card for many years because the picture teaches a valuable lesson: Don't live your life in regrets. Don't dwell on the past, even on the good things that you could not or chose not to do. My mother taught me, "If the Lord wants you to be a ball player, you will be. Follow where the Spirit takes you!"

There will be times in our lives when things don't go as we plan, but the Lord's plan is greater than we can even dream. When disappointments come into our lives, it is well to remember that we should learn from our experiences, both successes and failures, and be grateful for being able to move joyfully forward with faith and hope.

I have often pondered what would have happened in my life if I had chosen to pursue a baseball career. If I had been successful in that athletic career, I would never have had all of the other exciting opportunities I had to work for international companies and, most important, to serve the Lord to the extent that has been my privilege. Sometimes unrealized dreams or prayers not answered in the way we hoped are blessings in disguise that fulfill eternal purposes in our lives.

As we look to the future and leave behind what is past, secure in the guidance of the Spirit, we will find joy in our life well beyond what might have been. When we remember who we are and are true to ourselves and to our mission, we enjoy life as it is and are enabled to continue faithful to the end.

True and Faithful to the End

As sons and daughters of God, each of us left our heavenly home, having been called on a mortal mission for a noble purpose. Each of us should pray for guidance to know what we were sent to earth to accomplish—and for the strength and wisdom to remain true and faithful to the end.

It is part of the plan to have experiences that test, strengthen, and refine us. Most of these experiences can also distract us from completing our mortal mission by tempting us to let go of God's

word in the scriptures, in the teachings of the living prophets, and the promptings of the Holy Ghost. The Savior warned that "the cares of this world, and the deceitfulness of riches, and the lusts of other things" can "choke the word" (Mark 4:19).

May we listen to the Spirit and remember who we are and what we are here to do—to follow the Savior and His servants and return with honor. The Lord will direct us in our life's choices as we seek the guidance of His Spirit. Then, true to ourselves and our mission, we will be encircled in the arms of our loving Father and His Beloved Son and receive that sweet commendation, "Well done, thou good and faithful servant: . . . enter thou into the joy of thy lord" (Matthew 25:21).

CHECKPOINTS

✓ How well do I understand my mission in life?

✓ Do I seek the guidance of the Spirit in the choices I make to fulfill my mission?

✓ How much do I allow myself to be distracted from that mission by the vain things of the world or other temptations?

And Adam and Eve blessed the name of God, and they made all things known unto their sons and their daughters.

MOSES 5:12

CHAPTER TWENTY-FIVE

Strengthening Families

N O PARENT IS PERFECT. I find myself asking the question, How will my children remember me? Perhaps you have wondered how your children and grandchildren will remember you. Certainly parents make mistakes in their parenting, but through humility, faith, prayer, study, and continued effort, each of us can improve and in so doing bless the lives of family members now and for generations to come.

The calling of father or mother is sacred and carries with it great privileges and responsibilities. A parent assists Heavenly Father in accomplishing His plan for His children to come into this world to obtain bodies, to exercise their agency, and to learn, grow, and become like Him. A parent is also a servant of the Savior, teaching His gospel, and showing the way to follow Him in all things.

A significant part of a parent's responsibility is to represent Heavenly Father and exemplify who He is. Whether or not we realize it, our children naturally look to us to learn the characteristics of Heavenly Father. As they come to love, respect, and have confidence in us, they often unknowingly develop the same feelings towards their Heavenly Father. On the other hand, when children do not trust their parents, it is very difficult for them to trust in God.

As parents, we are invited to both emulate Heavenly Father and to seek His guidance in the way we raise His children. In the process, we find we are continually directed by His Spirit to make sacrifices to provide what our children need. The most important of those sacrifices is simply to obey God's commandments. In order to *lead* our children on the strait and narrow path back to Heavenly Father, we must walk that path ourselves. Even though we are not perfect, we are also responsible to occasionally provide, under the direction of the Spirit, loving course correction that will assist our children to stay on the path. Because they must choose for themselves whether to stay on that path, our correction must be inspired, understanding, and patient if we are to succeed in truly helping them.

PROACTIVE PARENTING

Part of helping our children is to proactively create an environment in which they can thrive spiritually. The key to that is to create a strong and supportive family.

Like Moses' mother, Jochebed, we raise our children in a wicked and hostile world, a world as dangerous as the courts of Egypt ruled by Pharaoh. But, like Jochebed, we also weave around our children a protective basket, a vessel called the family, through which they can safely return with honor. An important part of that safety is a clear signal that every family member is loved and belongs, even when they ignore parental teachings and make serious mistakes.

But Jochebed did not do her work alone. Moses' sister, Miriam, watched over the basket as it lay "in the flags by the river's brink" (Exodus 2:3). As our children leave our homes and make their way in the world, the Lord will likewise provide Miriams for them—special third-party helpers such as priesthood and auxiliary leaders, teachers, extended family, and worthy friends. As parents, we are sometimes prompted by the Spirit to seek special help beyond ourselves through such resources as priesthood leaders, doctors, and qualified counselors. The Spirit will direct when and how such help should be obtained. In our parenting responsibilities, it will be wise to remember that "it is not meet that [the Lord] should command in all things" (D&C 58:26). He may not tell us directly everything we should do in order to help our family. Just as the brother of Jared did when faced with having no light for his vessels (see Ether 2–3), we must carefully consider our family's needs, make a plan, and then take that plan to the Lord in prayer. This will require faith and effort on our part, and He will help us as we seek His assistance and do His will.

BE THERE WHEN OUR CHILDREN NEED US

Because of the importance of the family to the eternal plan of happiness, Satan makes a major effort to destroy the family. Among other things, he seeks to discourage us as parents from making our children a high priority. To ensure our children's well-being, we must deliberately spend time with each of them individually, letting them choose the activity and the subject of conversation. This requires that we block out distractions, even some that may seem harmless or even worthwhile, and do things for their sakes that we might not otherwise choose to do.

As a means for making improvements, we may wish to prayerfully evaluate how we spend our time each week. Here is a valuable exercise: Take a planner or other organizing tool and keep track of how much time is spent on work, Church assignments, social and personal activities, and with our children. What do we learn? Are our families—and specifically our children—getting our best efforts? Are they getting enough of us? What are they learning about us and about the Church by the way we are spending our time? Will

Robert at age two with his family: brother, Jerry;
father, J. Rulon; mother, Vera Marie; sister, Janet

they resist marrying an active member of the Church because they have seen our example of actively serving everyone else *but* them?

I remember as a young boy lying on the ground with my father and my brother. We would look up into the clouds. My father, who was an artist, would invite us to study the fluffy white shapes and pick out the shapes of animals and objects. This was a kind of Rorschach inkblot test administered by Mother Nature. What was most valuable was not pointing out the shapes but talking about what we saw—together! To this day, those sweet moments are remembered and recalled, long after Father is gone.

I thank my Heavenly Father for a mother who was also there when I needed her, including when I was a young man and dating young women. When I'd return from an evening out, we would talk about where I had been and what I had done. Then she waited for a goodnight kiss, which I appreciated the opportunity to give.

It was many years later when our children started to become teenagers that my mother asked Mary and me, "Are you talking with your sons and giving them a goodnight kiss when they come home?"

Mary said, "There are times when we don't do that."

Mother said, "Well, it is a great Word of Wisdom check."

I never knew that I had been checked on during all those years! What I did know is that my mother loved me, cared about what I was doing, and wanted to hear all about it. Realistically, some mothers are in situations that prevent them from being home all of the time. But in choosing obligations and making plans, all parents should remember that for children there are very few moments more lonely, even fearful, than coming home to an empty house.

Meeting the needs of our children includes involving them in activities that they need to grow and develop. For example, children need to work with their parents, even if it may be faster and easier for parents to do the job themselves. As we work together, we have the opportunity to talk with our children in a safe and open setting. I had many such opportunities myself every Saturday with my father.

Eating together is perhaps the most effective opportunity for open and safe communication. I remember an incident that happened when I was about twelve years old and I was beginning to enjoy playing baseball with my friends. "I'd like you home at 6:00 for dinner when your father arrives," my mother cautioned me as I left.

"Just save my meal, and I'll eat it later," I pleaded. "We're playing ball."

That's when she sat me down. "You have to understand, it's not just the food. It's being together as a family. Will you do this one thing for your mother?"

What could I say?

My mother understood something that sociologists and others are now confirming: "According to research, eating together as a family on a regular basis has some surprising effects. When sharing a meal together family bonds become stronger, children are better adjusted, family members eat more nutritional meals, they are less likely to be overweight, and they are less likely to abuse alcohol or other drugs."[1] I am convinced that having meals together daily and tucking our children into bed each night are some of the most important things parents can do.

LEAD BY EXAMPLE

Our children will best remember us by our example. I remember experiences from my early childhood that taught me about the priesthood and about how priesthood holders respect womanhood. From my father's example of tenderly caring for my mother, my aunts, and my sister, I began to see my own responsibilities toward women more clearly. Father was the first to arise from dinner to clear the table. My sister and I would wash and dry the dishes each night at Father's request. If we were not there, Father and Mother would clean the kitchen together. It may sound like something out of a black-and-white movie, but I have warm memories of Mother and her tiny slippered feet on top of Father's feet as they danced around the kitchen. Their lives were an expression of their love.

I also remember my brother, my sister, and me sitting on the floor around our mother and father as they read the scriptures to us. Sometimes they would ask, "What does that scripture mean to you?" or "How does it make you feel?" Then they would listen to us as we responded in our own words.

My father and mother served a full-time mission to England

---

1. Larry Forthun, "Family Nutrition: The Truth about Family Meals," http://edis.ifas.ufl.edu/FY1061; accessed 26 February 2010.

later in life. As I visited them one day in their small flat in London, I watched my mother, with a shawl wrapped snugly around her shoulders, putting shillings in the gas meter to keep warm. I asked, "Why did you come on a mission, Mother?"

Mother said simply, "Because I have eleven grandsons. I want them to know that Grandma and Grandpa served."

In later years, after Mother had a stroke, Father faithfully met her every need. The last two years of her life she required twenty-four-hour-a-day care. Often he was called by Mother every few minutes, day and night. I will never forget his example of continually caring for his cherished companion. He told me it was small payment for more than fifty years of my mother's loving devotion to him.

My parents understood well that their example was the powerful gospel teaching that would stick with us the rest of our lives.

BE BOLD BUT NOT OVERBEARING

Spending time with our children provides a great foundation of love for those times when we will need to correct them. While we do not want to be so iron-fisted that we drive our children away from the Lord, we do not want to be so afraid of chastising them that we fail to give them the direction they need to succeed in their lives.

So many parents are afraid of their children—afraid to counsel with them for fear of offending them. They feel that correcting their children will strain relationships or exacerbate problems. They fear their child will say, "If I can't have it my way, I'm going to leave!" But Alma demonstrated the essence of being a loving father when talking to his sons and telling them about things as they really are. He taught Helaman and Shiblon, "Inasmuch as ye shall keep the commandments of God ye shall prosper in the land; and inasmuch as ye will not keep the commandments of God ye shall be cut off from his presence" (Alma 38:1; see also 36:30). Such words may be difficult for a father to say to his son, but in them are essential truths a son may need to hear.

Like Alma, we should always speak the truth to our children in love and with genuine concern for their well-being. I recall counseling with a mission president who led with a very firm hand. He had built his own business and had a reputation for being a tough businessman. In his calling he was dealing with a difficult situation in which some of his missionaries had publicly vilified him. When we talked by telephone, the first thing he said was, "Don't tell me to love them!" He had already heard me give that counsel on other occasions.

Some firm action did need to be taken, but I was concerned about saving his missionaries. With a little counsel, this good mission president took a gentler approach than he might have on his own. Years later he came to see me and said, "I want to tell you how much I appreciated what I learned in the mission field with you. I learned that the Lord's way is different from mine. It helped me in my whole life." He had become more caring and warm in the way he led and parented, and his children recognized it.

As much as we want to help our children, it is necessary to recognize that we cannot force or "will" them to have faith. When a teenager begins testing family values, parents need to go to the Lord for guidance about how to help them. As a general rule, when young people struggle, that is the time for added love and support and to reinforce scriptural teachings about how to make choices with Heavenly Father's help. It is frightening to allow children to learn from the mistakes they may make, but their willingness to choose the Lord and the values of His gospel is greater when the choice they make comes from within. The Lord's way of love and acceptance is better than Satan's way of force and coercion, especially in rearing teenagers.

Faith is not something we or they can take "off the shelf." Rather, it grows in us, based upon our desire to receive it and to exercise it in our lives. Having rigid rules, drumming in discipline, and being harsh intellectually or physically never really works. All of us have to come to certain conclusions on our own, and our children are no exception.

Of course, the manner in which children come to their own conclusions varies widely. I smile when I meet parents who have three well-behaved children and one child who is "out of the box." Such parents sometimes say to themselves and others, "I don't understand it. We did everything the same." But each child is unique and therefore may need a different approach from what we may have used on the others. Great parents are flexible, recognizing that Heavenly Father has endowed each of His children with unique characteristics. The Savior's Atonement allows all of us to "come in the unity of the faith" (Ephesians 4:13) without losing our distinct, divinely given differences.

Root Out Selfishness

Is there a way to completely prevent the difficulties we encounter in our own parenting relationships? No. But addressing our own selfishness can make a significant difference. The natural man would focus on his or her own interests at the expense of listening, understanding, and taking into account the other person's real feelings, needs, and concerns. Part of God's plan for the family is to learn and practice getting beyond oneself by developing a deep and abiding desire for the welfare of others (see Enos 1:9). Being a good parent is an intensive course in that plan. As we follow it, we discover that it requires much sacrifice from us, even as it provides us with many opportunities to grow.

One way in which our selfishness can hurt our children is when we become more concerned about our image as parents than about their well-being. I can still recall a stake conference in which one of our sons was really acting up during the prayer. He seemed to sense that I couldn't do much to control him in public, and he was taking full advantage of the situation. After the prayer, I quickly took my son out, upset enough to spank him. All of a sudden I realized that the greatest problem wasn't him but me. I was humiliated because he had embarrassed *me*.

Of course we should never let our fears about ourselves—about how our children's challenges reflect on us—keep us from getting them the help they need. There are situations in which children have mental, physical, or emotional conditions that require professional attention—situations in which talking with them and loving them just aren't enough. Whether the answer is counseling or medication, when help from medical professionals is available, we do our children a disservice if we are reluctant to admit they have problems. Their diagnosis is not a reflection on us.

I am not suggesting that we rush to medicate every child who is highly energetic or deeply discouraged. Many challenges can be addressed solely through our prayers, love, and priesthood blessings. But some conditions are so severe or persistent that inspired parents may themselves be prompted to seek professional help for their children. It would be a tragedy to deny our children the help that is available to them merely because we thought others would judge us adversely as parents.

A related challenge arises when parents resent the bishop's involvement in helping their children repent and make restitution for their sins. Sometimes our self-concerns blind us to this essential principle: Our bishop is our ally, and he has the keys to do some things that not even a parent can do for his or her child. When we murmur about our priesthood leaders and their counsel, we do our children a great disservice. We diminish our leaders' credibility in their eyes and therefore tempt them to be closed to counsel in the future.

Look for Opportunities to Teach

The best way to help our children with the trials they face is to teach them the gospel of Jesus Christ—and teach them so it will sink deep into their hearts. There is not enough time in formal meetings to teach our children everything they need to know. Therefore, we must take advantage of everyday teaching moments. These moments are priceless. They come when we are working, playing, and struggling together. When they come, the Spirit of the Lord can help us know what to say and how to help our children accept our teaching. Sometimes we are too intimidated to teach or testify to our children. I have been guilty of that in my own life. Our children need to have us share spiritual feelings with them and to teach and bear testimony to them.

My mother was a ward and stake Relief Society president in the New York Stake for many years. Our ward covered a large area. When I was sixteen I was allowed to get my driver's license on the condition that I would drive my mother to help her fulfill her responsibilities as Relief Society president. I remember running up three flights of stairs to deliver groceries and doing all kinds of errands to assist families in need. Through her teaching, I learned to understand and appreciate the joy of serving and caring for others.

My mother understood the counsel of the Lord recorded in Deuteronomy 6:6–7: "And these words, which I command thee this day, shall be in thine heart:

"And thou shalt teach them diligently unto thy children, and shalt talk of them when thou sittest in thine house, and when thou walkest by the way, and when thou liest down, and when thou risest up."

Our challenge—and our opportunity—is to have the courage of Lehi to teach, preach, exhort, and even prophesy to our children in every setting along life's path. Our objective is to interact with them so that everything we say and do beckons them to keep the commandments, stay on the path, and partake of the fruit of the tree of life.

LOVING OUR PRODIGAL CHILDREN

What can parents do to help their young children stay on the path now and in the future? Children who learn to pray by praying with their parents are more likely to pray when they are older. Children who are taught to love God and believe He lives will more often continue their spiritual development as they mature—their feelings of love and devotion to God will increase with time.

But even parents who are exemplary in loving and teaching may have one or more children who choose to ignore or resist the gospel taught them in their youth. How should we respond? What can we do to help them? May I suggest that most of our children still have deep testimonies of the gospel, even though they may not be living gospel standards. Oftentimes, they are looking for the right moment, the right person, or the right set of circumstances to come back. We can help them by learning and living the principle of agency—believing, deeply believing, that they have the capacity to choose for themselves to follow the Savior. Then we pray and fast and exercise our faith that their life's experiences will help them regain a desire and an ability to follow Him.

We can also help them by cultivating an enviroment in our homes and meetinghouses that will assure them they are welcomed, loved, and needed. When my sweetheart and I were sealed in the Salt Lake Temple, Elder Harold B. Lee gave us wise counsel: "When you raise your voice in anger, the Spirit departs from your home." We must never, out of anger, lock the door of our home or our heart to our children. Like the prodigal son, our children need to know that when they come to themselves, they can turn to us for love and counsel.

How do they know that? In the parable of the prodigal son

is a powerful lesson for families and especially for parents. After the younger son "came to himself" (Luke 15:17), he decided to go home. How did he know his father wouldn't reject him? Because he knew his father.

Through the inevitable misunderstandings, conflicts, and follies of the son's youth, I can visualize his father being there with an understanding and compassionate heart, a soft answer, a listening ear, and a forgiving embrace. We do not know what the father's parting words were to his son, but I am convinced they were not harsh or vindictive. I believe the father must have made it clear to the rebellious son that if he ever returned, the son would be loved and welcomed home by his father with open arms and willing hands, for the scriptures say, "When he was yet a great way off, his father saw him, and had compassion, and ran, and fell on his neck, and kissed him" (Luke 15:20). Not only was the father quick to embrace the son when he returned but he had been slow to give up hope.

Even as we love and pray and seek after our prodigal children, we have a responsibility to those who are still walking the gospel path. We help them by continually reminding them of the blessings they are already receiving through their faithfulness. We thank them, as well, for the joy they bring us through their obedience. This will remind them that misbehaving is not the only way to get our attention. We should regularly let all our children know of our love for them, whether they have wandered to a far country or stayed faithfully at home.

Sometimes when our children stray, the adversary seeks to compound our grief by tempting us to blame ourselves for our children's choices. We may feel that everyone else's children are perfect and only ours have rebelled. But my wife has taught me that if we think other families don't have any difficulties or any problems, we just don't know them well enough.

Each child comes with varying gifts and talents. Some, like

Abel, seem to have been given gifts of faith at birth. Others struggle with every decision they make. Parents are never failures when they do their best. Their faith, prayers, and efforts will be consecrated to the good of them and their children now and in the eternities.

As parents of struggling children, we should be careful that our hope does not falter and our faith does not waver. The choices of our children should never weaken our own commitment to the Savior. Our worthiness will not be measured according to their righteousness. Lehi and Sariah did not let disobedient children tarnish their devotion to God. Lehi did not lose the blessing of feasting at the tree of life because Laman and Lemuel refused to partake of its fruit.

Parents sometimes feel they cannot accept or fulfill a Church calling because one of their children is straying. Yet as we accept callings and do our best, we may have a profound spiritual effect on those we love the most. We also have the opportunity in our callings to help those who may be struggling with the same trial we are enduring.

Although we could all be better parents, none of us needs to raise our children alone. They are our Heavenly Father's children, and He has a great stake in their success. I testify that He leaves the door open for our children when they wander from the strait and narrow path. I also testify that it is never too late to open the door between us and our children with such simple words as "I love you," "I am sorry," and "Please forgive me." We can begin now to create a home they will want to return to—not only now but in the eternities.

To parents and families throughout the world, I testify that the Lord Jesus Christ is mighty to save. He is the Healer, the Redeemer, the rescuing Shepherd who will leave the ninety and nine to find the one. If we are seeking the salvation of special "ones" in our own families, I bear testimony that they are within His reach. We assist Him by reaching out in love to those who wander even as we continue to nurture those who have stayed at home. With the help of the Lord and His doctrine, all the hurtful effects from challenges a family may meet can be understood and overcome. Whatever the needs of family members may be, we can strengthen them as we follow the counsel given by prophets.

Jesus was able to complete his mission of the Atonement on earth because of the knowledge, example, and love of His Father. Likewise, each of us as parents, through our example, love, and care, may be remembered by our children to have the qualities that our Heavenly Father and our Savior have, so that we may endure to the end and someday return with our families to Their celestial presence.

Checkpoints

✓ How proactive am I in seeking guidance from the Lord as I try to protect my children?

✓ How willing am I to make sacrifices so that I can spend time with my children and be there when they need me?

✓ Do I live my life so that I would be happy if my children follow my example?

✓ How willing am I to give my children correction when needed?

✓ Do I correct my children in love?

✓ How well do I customize my approach for each child?

✓ Am I sometimes more concerned about my image than my children's welfare?

✓ Do I look for opportunities to apply gospel teaching throughout the day?

✓ If my children stray, how well do I keep the door to my heart and my home open to them?

Pray ye therefore the Lord of the harvest,
that he will send forth labourers into his harvest.

Matthew 9:38

CHAPTER TWENTY-SIX

Feed My Lambs, Feed My Sheep

W HEN THE SAVIOR MET Peter, he was a fisherman, along with his brother, Andrew, and their companions, James and John. Jesus issued a simple invitation that would change their lives: "Come ye after me, and I will make you to become fishers of men" (Mark 1:17). In Matthew we read that they "straightway left their nets, and followed him" (Matthew 4:20). Luke adds that these disciples "forsook all" in order to do so (Luke 5:11).

Their decision to follow the Savior was immediate, but it would take a lifetime of service for them to fully become the kind of fishers the Savior had called them to be. In the days immediately following Jesus' death, Peter forgot who he was—the senior apostle—and what he was about for just a moment. In such circumstances, we tend to do what we know how to do. "I go a fishing," Peter declared, and several other apostles joined him (John 21:3).

Lovest Thou Me?

Soon the resurrected Savior stood on the shore. When Peter realized this, he swam to meet his resurrected Lord. The Savior had prepared a meal of fish and bread for His apostles (John 21:4–9). Afterwards He asked His chief apostle a simple, penetrating question:

"Simon, son of Jonas, lovest thou me more than these?" (John 21:15). The Savior was gently reminding Peter that he had been called to leave behind fishing and other lesser things to become a fisher of men.

"Yea, Lord; thou knowest that I love thee," Peter answered.

The Savior then taught a profound lesson to all of us through Peter: "Feed my lambs." He repeated the exchange two more times, with one minor change: "Feed my sheep" (John 21:15–17).

There were times in my life when I was distracted by my business interests and I needed this same kind of reminder. I have felt moved so deeply by the Savior's exchange with Peter that I have wept. What the Lord taught Peter applies to all of His disciples and specifically to those who hold the priesthood.

After teaching and preaching to the multitudes and healing them, we read that the Savior looked on the multitudes and "was moved with compassion on them, because they fainted, and were scattered abroad, as sheep having no shepherd." To His disciples He commented, "The harvest truly is plenteous, but the labourers are few." He then invited his disciples to pray that "the Lord of the harvest [would] send forth labourers into his harvest" (Matthew 9:36–38).

The next verses, which come immediately after the chapter break, show the fulfillment of this prayer. The Savior is calling the Twelve and giving them priesthood authority, beginning with Peter (see Matthew 10:1–2). To me, the message is clear: Faithful children of God who love the Savior are called to be laborers in His harvest and to assist in shepherding His flock.

Understanding our responsibilities as shepherds may take time, as it did for Peter. Shortly before the Savior's death, He warned

Peter: "Simon, Simon, behold, Satan hath desired to have you, that he may sift you as wheat: but I have prayed for thee, that thy faith fail not: and when thou art converted, strengthen thy brethren" (Luke 22:31–32).

Conversion

What is this conversion that causes us to be concerned about strengthening others? It is a refocusing of our attention away from the world and onto the work of salvation. It requires all our gifts and talents, and it calls for all our hearts. It also requires sacrifice. The Lord did not say, "Tend my sheep when it is convenient; watch my sheep when you aren't busy." He said, in essence, "Feed my lambs and my sheep; help them survive in this world, keep them close to you. Lead them to safety—the safety of righteous choices that will prepare them for eternal life" (see John 21:15–17).

What do the references to lambs and sheep mean? Feeding the *lambs* can be taken to mean serving those who are new to the gospel, such as newly baptized members, who must be nurtured and given warmth and fellowship in the family of Saints. It may also remind us that we are all called to teach and lead the youngest members of the Church—the children. Feeding the *sheep* may refer to serving the long-time members of the Church, some active and some less active, who need to be loved and safeguarded in the flock through individual ministering, including home and visiting teaching. The Savior's inclusion of both lambs and sheep suggests that our responsibility is to *feed everyone.*

As converted members, our work to feed and strengthen the flock of God often requires more than we think we can give. I can still remember one occasion when we had just moved to California, where I was taking on a challenging new assignment for my company. The bishop met with us and asked me about my availability to serve. I told him that I was working about fourteen to sixteen hours a day and added—mostly in jest—that if he had anything from 4:00 to 6:00 in the morning, I'd take it. I should have known better. I was soon appointed to teach early-morning seminary every weekday morning at 6:00.

Fulfilling such a time-consuming assignment was far from easy, given my professional responsibilities at the time. But I was richly blessed in both my personal and my professional life by heeding the call to help shepherd some of the Savior's lambs. I taught the Book of Mormon that year and learned things that have been a doctrinal foundation for serving in callings throughout my life.

A conversion is a change. In sacrificing to serve, we discover that we are changed: The Lord blesses us with energy and resources we didn't know we had. When I was a Regional Representative of the Twelve and a business executive, I would sometimes collapse on the couch after returning home from a long and exhausting trip. After a few minutes, my wife would kindly remind me that shepherds do not rest until they have taken care of all the sheep. "Have you done your home teaching yet?" she would gently ask. Getting up off the couch, I discovered a principle that applies to all service in God's kingdom: By feeding the lambs and sheep, we too are fed by the Spirit of the Lord, and we find reserves of love, motivation, energy, and desire to bring souls unto the Savior.

TRUE SHEPHERDS

Filled with a desire to be true shepherds, we are not content merely to number the sheep. True shepherds know and care for them just as parents know and care for their children. And when one of the sheep is wandering or lost, a true shepherd cannot rest.

I once encountered an older Basque shepherd in northern

Spain who told me about an experience he had had as a young shepherd that changed his life. As he was watching over his sheep, he started to daydream and lost track of time and circumstance. He drank a little too much wine and dozed off. When he awoke, he discovered that his sheep had wandered away and a couple of them had been killed by predators. His lapse was almost more than he could bear. He rededicated himself to his shepherding. From that point on he never lost his focus or neglected the sheep that were in his care.

As converted members and shepherds, our lapses are not likely to come because we are daydreaming or dozing off but because we are doing good things. Even so, our worthwhile preoccupations may be the adversary's invitation to draw our brothers and sisters away from the fold of God. As converted members and true shepherds, our calling is to be vigilant about His sheep—to remember them, watch over them, and do all we can to keep them from wandering off and losing their way.

Making a Difference

Good examples of this vigilance are Don and Marian Summers, a senior missionary couple. They had been serving in the comfort of the London Temple Visitors' Center, but I asked them to serve the last six months of their mission in the Swindon Branch to teach and assist in activating members. For eighty years Swindon had limped along with only a few faithful members and with many good members becoming less active. Sister Summers actually broke out in hives when I extended the new assignment, so I gave her and her husband some time to pray about it. They soon returned and accepted the call. Years later Don and Marian wrote me, recalling the following:

"Our first visit to the Swindon Branch was a bit disheartening

*Elder and Sister Hales with President Spencer W. Kimball and Sister Camilla Kimball
on the banks of the River Ribble, near Preston, England, about 1976*

as we met with the Saints in a cold, rented hall. The congregation numbered seventeen, including President and Sister Hales and four missionaries. Still wearing our winter coats, we all huddled around a small, inadequate heater while we listened to a Sunday School lesson."

The letter continued: "A branch member approached me one day: 'Elder Summers, can I give you a bit of advice? Never mention the word *tithing* to the Swindon members; they really don't believe in it, and all you will do is upset them.'"

Brother Summers wrote, "We did teach tithing and all the other gospel principles. With example and the encouragement of a branch president, there was a change of heart, and faith and activity started to increase. The membership records were completely updated as

328

we visited every member's home. When the leaders started caring, the members began to respond, and a whole new spirit pervaded the branch. The members became excited again about the gospel and helping one another.

"Firesides were held in our homes, and we worked closely with members and proselyting missionaries. We made a promise to the Lord that we would not let one new or reactivated member fall into inactivity while we were in Swindon.

"One young couple had a difficult adjustment to make as their customs, manners, and dress were different. They became offended at suggestions for changes. The couple twice wrote to the bishop [by then it was a ward] and asked to have their names removed from the Church records. In the last letter they forbade any of the members to visit them, so Marian and I went to the florist and purchased a beautiful plant of chrysanthemums and had it delivered to the young couple. It was a simple note: 'We love you; we miss you; we need you. Please come back.' Signed, The Swindon Ward.

"The next Sunday was fast and testimony meeting and our last Sunday in Swindon. There were 103 members in attendance compared to 17 when we had first arrived about a year before. The young couple was there and, in bearing his testimony, the husband thanked the ward for not giving up on them."

Each of us can have similar experiences in our own wards and branches when we determine that we will care as much about our brothers and sisters as a shepherd cares about his sheep and as the Lord cares about us. Vigilantly watching over the flock of God, we discover the fulfillment of having "compassion, making a difference" (Jude 1:22), for we are bringing souls unto God. How great is our joy.

The Bishop as a Shepherd

In speaking about shepherds, I feel I must share a few words about the role of bishops, whom the Lord makes "overseers, to feed the church of God, which he hath purchased with his own blood" (Acts 20:28). I am a bishop at heart, having served in that office four times, including once as Presiding Bishop.

Elder LeGrand Richards once said: "Now, Brethren, I understand all that we discussed, but until the bishops move, nothing will happen. Everything above the bishop is all talk." It is in bishops' interviews with the youth and with other members—extending callings, showing compassion for the needy and the widows, teaching and ministering—that the important spiritual things happen in the lives of the Saints. The office of the bishop embodies the work of the Savior and invites those who hold it to become as He is.

I wish that every member of the Church would pray every night and morning for their bishop. He needs our help. He cannot carry the responsibilities on his shoulders without our help and prayers.

If you are serving as bishop, you may feel inadequate in this role. But the Lord knows you. You have been ready-made for your calling. Because the keys, power, and resources are yours, your service as a shepherd will be a joy.

Of course, the fact that you hold keys does not mean you have to do everything yourself. Too often, we think of a ward like a family-sized garden, with only one source of water—the bishop. When there are problems and challenges, we think he is the only one who can solve them. While the bishop's energy, desire, and inspiration may seem to be overflowing, there is not enough of him to get to the end of the row. There are some things that must be done by the bishop alone, but they are few. Almost everything else can and should be done by priesthood and auxiliary leaders working under the bishop's direction.

The bishop who uses the resources at hand—the auxiliaries, the priesthood—to fulfill the needs of his people is a true bishop. He does not slavishly follow the letter of the law without leaving room for inspiration. He uses councils to invite ward members to work together. In unity they look after the fold of God, including the vital work of fellowshipping, reactivation, and retention. Through the council, they ensure that every member has a friend, a responsibility, and is nourished by the good word of God.[1]

Bishops are charged with doing so many things. Among the most important are the interactions with youth, especially the one-on-one interview. Bishops, do not miss this sacred opportunity. It can be one of the most spiritual experiences in the life of a young person. Spiritually prepare yourself to perceive their needs and minister to them, even as the Good Shepherd. (If you're a young person who hasn't had the opportunity to have an interview with your bishop lately and feel you could be blessed by having one, ask if you can meet with him.)

Above all, feed the sheep. It is not enough to give well-prepared talks and lessons. You must spiritually nourish the members. Build their testimonies, instill the Spirit of the Lord in their hearts, and strengthen their commitment to live the gospel and serve others. I once had an excellent bishop in my home ward who told me about how efficient his executive secretary was and how effectively this faithful servant had scheduled his time. We lived in a predominantly Latter-day Saint area where the ward consisted of just a few blocks, so I gave my bishop one piece of counsel, which he took to heart: "Be sure you leave time to walk the ward." He got the message that

---

1. See Gordon B. Hinckley, "Find the Lambs, Feed the Sheep," *Ensign*, May 1999, 104–10.

he needed to make sure his time was not so fully scheduled that he had no time to follow the promptings of the Spirit to serve his ward members spontaneously.

Finally, bishops must be wise when they are released. After I was released as a bishop in Chicago, we moved from the ward. Some time later I returned and realized how differently I saw my brothers and sisters. I was no longer their bishop, and I no longer had the special spiritual gift of discernment for them. Once the mantle is taken from you, you can't do what you once did as a bishop. It would be a mistake to try, even if members seek your counsel.

A Mission for All Saints

We need not be bishops or full-time missionaries like Don and Marian Summers to be able to reach out as shepherds. Every member of the Church has the responsibility, even the obligation, to bear testimony of Jesus Christ to family, friends, and neighbors in mildness and in meekness. Fear of man often holds us back—fear that we will offend them or fear that we will not be able to answer their questions. But fear is a tool of the adversary, and "perfect love casteth out fear" (1 John 4:18). When we focus on how much we love our brothers and sisters, our fears melt away. Love fills us with the desire and courage to open our mouths. The light of our testimony pushes back the darkness. There is no greater gift we can give others than to bear our testimony to them. There is no greater joy we can have than to bring even one soul unto Christ.

Bringing Others to Him

Doing our work as converted members of the Church—bringing others to Christ and strengthening them—does not mean inviting them to come to us as friends. It means inviting them to come unto the Savior. We do not need to have all the answers to all their questions or convince them that the gospel is true. Our work is to introduce those we love to the Lord and His word, where they will be able to find the answers for themselves. When we instill this understanding in the hearts of our family, friends, and neighbors, they are energized by the opportunity to embark upon a personal quest—to search and study for themselves and through personal prayer seek their own personal testimony. Whether or not the missionaries stay in the area or we continue to live nearby does not matter. They have the scriptures, the testimonies of latter-day prophets, the gift of the Holy Ghost, and priesthood and auxiliary leaders to strengthen them. They have their own role to play in the body of Christ, their own calling to fulfill. In short, they have found their own place in the kingdom, and they can be secure even if we are not continually by their side.

THE IMPORTANCE OF FELLOWSHIP

How do new and returning members find this secure place? When our brothers and sisters come out of the world into the kingdom of God, they leave much behind. Sometimes they are rejected by family members and lifelong friends. Even in the best circumstances, they find that their old social network and way of life are not entirely compatible with the gospel they have embraced. In faith they step out of one world into a new one—a world that may be without family, friends, associations, memories, and life experiences shared with others.

These are some of the extraordinary sacrifices new and returning members make to come to the Lord. And so we ask ourselves, What sacrifices are we willing to make to welcome them into His kingdom and to fellowship them on His behalf?

Long experience demonstrates that without receiving a warm hand of fellowship immediately, new and returning members become discouraged and lose the Spirit that brought them to the waters of baptism. What was for a time the thrilling new centerpiece of their lives is gradually abandoned because of a perceived offense, more pressing matters, or the wave of daily demands. No wonder some wander back into familiar places, associations, and routines.

Amid the busyness of our own lives, we have the sacred opportunity and obligation to walk the strait and narrow gospel path, from the gate of baptism to the doors of the temple, with new and returning members. As we continually fellowship others, we may walk this path over and over again. It is a noble, joyful work to walk this path—a work that strengthens not only them but us as well.

Are we ready to walk this path with our brothers and sisters? We have learned well the message of President David O. McKay that every member is a missionary. Hopefully, we will respond to the equally urgent plea that every member should be a fellowshipper: a friend, a shepherd, a nurturing and caring fellow Saint who reaches out to everyone—active members, new members, and members returning to the fold.

SOME HAVE COMPASSION

In our work as shepherds, our concern is not only for the spiritual welfare of our Heavenly Father's children but for their total well-being. Several years ago, after returning home from an assignment abroad, I became very ill from an amoebic disorder. With pain, dehydration, fever, and total enervation, I learned an important welfare lesson—that one could suddenly be thrust into a condition of intense need. In such conditions we cannot rescue ourselves.

We need the help of others to regain our equilibrium and begin to meet our own needs once again.

As converted members charged to strengthen our brethren, we should be aware that a temporal, physical, and emotional crisis can create severe spiritual deficits. Being poor includes not only being without money but also having unmet physical, spiritual, mental, and emotional needs, which true shepherds are called to help meet.

Temporal challenges can become spiritual opportunities. It is a sobering thought that one purpose of our trials and tribulations is to awaken in us a deep and abiding concern for the needy. As we struggle to endure our own temporal challenges, we begin to have a greater desire to help others who are also afflicted.

Imparting of our substance to the poor, as we are able, is essential to our salvation. Too often rich and poor alike shut their hearts to the divine attributes of love and compassion (see Mosiah 4:16–18). We should seek out the poor and the needy and share from our abundance. "Think of your brethren like unto yourselves, and be familiar with all and free with your substance, that they may be rich like unto you" (Jacob 2:17).

Continue to Minister

Concerning those who were not numbered among His people, Jesus said to the Nephites, "Nevertheless, ye shall not cast him out of your synagogues, or your places of worship, for unto such shall ye continue to minister; *for ye know not but what they will return and repent,* and come unto me with full purpose of heart, and I shall heal them; *and ye shall be the means of bringing salvation unto them*" (3 Nephi 18:32; emphasis added). We never know who may be depending on us.

It is not enough to think or say that something needs to be done. My prayer is that we will all have a renewed appreciation of our role as shepherds and a renewed determination, through our prayers of faith and compassion, to bring at least one precious soul back to salvation and exaltation. May the prayer of Alma also be our prayer:

"O Lord, wilt thou comfort my soul, and give unto me success, and also my fellow laborers who are with me. . . .

"Wilt thou grant unto them that they may have strength, that they may bear their afflictions which shall come upon them. . . .

"O Lord, wilt thou grant unto us that we may have success in bringing them again unto thee in Christ.

"Behold, O Lord, their souls are precious, and many of them are our brethren; therefore, give unto us, O Lord, power and wisdom that we may bring these, our brethren, again unto thee" (Alma 31:32–35).

CHECKPOINTS

✓ Do I recognize that I am a shepherd, assisting the Savior in tending to His flocks?

✓ How fully am I converted?

✓ Do I leave sharing the gospel and shepherding to those with official assignments for doing so?

✓ How well do I let love overcome my fears and do everything within my power to bring others unto Christ?

✓ In sharing the gospel, how well do I lead others to the Lord and the scriptures rather than feeling that I need to be the source of knowledge myself?

✓ How well do I make time to reach out in fellowship to those who are new in the gospel and may have had to leave friends and family behind?

✓ How well do I address not only the spiritual needs of others but also their temporal needs?

✓ Do I seek to help others in the Lord's way?

Feast upon the words of Christ;
for behold, the words of Christ will tell you
all things what ye should do.

2 NEPHI 32:3

CHAPTER TWENTY-SEVEN

FEASTING UPON THE WORDS OF CHRIST

I WILL NEVER FORGET THE lessons I learned from a Sunday School teacher when I was about ten years old. For Christmas we were given a large card that had small, individual booklets inside, each with a story from the Bible—David and Goliath, the Creation, Daniel and the lion's den. These were part of a long series of wonderful Bible stories. We read each one at home and came to class prepared to discuss them. I can remember those teaching moments quite vividly to this day.

After discussing each story, we were asked such questions as, "What does that mean to you?" "How does this scripture or story or principle relate to your life?" "How do you feel about it?" We were asked to think. We were not learning the stories only. We were discovering how we could apply them in our lives. My teacher was planting the seed of faith and helping it grow within each of us. Years later as a father, I applied these same teachings with my own children. I found that once I asked these kinds of questions, my boys began to live and feel what they were being taught.

The importance of the scriptures to those who have been

obedient and faithful to the commandments is interesting to me. As Lehi searched the plates, he learned what all of us learn by studying the scriptures:

- Who we are
- What we can become
- Prophecies for us and for our posterity
- The commandments, laws, ordinances, and covenants we must live by to obtain eternal life
- How we must live in order to endure to the end and return with honor to our Heavenly Father

These truths are so vital that Heavenly Father gave both Lehi and Nephi a vision representing the word of God as a rod of iron. Both father and son learned that holding to this strong, unbending, utterly reliable guide is the *only* way to stay on that strait and narrow path that leads to eternal life and to enter into the presence of our Savior.

The Book of Mormon records how one civilization after another regarded or *dis*regarded the scriptures, beginning with Lehi's own family. The fate of these civilizations is a testimony to all the world: If we don't have the word of God or hold fast to it, we will wander off into strange paths and be lost as individuals, as families, and as nations.

The Bible Is the Word of God

I have heard a few members of the Church say they don't read the Bible because it is not translated correctly. They are missing out on a treasure. I love the stories from the Bible I learned as a child. As an adult, I have found the parables and teachings of the Bible to be essential. When we read the Bible with the help of the Spirit and apply its doctrines in our lives, we are enriched in unique and vital ways.

I am also grateful for the faithfulness of those who, through the dispensations, sacrificed so that God's children could receive and live by His word. Because of their selfless and sometimes incomparable efforts, the world has been gradually preparing to receive the restored gospel and be ready to welcome the Savior's Second Coming.

The First Step

Making the scriptures available and helping God's children learn to read them was the first step to the restoration of the gospel. Originally the Bible was written in Hebrew and Greek, languages unknown to common people throughout Europe. Then, about four hundred years after the Savior's death, the Bible was translated by Jerome into Latin. But still the scriptures were not widely available. Copies had to be written by hand, usually by monks, each copy taking years to complete.

Then, through the influence of the Holy Ghost, an interest in learning began to grow in the hearts of people. This renaissance, or "rebirth," spread throughout Europe. In the late 1300s, a priest named John Wycliffe initiated a translation of the Bible from Latin into English. Because English was then an emerging, unrefined language, church leaders deemed it unsuitable to convey God's word. Some leaders were certain that if people could read and interpret the Bible for themselves, its doctrines would be corrupted; others feared that people with independent access to the scriptures would not need the church and would cease to support it financially. Consequently, Wycliffe was denounced as a heretic and treated accordingly. After he died and was buried, his bones were dug up and burned. But God's work could not be stopped.

While some were inspired to translate the Bible, others were inspired to prepare the means to publish it. By 1455 Johannes Gutenberg had invented a press with movable type, and the Bible was one of the first books he printed. For the first time it was possible to print multiple copies of the scriptures and at a cost many could afford.

Meanwhile, the inspiration of God also rested upon explorers. In 1492 Christopher Columbus set out to find a new path to the Far East. Columbus was led by the hand of God in his journey. He said, "God gave me the faith, and afterwards the courage."[1]

These inventions and discoveries set the stage for further contributions. For example, in the early 1500s young William Tyndale enrolled at Oxford University. There he studied the work of Bible scholar Erasmus, who believed that the scriptures are "the food of [a man's] soul; and . . . must permeate the very depths of [his] heart and mind."[2] Through his studies, Tyndale developed a love for God's word and a desire that all God's children be able to feast on it for themselves.

At about this time, a German priest and professor named Martin Luther identified ninety-five points of error in the church of his day, which he boldly sent in a letter to his superiors. In Switzerland, Huldrych Zwingli printed sixty-seven articles of reform. John Calvin in Switzerland, John Knox in Scotland, and many others assisted in this effort. A reformation had begun. Meanwhile, William Tyndale had become a trained priest fluent in eight languages. He believed a direct translation from Greek and Hebrew into English would be more accurate and readable than Wycliffe's translation

---

1. Quoted in Mark E. Petersen, *The Great Prologue* (Salt Lake City: Deseret Book, 1975), 29.

2. Quoted in Benson Bobrick, *Wide As the Waters: The Story of the English Bible and the Revolution It Inspired* (New York: Simon and Schuster, 2001), 89.

from Latin. So Tyndale, enlightened by the Spirit of God, translated the New Testament and a portion of the Old Testament. His friends warned him that he would be killed for doing so because the church and monarchy of his day opposed such efforts, but he was undaunted. Once, while disputing with a learned man, he said, "If God spare my life, ere many years I will cause a boy that driveth the plough shall know more of the scripture than thou dost."[3]

Eventually Tyndale, like others, was killed for his efforts—strangled and burned at the stake near Brussels. But the belief for which he gave his life was not lost. Millions have come to experience for themselves what Tyndale taught throughout his life: "The nature of God's word is, that whosoever read it, . . . it will begin immediately to make him every day better and better, till he be grown into a perfect man."[4]

Turbulent political times brought change. Because of a disagreement with the church in Rome, King Henry VIII declared himself the head of the church in England and required that copies of the English Bible be placed in every parish church. Hungry for the gospel, people flocked to these churches, reading the scriptures to one another until their voices gave out. The Bible was also used as a primer to teach reading. Though martyrdoms continued across Europe, the dark night of ignorance was coming to an end. Declared one preacher before being burned, "We shall this day light such a candle, by God's Grace, in England, as I trust shall never be put out."[5]

I express my personal gratitude to all who lived in England and throughout Europe who helped kindle that light. By God's grace,

---

3. Quoted in S. Michael Wilcox, *Fire in the Bones* (Salt Lake City: Deseret Book, 2004), 47.

4. Quoted in Wilcox, *Fire in the Bones,* xv.

5. Quoted in Bobrick, *Wide As the Waters,* 168.

the light grew brighter. Aware of the divisions within his own country, King James the First of England agreed to a new official version of the Bible. It has been estimated that more than 80 percent of William Tyndale's translation of the New Testament and a good portion of the Old Testament (the Pentateuch, or Genesis through Deuteronomy, and Joshua through Chronicles) were retained in the King James Version.[6] In time, that version would find its way to a new land and be read by a fourteen-year-old plowboy named Joseph Smith. Is it any wonder that the King James Version is today the approved Bible in English of The Church of Jesus Christ of Latter-day Saints?

Religious persecution in England continued under James's son Charles, and many were prompted to seek freedom in new lands. Among them were the Pilgrims, who landed in the Americas in 1620, the very part of the world Columbus had explored more than one hundred years earlier. Other colonists soon followed, including those such as Roger Williams, founder and later governor of Rhode Island, who continued to search for Christ's true Church. Williams said that there was "no regularly-constituted church on earth, nor any person authorized to administer any Church ordinance; nor could there be until, new apostles are sent by the great Head of the Church, for whose coming, he [was] seeking."[7]

More than a century later, such religious feeling guided founders of a new nation on the American continent. Under God's hand, they secured religious freedom for every citizen with an inspired Bill of Rights. Fourteen years later, on December 23, 1805, the Prophet

6. See Wilcox, *Fire in the Bones,* 80, 125, 197.

7. *Picturesque America, or the Land We Live In,* ed. William Cullen Bryant (New York: D. Appleton, 1872), 1:502, quoted in LeGrand Richards, *A Marvelous Work and a Wonder,* rev. ed. (Salt Lake City: Deseret Book, 1976), 27.

Joseph Smith was born. The preparation for the Restoration was nearing its completion.

As a young man, Joseph "was called up to serious reflection" on the subject of religion (Joseph Smith–History 1:8). Because he was born in a land of religious freedom, he could question for himself which of all the churches was right. And because the Bible had been translated into English, he could seek an answer from the word of God. He read in the book of James, "If any of you lack wisdom, let him ask of God" (James 1:5), and he did as directed. In answer to Joseph's prayer, God the Father and His Son, Jesus Christ, appeared to him (see Joseph Smith–History 1:11–20). This humble farm boy was the prophet chosen by God to restore the ancient Church of Jesus Christ and His priesthood in these latter days. This Restoration was to usher in the last dispensation, or the dispensation of the fulness of times, bringing back a fulness of priesthood blessings—all the blessings possible for man to possess on earth. With this divine commission, Joseph Smith's work was not to reform nor was it to protest what was already on the earth. It was to restore what had once been on earth and had been lost.

THE BOOK OF MORMON

As a central element of the Restoration, the Book of Mormon was revealed to the world as another witness to testify of Jesus Christ's divine calling and ministry. The Book of Mormon is essential to knowing who we are and what we can achieve in this life and in the eternities.

The Book of Mormon is a history of ancient prophets bearing testimony of how we should live by the commandments to have joy in this life. It is clear that if we are obedient, we will have joy and prosperity; but if we are disobedient, we will suffer sadness in our trials and tribulations. This theme is taught and illustrated over and over in the Book of Mormon, not only for individuals but even for nations.

How important is the Book of Mormon? The Church was organized on April 6, 1830, just eleven days after the Book of Mormon was printed. Why is that important? Because, until the priesthood had been restored in 1829 and until the Book of Mormon had been published and printed, it was not possible to fully restore the true Church of Christ in these latter days. That is how important the priesthood and the Book of Mormon are. The Book of Mormon is the keystone of the Restoration through Joseph Smith in these latter days.

Teaching Our Children from the Book of Mormon

All of us reflect on powerful teaching and learning experiences, and we talk about how to provide the same kinds of experiences for our children, but how do we actually give them those experiences?

Many years ago I was teaching our young son about the life and experiences of the brother of Jared. Although the story was interesting, he was not engaged. I then asked what the story meant to him personally. As I learned from my parents and that special Sunday School teacher, it means so much more when we involve our children by asking them to share their feelings, insights, and ideas.

He said, "You know, it's not that different from what Joseph Smith did in the grove when he prayed and got an answer."

I said, "You're about Joseph's age. Do you think a prayer like his would be helpful to you?" Suddenly, we were no longer talking about a long-ago story in a faraway land. We were talking about him—about his life, his needs, and the way prayer could help him.

As parents, we have the responsibility to help our children to "liken all scriptures"—indeed, every part of the gospel of Jesus Christ—unto themselves for their "profit and learning" (1 Nephi 19:23).

These teaching moments are priceless. They come in the course of our daily lives when we are engaged together in real life activities. When such teaching moments come, the Spirit of the Lord can help us know what to say and help our children to accept our gospel teachings.

Personal Revelation

The most important gospel learning and teaching comes through the process of seeking and receiving personal revelation.

This process begins by bonding scripture study with personal prayer. Why are these two activities so important and dependent upon each other? They open the channel of two-way communication with our Heavenly Father. When we want to speak to God, we pray. And when we want Him to speak to us, we search the scriptures, for His words are spoken through His prophets. When we are engaged in both, we invite the personal revelation that comes through the promptings of the Holy Spirit.

To truly feast upon the words of Christ and be nourished in prayer, however, we cannot ignore the third element of personal revelation: pondering. It is by pondering that we make what is revealed to us part of our every thought and action. The Lord commanded Joshua, "This book of the law shall not depart out of thy mouth; but thou shalt meditate therein day and night, that thou mayest observe to do according to all that is written therein: for then thou shalt make thy way prosperous, and then thou shalt have good success" (Joshua 1:8).

THE TIME FOR SCRIPTURES IS NOW

Some wonder how relevant ancient scripture is today. More than two millennia ago, Isaiah wrote of the word of God, "Now go, write it before them in a table, and note it in a book, that it may be for the time to come for ever and ever" (Isaiah 30:8). That time is now. This world needs the scriptures today. We boldly declare that the answer to the terror, destruction, and even genocide of these last days is found in the scriptures.

If we will look at the history of the Jaredites, if we will look at the record of the Mulekites, if we will look at the record of the Lamanites, we will see that all these nations, and even the Nephites, fell away when they did not have, study, or follow the holy scriptures. They wandered away from the gospel path, and they were lost or destroyed.

I testify that throughout time, the holy scriptures are the word of God given for the salvation of God's children. If you have not heard His voice speaking to you lately, return with new eyes and new ears to the scriptures. They are our spiritual lifeline.

As with voices from the dust, the prophets of the Lord cry out to us on earth today: Take hold of the scriptures! Cling to them, walk by them, live by them, rejoice in them. Resist the urge to merely nibble at them. The prophets enjoin us to "feast" on them. And, to use the words of Joseph Smith, the doctrine of the scriptures "tastes good" and is nourishing to the soul.[8] Truly, His word, taken into our hearts and put to work in our lives, is "the power of God unto salvation" (D&C 68:4), and it will lead us back to our Savior, Jesus Christ.

---

8. Joseph Smith, *Discourses of the Prophet Joseph Smith,* comp. Alma P. Burton (Salt Lake City: Deseret Book, 1977), 349.

Checkpoints

✓ Do I hold fast to the word of God, or do I wander off into strange paths?

✓ How much do I appreciate the individuals who sacrificed their time and even their lives to bring us the Bible?

✓ How well do I liken the scriptures unto myself?

✓ How well do I help bring the scriptures to life for my children and others I teach?

✓ How well do I use the scriptures as a vehicle for receiving personal revelation?

Believe in the Lord your God, so shall ye be established;
believe his prophets, so shall ye prosper.

2 CHRONICLES 20:20

CHAPTER TWENTY-EIGHT

Following God's Prophets

B ASEBALL WAS A BIG part of my life in high school. I
was fortunate enough to be taught by a wonderful coach,
Art Smith, a man I'll never forget. He had played for the
Chicago White Sox, and he taught me how to throw a fastball
that curves away from a right-handed batter. But I'm even more
grateful for some lessons he taught me about life. He was a man
of integrity.

In one key game when I was a sophomore, I found myself on
the mound in the bottom of the ninth with two outs, the bases
loaded, and the game on the line. The catcher kept flashing signs
telling me to throw a fastball. It was my first big game, and the
batter was a .350 hitter, one of the best players on Long Island.
It was late in the game, and I wasn't sure if I had enough arm
strength left to throw a really good fastball, so I kept ignoring the
catcher's signals. Finally, in frustration he threw his glove down in
front of hundreds of people at the game, and hollered as loud as he

Robert at fifteen, pitching for his high school team

could, "Throw what you want!" I think he did this for the coach's benefit.

That's when Coach Smith came out to the mound and taught me an important lesson. "Do you know the kid behind the plate is tough? He's one of the finest catchers we've ever had. He's played against all these fellas in summer ball. He knows them—he knows where the location of the pitch should be. If you're half smart, you'll listen to him." He started back toward the bench and then turned around with one last comment: "By the way, I'm the one signaling to him for you to throw a fastball. That's why he keeps giving you the sign to throw a fastball. What got you here is gonna keep you here." He wanted me to throw my fastball—what had gotten me here—but I was afraid it wouldn't work as well late in the game as it had early on.

So I set up to pitch, and the catcher didn't even have his mitt on. He was egging me on, and it worked. I wanted to break his hand. So I reached back and threw as hard as I could throw. I don't know if I ever threw that fast again. I struck the guy out, and we won the game.

I thought I knew better than my catcher, but I didn't. He was getting his signals from the coach, and they both knew things I didn't know. In my reluctance to follow his signs, I nearly lost the game.

Following Counsel

We, too, are blessed with someone who knows things we do not know, who gives us counsel that will help us prevail in the challenges of life. There has always been a desperate need for the steady and reassuring voice of a living prophet of God: one who will speak the mind and will of God in showing the way to spiritual safety and personal peace and happiness. When we ignore his counsel because we think we know better, we are following an unfortunate pattern that is frequently detailed in the scriptures. We are risking losing not just a game but our very salvation.

In the Old Testament we find a story about Miriam and Aaron, who questioned the judgment of Moses. Moses had become the leader of his people, Miriam was his older sister, and Aaron was his older brother. What complicates this story is that Aaron became the spokesman for Moses because Moses considered himself "slow of speech, and of a slow tongue" (Exodus 4:10). Unfortunately, Aaron and Miriam began to question why only

Moses was receiving revelation. After all, they too had been faithful. They began to think they knew better than God's prophet.

"And Miriam and Aaron spake against Moses because of the Ethiopian woman whom he had married" (Numbers 12:1). In other words, they questioned his judgment, and in doing so they were speaking against the prophet.

They said, "Hath the Lord indeed spoken only by Moses? hath he not spoken also by us? And the Lord heard it.

"(Now the man Moses was very meek, above all the men which were upon the face of the earth.)

"And the Lord spake suddenly unto Moses, and unto Aaron, and unto Miriam, Come out ye three unto the tabernacle of the congregation. And they three came out" (Numbers 12:2–4). The tabernacle of the congregation was a type of a tent with the tabernacle built inside it.

"And the Lord came down in the pillar of the cloud, and stood in the door of the tabernacle, and called Aaron and Miriam: and they both came forth" (Numbers 12:5). I imagine that perhaps they thought He was going to say something like, "Yes, I do speak to everyone," but He didn't.

"And he said, Hear now my words: If there be a prophet among you, I the Lord will make myself known unto him in a vision, and will speak unto him in a dream" (Numbers 12:6). In other words, if someone is going to speak to the prophet or have someone speak for him, *I'll* speak to him. I'll come to him in a vision. I'll come to him in a dream.

And then the Lord says: "My servant Moses is not so, who is

faithful in all mine house" (Numbers 12:7). The Lord is asking, Isn't Moses the most faithful of all?

"With him will I speak mouth to mouth, even apparently, and not in dark speeches; and the similitude of the Lord shall he behold: wherefore then were ye not afraid to speak against my servant Moses?

"And the anger of the Lord was kindled against them; and he departed" (Numbers 12:8–9).

When He departed, Miriam was left leprous, white as snow, as though she were dead. Aaron repented and recognized his sin and appealed to Moses to heal her. Moses cried to the Lord on behalf of his sister, and she was healed. But before the camp could move on, Miriam had to be shut out for seven days (Numbers 12:10–15). Miriam's rebellion had slowed the progress of Israel for a time, and she had jeopardized her own spiritual progress. But by following the prophet again, she found mercy and was restored.

EVEN AS MOSES

In the Doctrine and Covenants, the Lord refers to this story when He corrects Hiram Page and Oliver Cowdery. Hiram Page, a recent convert to the Church, claimed to have a stone through which revelations could be received for the building up of Zion. I can only imagine that his ego led him to believe that if Joseph Smith could have a stone to receive revelations, so could he.

Hiram Page was a cunning man who was able to deceive Oliver Cowdery, despite what Oliver had experienced with the Prophet Joseph Smith, including the experiences of witnessing the plates and receiving the Aaronic Priesthood at the hands of John the

Baptist. But these sacred experiences occurred in the company of the Prophet. The deception of Hiram Page occurred when the Prophet was away in Fayette, New York, and Oliver was on his own. Oliver didn't have the Prophet to help him. When Joseph returned to Fayette, he was concerned for Oliver and inquired of the Lord. The Lord answered the Prophet's prayer with this revelation for Oliver:

"I say unto thee, Oliver, that it shall be given unto thee that thou shalt be heard by the church in all things whatsoever thou shalt teach them by the Comforter, concerning the revelations and commandments which I have given.

"But . . . no one shall be appointed to receive commandments and revelations in this church excepting my servant Joseph Smith, Jun., for he receiveth them *even as Moses.*

"And thou shalt be obedient unto the things which I shall give unto him, even as Aaron, to declare faithfully the commandments and the revelations, with power and authority unto the church. . . .

"And thou shalt not command him who is at thy head, and at the head of the church;

"For I have given him [the President of the Church] the keys of the mysteries, and the revelations which are sealed, until I shall appoint unto them another in his stead.

" . . . Thou shalt have revelations, but write them not by way of commandment" (D&C 28:1–8; emphasis added).

Oliver was still going to have revelations. He was going to be a witness. And the Lord taught Oliver this great lesson because Oliver would become a very important man in the next year or so.

Then the Lord said to Oliver: "Take thy brother, Hiram Page, between him and thee alone, and tell him that those things which he hath written from that stone are not of me and that Satan deceiveth him; for, behold, these things have not been appointed unto him, neither shall anything be appointed unto any of this church contrary to the church covenants" (D&C 28:11–12).

If we have an associate, or a friend, or one of our family, who claims to receive revelations about how the Church should be run, we should do as Oliver Cowdery was told to do and meet with that person alone. We should have a prayer with him or her and teach this doctrine.

The history of the Church tells us what finally happened to Hiram Page. He listened to the Brethren, followed them for a while, and then eventually fell away from the Church because his soul was cankered and he would not listen to the Brethren. Unlike Miriam, he did not take to heart the lesson the Lord taught about the importance of following prophets.

So Shall Ye Prosper

Another Old Testament story teaches us just how important it is to follow living prophets. King Jehoshaphat had several great armies coming to battle against him in an attempt to possess his land. Understandably, he was seized with dreadful fear, so he proclaimed a fast throughout all his kingdom and gathered the people of Judah together to plead for guidance from the Lord. Jehoshaphat humbly and earnestly prayed:

"O our God, . . . we have no might against this great company that cometh against us; neither know we what to do: but our eyes are upon thee" (2 Chronicles 20:12).

Then came the answer of the Lord through the prophet Jahaziel: "Hearken ye, all Judah, and ye inhabitants of Jerusalem, and thou king Jehoshaphat, Thus saith the Lord unto you, Be not afraid nor dismayed by reason of this great multitude; for the battle is not yours, but God's. . . . Fear not, nor be dismayed; . . . for the Lord will be with you" (2 Chronicles 20:15–17).

Jehoshaphat and all the inhabitants of Jerusalem fell in thankful prayer before the Lord. Jehoshaphat then gave very important counsel that we today would do well to obey. Indeed, just as with the people of Judah, our lives may depend upon it—even our eternal lives: "Believe in the Lord your God, so shall ye be established; believe his prophets, so shall ye prosper" (2 Chronicles 20:20).

As promised, the Lord protected the good people of Judah. As Jehoshaphat's forces looked on, the armies that came to battle against them fought so fiercely among themselves that they completely destroyed one another before they ever reached the people of Judah. They who followed the prophet's counsel prospered.

Not of This World

Taking our signals from prophets may not always be easy, because they sometimes ask us to do things that are hard—that is, they call us out of the world and put us out of step with society. In fact, a characteristic of prophets throughout the ages is that, regardless of the consequences, they have had the strength to plainly and boldly warn of the consequences of violating God's laws. They do not preach that which is popular with the world. President Ezra Taft Benson taught that "popularity is never a test of truth."[1]

---

1. Ezra Taft Benson, "Fourteen Fundamentals in Following the Prophet," in *1980 Devotional Speeches of the Year* (Provo: Brigham Young University Press, 1981), 29.

Why do prophets proclaim unpopular commandments and call society to repentance for rejecting, modifying, and even ignoring the commandments? The reason is very simple. Upon receiving revelation, prophets have no choice but to proclaim and reaffirm that which God has given them to tell the world.

Prophets do this knowing full well the price they may have to pay. Some people who choose not to live the commandments make every effort to defame the character of the prophets and demean their personal integrity and reputation. In response, the prophets remain silent and turn the other cheek. The world may see this as weakness, but it is one of the greatest strengths a man can have—to be faithful, unyielding, and unwavering to that which he knows to be true, accepting whatever consequences may follow.

Each of us is free to accept or reject the prophets and the commandments they reveal, but none of us is free to modify those commandments to suit our personal preferences. Church members do not have the right to change revealed truths just for the sake of being popular with the world. Nor do prophets have the authority to alter God's commandments in order to make them more palatable to those who are weak in their resolve to live worthily.

COME, LISTEN TO A PROPHET'S VOICE

As Latter-day Saints, we strive to answer the call, "Come, listen to a prophet's voice / And hear the word of God."[2] We do so believing that we enjoy "the same organization that existed in the

---

2. "Come, Listen to a Prophet's Voice," *Hymns of The Church of Jesus Christ of Latter-day Saints* (Salt Lake City: The Church of Jesus Christ of Latter-day Saints, 1985), no. 21.

Primitive Church, namely, apostles, prophets, pastors, teachers, evangelists, and so forth" (Article of Faith 6). With the restoration of the priesthood in 1829, we know there was a restoration of prophets to the earth. Our greatest security comes from following these prophets and their predecessors from the foundation of this world.

Understanding the role of prophets, we recognize that we make a terrible mistake whenever we disregard their counsel, thinking we know better. We believe that if we see with the eye of faith, and patiently wait for all things to be revealed, we will understand that prophetic teachings are preparing us not for this world but for God's kingdom. With that assurance, we humbly and willingly seek prophetic direction.

I testify that living prophets are leading The Church of Jesus Christ of Latter-day Saints today. The prophet and President of the Church is ordained and holds all the keys to lead the Church. He faithfully takes counsel with his counselors and with the Quorum of the Twelve Apostles, all of whom are ordained and sustained as prophets, seers, and revelators. God's work rolls on through the work of these chosen servants. This has been true in the past and continues to be true today. We give thanks for the blessing of following God's prophets.

CHECKPOINTS

✓ How willing am I to humble myself to follow the counsel of prophets and other wise leaders?

✓ How often do I rebel against the counsel of prophets, believing I know better?

✓ When prophetic counsel is inconvenient for me or puts me out of step with society or friends, does my willingness to follow the prophet waver?

*Whatever principle of intelligence we attain
unto in this life, it will rise with us in the resurrection.*

DOCTRINE & COVENANTS 130:18

CHAPTER TWENTY-NINE

THE JOURNEY OF LIFELONG LEARNING

O UR QUEST FOR KNOWLEDGE began long before we were born. In our premortal existence we learned about our Heavenly Father's plan for us, including the tremendous learning opportunity that mortality would provide. Then, with knowledge and understanding, we chose to come to the earth in order to learn, grow, develop, and progress—to become like our Heavenly Father. Here on earth, then, as Brigham Young once observed, "we are in a great school."[1]

EDUCATION FOR ETERNITY

The purposes of this "school" go far beyond the bounds of mortality. The Lord revealed: "Whatever principle of intelligence we attain unto in this life, it will rise with us in the resurrection.

"And if a person gains more knowledge and intelligence in this life through his diligence and obedience than another, he

---

1. Brigham Young, *Discourses of Brigham Young*, sel. John A. Widtsoe (Salt Lake City: Bookcraft, 1998), 248.

will have so much the advantage in the world to come" (D&C 130:18–19).

While life on earth is only a small moment in eternity, what we learn here is an essential part of our eternal education and eternal progression. When we understand this, our reasons for learning become clear: We search and study for the joy of being edified rather than for the pleasure of being entertained. Our educational goals are not to impress others but to serve them. Our learning objective is not to succeed in the eyes of men but to grow, improve, and return to our heavenly home with honor, prepared to receive greater responsibility and opportunity than we now have.

In other words, when our view of education is not a destination, such as passing a course or completing a degree, then everything about our approach to learning is different. We begin to see our education as a lifelong journey. Seen that way, the curriculum outlined by the Lord not only makes sense to us but thrills us "that [we] may be instructed more perfectly in theory, in principle, in doctrine, in the law of the gospel, in all things that pertain unto the kingdom of God, . . . of things both in heaven and in the earth, and under the earth; things which have been, things which are, things which must shortly come to pass; things which are at home, things which are abroad; the wars and the perplexities of the nations, and the judgments which are on the land; and a knowledge also of countries and of kingdoms" (D&C 88:78–79).

For all of us, our journey of lifelong learning began in our homes, which are the centers of our mortal tutelage and the incubators for our eternal growth. The first verse of the Book of Mormon provides the pattern: "I, Nephi, having been born of goodly parents, therefore I was taught somewhat in all the learning of my father"

(1 Nephi 1:1). Just as Nephi's field of study was *all* that his father knew, so lifelong learners desire to know all about everything, and their desire to understand and grow is unbounded. Perhaps that is why Brigham Young said, "Should our lives be extended to a thousand years, still we may live and learn."[2]

Attributes of Lifelong Learners

Lifelong learners, like Nephi, share several attributes, some of which they may always have had, but most of which were developed through seeking wisdom and knowledge "by study and also by faith" (D&C 88:118). Here are a few of them:

Courage. Lifelong learners have the courage to go beyond the limits of their educational comfort zone and learn about what is unknown and unfamiliar to them. They are not too proud to say "I don't know" and to ask "why?" They are not afraid of starting at the beginning and learning "line upon line, precept upon precept" (2 Nephi 28:30).

Too often we focus only on our educational strengths and avoid overcoming our educational weaknesses. Thus our strengths in a sense *become* our weaknesses. When this occurs, we find ourselves dwelling in the security of the past and unwilling to venture into the future.

But lifelong learners take the long step of faith into the unknown and unfamiliar. As they do, they recognize that the light of truth goes before them. For instance, they may have had a nagging fear of mastering the computer, but as they move forward and apply themselves, they learn the wonderful ways in which God's work is accomplished through computer technology. This work includes

2. Young, *Discourses of Brigham Young,* 345.

researching genealogical lines, preparing personal and family histories, communicating with family members, sharing the gospel, and so on. Lifelong learners discover sacred purposes in their learning and prepare themselves to serve others with the knowledge they gain.

Faithful desire and curiosity. Lifelong learners have an insatiable, unselfish, deep desire to acquire a wide spectrum of knowledge across many disciplines. For example, a mother desires that her seriously ill child be properly diagnosed and treated. Rather than just sitting home worrying, she researches medical books and journals to increase her understanding. Along the way, she is able to identify several clues to help doctors find a cure. Lifelong learners are filled with desires for knowledge that will help them to be better helpmeets, better mothers, better fathers, better citizens, and better servants in the Lord's kingdom so "that [they] may learn and glorify the name of [their] God" (2 Nephi 6:4).

Lifelong learners are also curious at heart. When we are children, our curiosity is instinctive, but our formal education tends to confine us and define the boundaries of acceptable inquiry. Lifelong learners retain their God-given sense of wonder and delight and their childlike curiosity in everything around them. They still feel the exhilaration and satisfaction of comprehending a new idea or mastering a new skill.

Humility and patience. Lifelong learners recognize that the source of all knowledge is our Heavenly Father and that the capacity and opportunity to learn are gifts from God. They regularly experience the fulfillment of Alma's promise: "He that truly humbleth himself, . . . the same shall be blessed" (Alma 32:15). Because lifelong learners believe that intelligence comes from Heavenly Father, they do not glory in their intelligence quotient or their own accomplishments. They freely acknowledge that "to every man is given a gift by the Spirit of God" and that all gifts are given so that we can lift and strengthen others, "that all may be profited thereby" (D&C 46:11–12).

In their quest for knowledge and understanding, lifelong learners also acquire patience. They do not give up when the learning becomes hard or when it requires marked growth. Thomas Edison was a lifelong learner. He is reported to have said, "I have not failed 700 times. I have not failed once. I have succeeded in proving that those 700 ways will not work. When I have eliminated the ways that will not work, I will find the way that will work."[3]

Communication. Lifelong learners are teachers at heart. As classmates, they help others succeed. As mentors and teachers, they delight in others' gifts and rejoice to see them progress. They believe in others' unique gifts and talents and are not afraid of helping others surpass them in their level of skill and accomplishment.

They pray for guidance and understanding in working with others and seek to follow the Spirit in all they share and teach. Their communication is always an open, balanced exchange that is mutually beneficial, so that they may be "edified and rejoice together" (D&C 50:22). They do not dominate; their special gift is to genuinely listen.

Because of their example, lifelong learners promote lifelong learning in others. They do not presume to provide all the answers. By what they do and say, they inspire others to drink deeply from the fount of knowledge for themselves.

For example, President Boyd K. Packer was once leading a question-and-answer session when a learned man asked about President Packer's teachings on the Atonement. How did President

---

3. http://www.quotableedison.com/allquotes.php; retrieved 21 April 2010.

Packer, a prophet, seer, and revelator, and a true lifelong learner, respond? I imagine the learned man expected a great oration on the subject, but President Packer's answer was a powerful example of how lifelong learners influence others. President Packer replied, "Read the Book of Mormon a few times, searching for teachings about the Atonement. Then write a one-page summary of what you have learned. Then, my dear brother, you will have your answer." Lifelong learners naturally desire that others also enjoy a lifetime of thought, exploration, discovery, and personal growth.

LIFELONG LEARNING AND THE SCRIPTURES

Nowhere is the benefit of lifelong learning more clear than in the regular study of the scriptures. Regardless of how many times lifelong learners may read them, the scriptures always provide new insight and understanding. In fact, the more we read the scriptures, the more meaningful our learning becomes. That is because scriptural learning is cumulative. Everything we learn becomes the foundation for greater learning. But for this cumulative effect to occur, the scriptures must be read regularly, even daily. President Ezra Taft Benson taught: "Yesterday's meal is not enough to sustain today's needs. So also an infrequent reading of [the Book of Mormon,] 'the most correct of any book on earth,' as Joseph Smith called it, is not enough."[4]

The primary purpose of daily scripture study is not to collect facts but to gain deep gospel understanding and spiritual strength. As we read the scriptures, our knowledge increases, and we become

---

4. Ezra Taft Benson, "A New Witness for Christ," *Ensign,* November 1984, 6–7, quoting Joseph Smith, *History of The Church of Jesus Christ of Latter-day Saints,* 2d ed. rev., ed. B. H. Roberts (Salt Lake City: The Church of Jesus Christ of Latter-day Saints, 1932–51), 4:461.

spiritually stronger, which then qualifies us for greater learning—for greater vision and even deeper understanding of gospel truths. This is the gospel pattern of learning: "line upon line, precept upon precept" (2 Nephi 28:30).

Learning in this way does not require years of formal training. This is illustrated by the experience of Peter and John in the book of Acts. The Jewish rulers of their day were surprised at these two unlearned Apostles. The Jews assumed that gospel knowledge required exhaustive study and formal training. Yet the scriptures tell us: "Now when [the Jews] saw the boldness of Peter and John, and perceived that they were unlearned and ignorant men, they marvelled; and they took knowledge of them, that they had been with Jesus" (Acts 4:13).

Unlearned and ignorant in the eyes of the world, Peter and John had gained great gospel knowledge from listening and hearkening to the words of our Savior. The same can be true for us. In our gospel study, a master's degree in theology is far less valuable than the degree of knowledge we obtain from the simple teachings of the Master Himself. Virtually all of us can obtain this advanced "degree."

The key to obtaining scriptural knowledge is not merely memorizing verses and comprehending them but to follow the Spirit by putting them into practice. We may say we have learned a gospel truth, but we do not know it until we have acted upon it. In other words, the scriptures are less an encyclopedia and more an instruction manual. To truly study the scriptures, we must soar beyond names and places and abstract principles and doctrines. Our study must produce a change in us, a mighty change in our hearts, until the way we feel and think and act is a reflection of the Creator Himself. The result of our lifelong learning is reflected not in the honors we receive but in who we become. And our aim is to become like God and inherit all He has. This is why we learn and what we most deeply want to achieve.

Past, Present, Future

As lifelong learners we see the connection between what we have learned in the past, what we are learning now, and what we can learn in the future. We draw on all we have learned in the past to help us continue learning and growing. Yet we do not dwell in the past. We are always open to new concepts that are endorsed by the Spirit of Truth. We seek this new knowledge and welcome it, even when it requires us to change and grow.

That change might be expressed in this way: We spend our lives doing better than our best! Our best today is not our best tomorrow. Our best today is never our best tomorrow, for what we learn and do today changes our capacity. Our progress depends upon doing better today, even though yesterday's "better" seemed all that was possible at that time.

How does a person do better than he thought possible? In the 2004 Olympics, American swimmer Michael Phelps won the bronze medal in the men's 200-meter freestyle with a time of 1 minute and 45 seconds. In 2004 that was his best. But he knew that to win the gold medal in that event in 2008 he would have to do better than his best, so he set about training to meet that goal. Millions had the opportunity to watch the Olympic saga that unfolded as he did better than his previous best, setting a new world record of 1 minute and 42 seconds and winning a gold medal. In Beijing he shattered his own previous world record by a full second and improved upon Mark Spitz's winning time of 1972 by 10 seconds. Think how fast that is! In fact, he shaved off more than a full minute from the 1904 gold medal winning time of 2 minutes and 44 seconds. Just imagine, today in just a minute they swim two laps of the pool! That's how far he would have finished ahead of the winner in 1904. It is remarkable that of Michael Phelps's 2008 gold medals, seven of his times beat world records—not only his own records but also *world* records. The other, his eighth medal, set an Olympic record. Can you imagine being able to do that and doing better than your best?

As we strive to become better than yesterday's best, we can determine never to dwell on the past or to "protect" ourselves from the inevitable learning and growth necessary to move forward and meet new challenges. If we fail to learn and grow, our personal best of yesterday will not meet the demands of tomorrow's opportunities. In both spiritual and temporal matters, doing better than our best means following the example of the Savior, who continued "from grace to grace" (D&C 93:13). For "he that receiveth light, and continueth in God, receiveth more light; and that light groweth brighter and brighter until the perfect day" (D&C 50:24).

Lifting Our Sights

Sometimes attaining the next magnificent vista in our journey of lifelong learning means lifting our sights. When we reach a milestone we thought was our ultimate goal, we may find ourselves both elated and depressed. For example, how do we feel as a child when Christmas morning has come and gone? Or later, when our full-time mission is completed, or our wedding and honeymoon are over, or our long-awaited vacation has come to an end? There is a moment when the stark reality of accomplishment leaves us wondering, What's next? What do I do now?

As we stand atop any peak, let us enjoy the moment of satisfaction in the present. Look at the remarkable view and the progress we have made. Then turn around to see what new peaks are now in sight and set a course to climb higher in the future. When we do this, we see clearly how the achievement of one goal paves the way to higher achievement in the future.

Looking back and contemplating the sacrifice and hard work that were required to achieve past goals, we gain confidence and determination that we can do more and climb even higher. The real meaning of lifelong learning takes shape in the cycle of past, present, and future—with each old step becoming a foundation for the new.

Motherhood, a Study in Lifelong Learning

The work of motherhood, accomplished by the motherly influence of sisters, aunts, grandmothers, Primary and Young Women leaders, as well as mothers in the home, is an ideal opportunity for lifelong learning. Just think of the learning process of a mother throughout the lifetime of her children. Each child brings an added dimension to her learning because each child's needs are unique and continually changing as each child grows.

In the process of rearing children, a mother will find that her studies include such topics as child development, nutrition, health care, physiology, psychology, nursing with medical research and care, and educational tutoring in many diverse fields, such as math, science, geography, literature, English, and foreign languages. She develops gifts in such areas as music, athletics, dance, and public speaking. The examples of her learning go on and on. Even more impressive is the spiritual learning she gains as she teaches gospel principles to her children, lessons in family home evening, and classes in Primary, Relief Society, Young Women, and Sunday School. Her most effective teaching occurs in quiet, private moments between herself and her children. Her most effective classroom is at her knee. A mother's opportunities for lifelong learning and teaching are greater in magnitude than any other, for the growth and development of children is by far the most important and demanding work in the universe!

With this in mind, it never ceases to amaze me that in many cultures the choice to be a mother is considered a form of servitude that does not allow women to develop their gifts and talents. Nothing, absolutely nothing, could be further from the truth. However, lifelong learning that centers on rearing children may not bring the honors of men. To the extent that we allow the world's values to define us and our achievements, it may be hard to appreciate the achievement of bringing up children in light and truth. We must not let the world define, denigrate, or limit the value of our lifelong teaching and learning in the home and family, both in mortality and throughout the eternities.

GETTING UNDERSTANDING

For all of us, gaining knowledge is essential to gaining not only eternal salvation but also happiness in this life. "Happy is the man that findeth wisdom, and the man that getteth understanding" (Proverbs 3:13).

How do we get this understanding? We start with basic intelligence, or an IQ, which is God-given as one of the gifts bestowed on mankind. "The glory of God is intelligence, or, in other words, light and truth" (D&C 93:36). To basic intelligence we add knowledge, which comes to us through learning and experience. The sum of basic intelligence plus knowledge and experience equals wisdom.

"Wisdom is the principal thing; therefore get wisdom: and with all thy getting get understanding" (Proverbs 4:7). The world stops at the level of wisdom, but the scriptures teach, "The Lord by *wisdom* hath founded the *earth;* by *understanding* hath he established the *heavens*" (Proverbs 3:19; emphasis added).

Wisdom plus the gift of the Holy Ghost provides understanding. With understanding, our hearts are softened and made pure, our minds are enlightened and expanded, and our souls are enlarged. Our whole desire becomes for the welfare of our brothers and sisters, and we willingly lose our lives in their service. As our understanding grows, we are forever changed, until we have "no more disposition to do evil, but to do good continually" (Mosiah 5:2). In this way, our lifelong learning develops in us "an eye single to the glory of God" (D&C 82:19), and our calling to return with honor to Him and His Son, Jesus Christ, is made sure.

CHECKPOINTS

✓ Why do I learn? What can I do to raise my sights for learning so that my aims are more eternal and less temporal?

✓ How much is fear inhibiting my ability and willingness to learn?

✓ How can I cultivate greater curiosity?

✓ How patient and humble am I in my quest for knowledge?

✓ How well do I communicate, both in seeking and in sharing knowledge?

✓ How well do I apply what I learn in the scriptures to becoming a better person?

✓ How well do I build upon past successes to do even better in the future?

✓ How well do I seek knowledge to improve as a parent?

PART 4

Decades of Serving and Enduring to the End

And then, if thou endure it well,
God shall exalt thee on high.

DECADES OF SERVING AND ENDURING TO THE END

According to the Lord's timetable, our decades of serving and pressing forward may ease us gently (or sometimes catapult us suddenly) into the final season of our mortal life—a time in which we are often presented with unique tests of our faith, along with continuing opportunities to serve. I have called this time the *Decades of Serving and Enduring to the End*.

Growing old is never easy, and facing death for our loved ones and ourselves can be challenging. But a sure knowledge of the Savior's Atonement removes the sting of separation as it offers the promise of renewal and reunion, helping us endure well to the end. Along the way, we will come to understand that though our challenges may be temporary, how they shape us will be eternal. They can be priceless opportunities to discover how deeply the Savior cares about us and how eager He is to help us make a joyful transition from this life to the next.

Of course, there is much more to endurance than just surviving until the end. The *Decades of Serving and Enduring to the End* are a precious season of life that can be filled with opportunities for service and for leading by example, though perhaps in a more subdued fashion than in earlier, more vigorous years. And who would discount the blessings of those quiet, peaceful moments when we "let the solemnities of eternity rest upon [our] minds" (D&C 43:34) as we prepare for the great adventure of immortality?

The Lord's plan is perfect and complete, from preparation to fulfillment. How grateful we are to be able to spend our lives in His service.

Behold, I have refined thee, but not with silver;
I have chosen thee in the furnace of affliction.

ISAIAH 48:10

CHAPTER THIRTY

LEARNING FROM LIFE'S TRIALS

E ACH OF US MUST GO through certain experiences to become more like our Heavenly Father and His Son, our Savior, Jesus Christ. In the school of mortality, the tutor is often pain, disappointment, failure, and tribulation. Sometimes failure teaches us the greatest lessons of all and becomes the sure foundation of future success.

As we progress, we learn that while suffering in this life is a universal condition, how we respond to it is a matter of individual choice. And the way we answer life's trials is the basis of our personal growth and discipleship. Simply stated, it is not the obstacle that makes us who we are but how we overcome it.

Our suffering offers us two paths. If we travel the path of faith, our suffering motivates us to draw close to and rely upon the Lord. When this happens, our suffering strengthens us, purifies us, and helps us become like Him. If we travel the other path—the path in which we rely on our own understanding (see Proverbs 3:5)— instead of "relying wholly upon the merits of him who is mighty to save" (2 Nephi 31:19), our suffering is a great burden. It can tarnish our peace, diminish our happiness, and lead us to cynicism, apathy, and bitterness. Which path will we choose for ourselves? I know and testify that the choice truly is ours, for the power is in us, wherein we are agents unto ourselves (see D&C 58:28).

The truth is, "when the very jaws of hell gape open the mouth wide after [us]" (see D&C 122:7), turning to the Lord helps develop in us a kind of spirituality that can be gained only in extremity. That spirituality is necessary to our salvation. We remember that Paul taught, "God . . . provided some better things for them through their sufferings, for without sufferings they could not be made perfect" (JST Hebrews 11:40).

Though our own suffering cannot be compared to the Savior's agony in Gethsemane, through it we can begin to understand the magnitude of His Atonement, by which we are made perfect. In His time of agony, He prayed to His Father, "If it be possible, let this cup pass from me: nevertheless not as I will, but as thou wilt" (Matthew 26:39). For us, it is one thing to understand the words "Thy will be done" (Matthew 6:10), and it is another to live them. When we do, we begin to become perfect, "even as I, or your Father who is in heaven is perfect" (3 Nephi 12:48). This perfection includes accomplishing one of our principal objectives in mortality: to endure faithfully to the end.

Submitting to God's Will and Timing

How do we endure to the end? We begin by first learning to submit to the Lord's will and His timing in all things. On a few occasions, I have cried out in prayer, wanting to know what I should learn from my suffering. Such entreaties were of no avail. As Heavenly Father desires for all of us, He wanted to teach me through my hard experiences and suffering, and when I was willing to submit to His will and timing, I began to learn.

Years ago I was left alone to ponder this very idea in the stark white, sterile environment of a hospital room. My dear wife, Mary, had just been wheeled away to have a serious operation. My first response was to pray for her to be returned to me alive and well. My prayer was almost one of demanding her return because of the good life she had lived, because her husband and children needed her care, and because our lives of service had, in some way, qualified us for the blessing of her being healed. I felt as if her health was a debt owed to us. Upon concluding the prayer, I felt a heavy feeling come upon me. I did not have the peace, comfort, or reassurance that I had anticipated. What was wrong? Why hadn't I been comforted? Why did I still have so much anxiety and fear?

After a few minutes of apprehension and deliberation, I knelt to pray for a second time. This time, however, I acknowledged the Lord's hand in our lives, gave thanks for the many blessings we had received together as companions in more than twenty years of marriage, and expressed that I would put the outcome of the operation into Heavenly Father's hands in order that His will would be done. After offering the prayer, I was ready to accept the will of God as it affected Mary's life, my life, and the life of our family.

As I concluded, a sweet, comforting spirit of peace rested upon me. Not because I was assured of Mary's safe return to health, but because I knew I would be able to accept Heavenly Father's will and trust in Him and His Son, Jesus Christ, to give me the strength to do whatever They wanted me to do.

This kind of faith is a gift, a blessing from God. When we exercise that faith to say, as the Savior did, "Not as I will, but as thou wilt" (Matthew 26:39), we are strengthened to faithfully endure. Some may wonder whether the purpose of faith is to change the circumstances that are causing us to suffer. But if the only reason for our faith were to change circumstances, what blessings we would miss! The purpose of our faith is also to strengthen us to face our trials and endure them well (see D&C 121:8). It is a privilege for all of us to say, as the Savior did, "thy will be done" (Matthew 26:42) and to learn by experience that God "doeth not anything save it be for the benefit of the world" (2 Nephi 26:24). When we willingly submit to God's will and timing in our lives, we lay the foundation for enduring to the end in righteousness.

OBTAINING AND KEEPING AN ETERNAL PERSPECTIVE

Our strength to endure increases when we obtain and keep an eternal perspective of our trials. This perspective includes an important truth about us: We wanted to come to this earth to receive a physical body and to live in this estate with all of its blessings and hardships. We wanted to keep the Lord's commandments and to learn by experiencing opposition in all things. Without the trials of our lives, we could not accomplish these and other purposes for which *we* desired to come to the earth, including the ultimate purpose of becoming like our Savior and returning to live with Him and our Heavenly Father eternally.

We keep this perspective as we continue to draw close to the Lord and reflect on the trials and tribulations that have already strengthened us and helped us become who we are. As we recognize how the Lord has developed us through tribulation, we realize that our suffering is essential to fulfilling the gospel plan in our lives. We also realize that we need the opposition to make us strong; we need the fire to temper our spiritual steel. With this eternal perspective, we have confidence in His promise: "If you keep my commandments and endure to the end you shall have eternal life, which gift is the greatest of all the gifts of God" (D&C 14:7).

Heavenly Help

Is there such a thing as too much suffering—suffering more than we can bear? Paul assured us: "There hath no temptation taken you but such as is common to man: but God is faithful, who will not suffer you to be tempted above that ye are able; but will with the temptation also make a way to escape, that ye may be able to bear it" (1 Corinthians 10:13).

Our Savior knows our hearts—each one. He knows the pains of our souls, and He will succor us in our time of need. Not only will He not tempt us more than He can strengthen us to resist that temptation but He will not allow us to suffer more than He can strengthen us to bear that suffering. In my own times of affliction I have learned that I was not left alone but that guardian angels were sent to attend me. Some of these were doctors, nurses, and especially my eternal companion, Mary. On occasion, when the Lord so desired, I was also comforted with visitations of heavenly hosts that brought comfort and eternal reassurances in my time of need.

Don't Retreat or Give Up

When our suffering wounds us spiritually or physically, our first reaction may be to retreat into the dark shadows of depression, to shut out the impulses of hope and joy, and to give up on the light of life, which comes when we try to live the commandments of our Father in Heaven. When we retreat, we may begin to focus on such questions as *Why? What if?* and *If only*—for which Heavenly Father, in His wisdom, does not always provide immediate answers. To receive the Lord's comfort, we must exercise faith, and it is His will that through our mortal suffering, our faith will have an opportunity to grow. For this reason, the questions *Why me? Why our family? Why now?* are usually unanswerable, at least for the moment. Even asking them can be a way of retreating or giving up on faith and rejecting our family and our friends, those who can help us most. When these questions take center stage, they can lead us to reject this eternal truth about ourselves: We are able to overcome all things through Christ. When we reject that truth, we feel justified in committing sin—turning away from the teachings of the Savior and His plan to help us grow through our earthly experiences.

Rather than retreating and giving up, we should accept the Lord's invitation to focus on increasing our faith in Him. This we do by turning to Him and asking Heavenly Father for strength to overcome the pains and trials of this world and continuing to seek greater understanding. He invites us to endure in righteousness to the end.

One way to build our faith is to follow the example of our Savior when He was suffering on the cross. In the midst of His greatest trial, He was concerned that His mother be cared for and that His tormentors be forgiven. We too can focus our concern on caring for the needs of others. Reaching out to help others can quickly dispel feelings of loneliness and imperfection—and replace them with feelings of hope, love, and encouragement.

BE UP AND DOING

President Harold B. Lee brought to my attention the story of Henry Wadsworth Longfellow and how he responded to the tragic death of his wife. Historical accounts tell us that his wife's dress caught fire, and he was badly burned trying to save her. She died a short time later. He was too injured to attend her funeral, which was held on the anniversary of their wedding day. As time passed, his grief intensified. Three years later he felt increasingly isolated and hopeless. President Lee wrote: "Time had not softened his grief nor eased the torment of his memories. He had no heart for poetry those days. He had no heart for anything, it seemed. Life had become an empty dream. This could not go on, he told himself. He was letting the days slip by, nursing his despondency. Life was not an empty dream. He must be up and doing. Let the past bury its dead.

"Suddenly Longfellow was writing in a surge of inspiration, the lines coming almost too quickly for his racing pen . . . :

Tell me not, in mournful numbers,
Life is but an empty dream!
For the soul is dead that slumbers,
And things are not what they seem.

Life is real! Life is earnest!
And the grave is not its goal;
Dust thou art, to dust returnest,
Was not spoken of the soul.[1]

1. Harold B. Lee, "From the Valley of Despair to the Mountain Peaks of Hope," *New Era*, August 1971, 8.

Longfellow continues in the sixth stanza with words that have helped many a sorrowing soul:

> *Trust no Future, howe'er pleasant!*
> *Let the dead Past bury its dead!*
> *Act,—act in the living Present!*
> *Heart within, and God o'erhead!*

Finally, in the ninth verse he gives the following profound counsel and inspiring advice to all who would receive it:

> *Let us, then, be up and doing,*
> *With a heart for any fate;*
> *Still achieving, still pursuing*
> *Learn to labor and to wait.*[2]

Earlier I told the story of how lacing up my boots helped save my ankles when I had to jump from the cockpit of my F-100 onto the tarmac. As I crawled away from my burning plane, my commander drove up and taught me a lesson I will never forget. First he asked if I was all right. I told him I was, although that was a bit of a stretch. Then he asked, "Lieutenant, when are you going to fly again?"

"If I can get my ankles taped up, tomorrow, sir," I replied.

"Good," he approved and began to drive away. His car stopped a few feet later, and he rolled down his window to make one last comment. "Hales, you owe me fifteen million dollars for the plane."

My commander was concerned about my physical safety, but he

---

2. Henry Wadsworth Longfellow, "A Psalm of Life," in *The Complete Poetical Works of Longfellow*, ed. Horace E. Scudder (Boston: Houghton Mifflin, 1893), 3.

The damage sustained by Lieutenant Hales's F-100 aircraft

was more concerned about my mental and emotional well-being. He wanted to make sure that I would mentally leave behind the fiery wreckage of that day and move forward—that I would be up and doing. That was a valuable lesson I have kept with me throughout my life. We will all suffer setbacks and losses. But we must make sure we don't become bogged down by the hardships of our past. Like Longfellow, we must leave our sorrows behind us and be up and doing.

That is true even when we bring our hardships upon ourselves. While some tribulations come unbidden, there are certainly others we inflict upon ourselves by thoughtlessness, carelessness, and disobedience. Even so, because of the everlasting mercy of our Heavenly Father, these "failures" can be our greatest teachers if we have the humility to learn from them and the faith to be up and doing, filled with hope.

Closeup of the damage

I testify that the Savior is the source of that hope. Reconciliation, recompense, healing, and peace come only through Him and because of Him—and always in His time and His way. So let us be patient in Him, that He may accomplish His glorious purposes in us, and fulfill the deepest and fondest desires of our hearts—to become like Him and return to Him with honor.

CHECKPOINTS

✓ In times of trial, do I seek counsel from the Lord or seek to counsel Him?

✓ How well do I keep my eye on the eternal prize when suffering in the moment?

✓ How well do I seek and recognize help from heaven in the midst of my afflictions?

✓ Do I use adversity as an excuse to retreat from life or as a reminder to reach out to help others in need?

✓ After persevering through hardships, how well do I leave the past behind and move forward with my life?

Wherefore, if ye shall press forward, feasting upon the word of Christ, and endure to the end, behold, thus saith the Father: Ye shall have eternal life.

2 NEPHI 31:20

CHAPTER THIRTY-ONE

LIKE SIMEON AND ANNA

H OW WE FINISH LIFE matters, just as it matters how we finish a race or finish a mission. After all, Heavenly Father's greatest reward, eternal life, is only for those who endure to the end (see D&C 14:7). Enduring to the end is one of life's greatest challenges and greatest accomplishments. It is critical to our salvation.

There is more to endurance than just surviving and waiting for the end to arrive. To endure to the end takes great faith because the final season of our lives often presents us with unique tests of our faith. To endure these tests well depends on our commitment to accept the Lord's will and remember that our adversity and our afflictions shall be "but a small moment" (D&C 121:7) and will be for our good (see D&C 122:7). As we endure, we will discover that though our challenges are temporary, how they shape us will be eternal. In fact, as seasoned Saints, we will discover that some of the challenges we encounter are priceless opportunities to discover how deeply the Master cares about the welfare of our souls and how willing He is to help us endure to the end.

I admire those who valiantly endure to the end despite failing health and other challenges. I think of how President Gordon B. Hinckley was helped into the room for one of the last meetings he attended. He was weak and frail, but he still came. All of us who witnessed how hard he worked until the last moments of his life learned lessons about enduring to the end that we will never forget.

I want to give encouragement to all who are struggling to endure through the later seasons of their lives. Despite the effects of age—and sometimes *because* of those effects and the positive impact your needs have on others—you are making an essential contribution. Be assured, the challenges of your growing older may be the very opportunities others need to grow and progress. For this reason, your willingness to finish the race strong is an integral part of Heavenly Father's plan for you and for those you love. I also want to invite all of us to be more diligent in learning from and honoring these seasoned Saints among us.

Fighting On

Getting old isn't easy. (You don't need to ask how I know.) I have now had three heart attacks, not to mention other conditions that have threatened my life. I was serving as the Presiding Bishop of the Church when I suffered my first heart attack, and I had been working hard seven days a week in my calling at the time. Suddenly I was confined mostly to my hospital room or bedroom for several months. I felt frustrated and even useless. I measured time by the sun going across the wall.

I experienced similar emotions as I recovered from subsequent heart attacks and illnesses. I particularly remember one incident after about two years of being unable to go regularly to the office and to handle my usual duties. I had been struggling with feelings of despair when my wife left this poem on my pillow:

"Fight on, my men!" says Sir Andrew
   Barton,
"I am hurt, but I am not slain;
"I'll lay me down and bleed awhile
"And then I'll rise and fight again."[1]

As I read and pondered those words, I began to better understand my unique responsibility and opportunity. The Savior has commanded us to "let the solemnities of eternity rest upon your minds" (D&C 43:34). With my physical activity severely restricted by intense pain, and in my weakened and disabled body, I could experience the joy of pondering my experiences in mortality. With my calendar wiped clean of meetings, tasks, and appointments, I had the privilege of turning my attention away from matters of time toward matters of eternity.

During this period of new growth, I discovered that if I dwelt only upon my pain, my healing process was inhibited. But if I freed my mind to contemplate more important matters, an essential part of the healing process began to take place—both in body and soul. That is possible in part because pain brings about the very humility that allows us to truly ponder. Constant, intense pain is a great consecrating purifier that draws us closer to the Holy Ghost and makes us more capable of receiving His sanctifying, enlightening, enlarging influence.

During this harrowing period, I became even more drawn to the scriptures—the accounts of those who had suffered even more severe trials than I was suffering and the saving doctrines they helped to bring forth. As I studied, the veil was especially thin, and answers given to them were also revealed to me—along with insights specially tailored for my situation. Dark moments of depression were quickly

---

1. "The Ballad of Sir Andrew Barton," *The Oxford Book of Ballads,* sel. and ed. James Kinsley (Oxford: Oxford University Press, 1969), 517; spelling modernized.

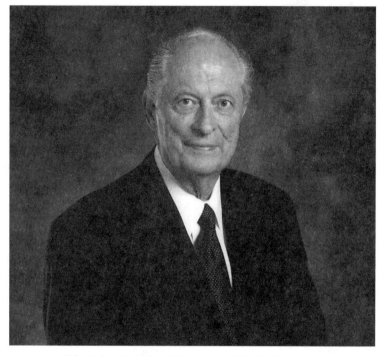

Elder Robert D. Hales of the Quorum of the Twelve Apostles

dispelled by the light of pure doctrine and personal revelation. And through it all, the peace of the Spirit of God was poured out upon me, with continual comfort and assurances that all would be well.

It is an experience I am grateful to have endured. While I was unable to serve in the way to which I had been accustomed, the Lord allowed me to grow and learn in ways that would otherwise have been impossible.

Not Where but How

My experience with the challenges of advancing years has also taught me that we cannot endure to the end alone. Indeed, we are not meant to endure alone. All of us have the opportunity to help others by lifting and strengthening them, even if just by having a cheerful attitude and saying hello. Our responsibility is not only to continue serving others but to allow them—by our patience and graciousness—to serve us.

Regarding service to others, one very real challenge many of us face could be termed *withdrawal.* There is a certain joy that comes from serving in callings that demand much of our time and attention. As priesthood and auxiliary leaders, we have wonderful opportunities to experience new challenges, rely upon the Lord, work with others, and grow. We get to know the members of our wards well and are in a unique position to help them. And even though we do not serve in order to validate ourselves, we may naturally enjoy the feeling of being needed and being busy—being in the middle of things. As we age, however, most of us move on to a different stage of our discipleship. To the extent that our health allows us to serve in callings, we are more likely to serve in the quiet, unnoticed corners of the kingdom. We are not as busy, and we are no longer in the center.

If we are not careful, we may find ourselves floundering in our commitment to serve the Savior. Yet how we serve when we no longer find ourselves in the gospel limelight may be even more important than how we served when the whole ward or stake seemed to be watching us. As the years go on, we become more concerned with God watching us. It becomes clear to Him and to us that the way we serve Him in our golden years reveals the true riches of our souls.

We now have many former General Authorities serving throughout the Church as Sunday School teachers, ward mission leaders, and in other positions we do not sustain in general conference. Their humble, dedicated service in these callings is just as important to their eternal progress as was their devoted ministry as General Authorities. They and all of us have the opportunity to learn that in our service to the Savior, what matters is not where we serve but how.[2]

---

2. See J. Reuben Clark Jr., in Conference Report, April 1951, 154.

Cultivating New Desires

As seasoned Saints, we face another challenge in having reduced capacity. Our declining health may make it difficult for us to serve as we have in the past and as we want to do now. Someone who has been an effective gospel teacher for years may struggle to recall scriptures that once came quickly to mind. Some who have always been physically strong and mobile may find themselves confined to a wheelchair, making them more dependent on others' help in order to serve and bless others. No longer called upon to serve in demanding callings as we once were, and in some cases no longer able to serve as we wish we could, we may be tempted to check out—to sit down and wait out the race. But there is no such thing as spiritual retirement.

It is for the Lord, not us, to decide the terms of the race of life, including when the race should be over. As long as he lends us breath in mortality, we are to run, even if that means shuffling breathlessly along.

There is much we can do in our advanced years, even without high profile callings and the physical vitality we once had. Liberated from the more time-consuming callings, we are often better able to focus our efforts as home and visiting teachers and neighbors. Spared of the need to attend hours of meetings in leadership positions, we can write our own life histories for our children and grandchildren. Limited in our mobility, we may discover we can still provide invaluable service to ancestors beyond the veil by using our computers to do family history. Without children of our own at home, we can provide love, support, and guidance to our grandchildren and great-grandchildren. Without the demands of school or career, we are free to study the gospel and gain wisdom from the best books.

In fact, when we watch some of our children or grandchildren try to juggle the demands of parenthood, challenging careers, and taxing callings, we can be grateful for this season of our lives. Spiritually, it is as if we are in the independent study phase of our eternal education. We may not have the rigorous, structured coursework of our youth, but in some ways we have more opportunity to follow a course of spiritual improvement charted for us by the Spirit. This phase of our spiritual schooling requires more self-discipline and initiative than earlier phases, but the opportunity for growth is even greater.

Two Examples

Two shining examples of seasoned Saints who served nobly to the end are Simeon and Anna. Luke tells us that Simeon was a "just and devout" man, a man who enjoyed the companionship of the Holy Ghost, a man who had been awaiting the Savior, "the consolation of Israel" (Luke 2:25). The Holy Ghost had revealed to him that "he should not see death, before he had seen the Lord's Christ" (Luke 2:26). Guided by the Spirit, he came to the temple just as Mary and Joseph brought the infant Jesus, as was the custom. With no official calling apart from being a disciple, Simeon took the baby in his arms and blessed him, causing Mary and Joseph to marvel (see Luke 2:27–33).

Anna too was filled with the spirit of prophecy. At age eighty-seven she had been a widow most of her life, but she had not succumbed to despair. Instead, Luke tells us, she "departed not from the temple, but served God with fastings and prayers night and day" (Luke 2:37). Like Simeon, Anna also rejoiced that she was able to see the Savior with her own eyes. She then spoke "of him to all them that looked for redemption in Jerusalem" (Luke 2:38).

I often see seasoned Saints in the temple today who remind me of Simeon and Anna. With their frail bodies, some move with great effort as they perform a work that cannot be performed by those who have passed beyond the veil and no longer have bodies at all. Surely they would be more comfortable relaxing at home in an easy chair, but they are pressing forward for an eternal throne. They understand that they still have something invaluable to offer.

I sometimes wonder if we understand the examples of Simeon and Anna as well as we should. I hope we regard our own parents and other elderly members as highly as we regard Simeon and Anna, seeking their counsel and listening to their direction.

Once my two boys and I were standing in the kitchen with my father, who was about seventy-five at the time. I was a Regional Representative of the Twelve, and general conference was coming up. As we were standing in the kitchen, my father turned to me and said, "Bob, you need a haircut." My two sons were shocked; they couldn't believe it. They were practically rolling on the floor, trying to contain their amusement.

You might ask, Well, what did you do?

I went to the barber and got a haircut!

As grown children, do we counsel with our parents? As grandchildren, do we realize what a wealth of wisdom our grandparents have stored through a lifetime of experience and service? Do we make the effort to visit and attentively, gratefully, listen to what they have to say, just as young Joseph and Mary savored the words of Simeon and Anna? Have we interviewed them to learn about their childhood, their parents, their testimonies, and their lives? As priesthood and auxiliary leaders, do we take advantage of their expertise to bless the lives of those for whom we have stewardship? By doing so, not only will we be blessed but we will help them endure to the end and prepare to receive eternal life (see 2 Nephi 31:20).

When we persevere in humility and faith, the promised blessings are great. "And then, if thou endure it well, God shall exalt thee on high; thou shalt triumph over all thy foes" (D&C 121:8). As the

Lord declared to John the Revelator, "Him that overcometh will I make a pillar in the temple of my God, and he shall go no more out" (Revelation 3:12).

I pray that as seasoned Saints, we can follow the example of Simeon and Anna, pillars of the temple, who served faithfully to the end. May we continue to offer all that we have in the service of our Heavenly Father so that when He finally declares the race over for us, we will be able to return to Him with honor. With Paul, we will be able to say, "For I am now ready to be offered, and the time of my departure is at hand. I have fought a good fight, I have finished my course, I have kept the faith: Henceforth there is laid up for me a crown of righteousness, which the Lord, the righteous judge, shall give me at that day" (2 Timothy 4:6–8).

CHECKPOINTS

✓ How do I learn from my pain and affliction so that I am not simply suffering?

✓ How diligently do I serve when I am no longer in the calling limelight?

✓ How well do I resist the urge to spiritually retire?

✓ Do I relax in my easy chair or press forward for an eternal throne?

✓ How well do I seek counsel from seasoned Saints and treat them with the respect they deserve?

O death, where is thy sting?
O grave, where is thy victory?

1 CORINTHIANS 15:55

CHAPTER THIRTY-TWO

FACING DEATH

W HILE I WAS SERVING in the Air Force in my early twenties, one of the pilots in my squadron crashed on a training mission and was killed. I was assigned to accompany my fallen comrade on his final journey home to be buried in Brooklyn. I had the honor of standing by his family during the viewing and funeral services and of representing our government in presenting the flag to his grieving widow at the graveside.

The funeral service was dark and dismal. No mention was made of his goodness or his accomplishments. His name was never mentioned. At the conclusion of the services, his widow turned to me and asked, "Bob, what is really going to happen to Don?" I was then able to give her the sweet doctrine of the Resurrection and the reality that, if baptized and sealed in the temple for time and all eternity, they could be together eternally. The clergyman standing next to her said, "That is the most beautiful doctrine I have ever heard."

In moments like this we become aware of the power of the eternal perspective offered us in the doctrine of the plan of salvation, and we truly appreciate the restored gospel in our lives.

THE IMPORTANCE OF AN ETERNAL PERSPECTIVE

Of course, there is never a good time to lose those we love to death. Sorrow at their passing is understandable; in fact, it is commanded: "Thou shalt live together in love, insomuch that thou shalt weep for the loss of them that die" (D&C 42:45). Yet when we understand the plan of salvation, our grief is tempered by the knowledge and hope of what is to come for our departed loved ones. Their passing may be painful for us, but we are promised by the Lord that "those that die in me shall not taste of death, for it shall be sweet unto them" (D&C 42:46).

When the Savior died, there was darkness and sorrow on earth but joy in the spirit world (see D&C 138:18). We mourn the loss of those we love, but we know they are passing "beyond this vale of sorrow into a far better [place]" (Alma 37:45). Joseph Smith, who faced the prospect of death repeatedly during his own short life, taught, "The only difference between the old and young dying is, one lives longer in heaven and eternal light and glory than the other, and is freed a little sooner from this miserable, wicked world."[1] I testify of the extraordinary peace and tranquillity that await those beyond the veil who have followed the light and knowledge they received in this life. If we could experience, even momentarily, the scene that awaits the righteous there, we would find it difficult to return to mortality. I know this from experience.

Facing death for ourselves or our loved ones is never easy, but consider the contrast between the funeral for my fallen Air Force comrade and the attitude of faithful disciples who mourn the loss of their loved ones. Some time ago I had the opportunity of visiting a man who had been diagnosed with a terminal illness. A devoted

---

1. Joseph Smith, *History of The Church of Jesus Christ of Latter-day Saints,* 2d ed. rev., ed. B. H. Roberts (Salt Lake City: The Church of Jesus Christ of Latter-day Saints, 1932–51), 4:554.

priesthood holder, he was confronted with the realities of mortality. He found strength, however, in the example of the Savior, who said, in the Lord's Prayer: "After this manner therefore pray ye: . . . Thy will be done in earth, as it is in heaven" (Matthew 6:9–10). My friend took courage in knowing that as Jesus was required to endure great pain and agony in the Garden of Gethsemane while completing the atoning sacrifice, He uttered the words, "O my Father, if this cup may not pass away from me, except I drink it, thy will be done" (Matthew 26:42).

My friend came to accept the phrase "Thy will be done" as he faced his own poignant trials and tribulations. As a faithful member of the Church, he now turned away from the daily concerns of mortality and began to let the solemnities of eternity rest upon his mind (see D&C 43:34). Particularly touching were his questions: Have I done all that I need to do to faithfully endure to the end? What will death be like? Will my family be prepared to stand in faith and be self-reliant when I am gone?

We had the opportunity to discuss all three questions. They are clearly answered in the doctrines taught by the Savior. We discussed how he had spent his life striving to be faithful, doing what God asked of him, being honest in his dealings with his fellowmen, and caring for and loving his family. We talked about what happens immediately after death, about what we have been taught about the world of spirits. We discussed the place of paradise and happiness for those who have lived righteous lives. We reminded ourselves of the doctrine that death and what awaits us is not something to fear.

After our conversation, he called together his wife and children and grandchildren to teach them again the doctrine of the Atonement and that all will be resurrected. Everyone came to understand that just as the Lord has said, while there will be mourning at the temporary separation, there is no sorrow for those who die in the Lord (see Revelation 14:13; D&C 42:46). A special priesthood blessing gave him comfort, reassuring him that all would be well, that he would not have pain, that he would have additional time to prepare his family for his departure—including the rare and sacred blessing that he would know the time of his departure. The family related to me that on the night before he passed away, he said he would die the next day. He passed away the next afternoon, at peace, with all his family at his side. This is the solace and comfort that comes to us when we understand the gospel plan and know that families are forever.

I was also impressed by a young man I knew who passed away from a terminal illness. He knew that his illness would first take away his manual dexterity and his ability to walk, its progression would take his ability to speak, and finally his respiratory system would cease to function. But he also had faith that families are forever. With this knowledge, he spoke to each of his children through video recordings for them to view when he was gone. He produced recordings to be given to his sons and daughters at important, sacred occasions in their lives, such as baptisms, priesthood ordinations, and weddings. He spoke to them with the tender love of a father who knew that even though he would not physically be with them for a time, he would spiritually never leave their side. He knew and bore witness that families are, literally, forever.

The examples shown by those who face death with faith are an inspiration to all of us. Great lessons can be learned as we observe how the restored gospel brings light where there is darkness and a calming influence where there is turmoil. It gives eternal hope where there would otherwise be despair. It is more than just beautiful doctrine. It can be a reality in our lives, based on our obedience. Because of our Savior's Atonement, in the apparent strike of death there truly is no sting. Because of the Savior's Resurrection, in the apparent triumph of the grave there truly is no victory. His resurrected light dispels the darkness, defeating the prince of darkness. His eternal light brings a perfect brightness of hope, thwarting the one who wants all to be miserable like unto himself. The knowledge and understanding of the doctrine that God lives and Jesus is the Christ makes it possible to endure all things, including death.

DIFFICULT DEATHS

Whenever we lose loved ones at a young age, death becomes an especially great trial. It is a supernal blessing to know that "all children who die before they arrive at the years of accountability are saved in the celestial kingdom of heaven" (D&C 137:10). Faithful family members feel the pain of separation but are comforted by the peace that comes from priesthood blessings, family prayers, and the knowledge of the Resurrection that assures them they will be reunited with their loved one in the not-too-distant future. Their faith and putting their trust in the Lord help them put the whys and ifs behind them and feel the comfort of the Spirit of the Lord.

Our hearts are especially tender at the passing of those who have attained the age of accountability but did not necessarily "die in the Lord" (D&C 63:49). The Savior acknowledged the difficulty of death under such circumstances when He said that we should "weep for the loss of them that die, and more especially for those that have not hope of a glorious resurrection" (D&C 42:45). Yet even for such individuals we can rejoice that they will eventually be literally resurrected. Amulek taught, "This mortal body is raised to an immortal body, that is from death, even from the first death unto life, that they can die no more; their spirits uniting with their bodies, never to be divided; thus the whole becoming spiritual and immortal, that they can no more see corruption" (Alma 11:45). All of us who came to earth will receive this extraordinary gift of immortality (see

1 Corinthians 15:22). The path to receive that gift may be longer and more painful for some than for others, but ultimately everyone will be redeemed by a loving Savior and will be "heirs of salvation" (D&C 76:88).

Our grief is also more poignant when a young person dies before fully embracing the ways of the Lord. It is true that "this life is the time for men to prepare to meet God" (Alma 34:32). Yet Joseph Smith had few truths revealed to him that were more merciful and comforting than this one: "All who have died without a knowledge of this gospel, who would have received it if they had been permitted to tarry, shall be heirs of the celestial kingdom of God" (D&C 137:7). This verse speaks only of those who died without a knowledge of the gospel, but it is my personal belief that the God who knows the thoughts and intents of our hearts will not deny eternal blessings to any who would have lived worthy of such blessings "if they had been permitted to tarry."

Losing a loved one to suicide is a uniquely heart-wrenching trial. Knowing that the Lord commands us not to take our lives, we understandably worry about the fate that awaits loved ones who succumb to such a temptation. Nonetheless, we are commanded not to judge unrighteously, and Church leaders have counseled us not to judge those whose physical, mental, and emotional conditions are not known to us, as in the case of those who take their own lives. I am absolutely convinced of the rightness of that counsel.

In all matters of individual salvation, I take great hope in the knowledge that all of us will be judged by the Savior, who knows our circumstances perfectly because He has suffered our individual pains, afflictions, sicknesses, and infirmities (see Alma 7:11). As Paul wrote, "For we have not an high priest which cannot be touched with the feeling of our infirmities" (Hebrews 4:15). We may be surprised at just how much mercy will be available from the Savior, who was "made like unto his brethren, that he might be a merciful and faithful high priest" (Hebrews 2:17).

SURVIVORS' GUILT

Besides sorrowing for the passing of loved ones, sometimes we experience the sorrow of guilt for what we might have done to prevent death or better support and comfort the dying in the twilight of their lives. Some may even wonder whether they might have saved their family member or friend if they had only been more diligent or exercised more faith in their behalf.

We should not blame ourselves or let guilt compound our grief when a loved one passes away. I once heard President Spencer W. Kimball teach that while we can shorten our lives by our actions, we cannot lengthen our lives one second more than the time that is granted to us to be on earth. There is a time appointed for each of us to leave this world (see D&C 42:48), which means that as long as no unrighteousness is involved, there is nothing we can do to prevent death or forestall it when the appointed time has come. We should leave the burden of such groundless guilt at the feet of the Savior and "bear a song away," focusing on past joys and lessons learned rather than on facts we cannot and need not change.[2]

TRUSTING THE LORD'S TIMING AND PURPOSES

Some whose loved ones suffer from prolonged and painful illnesses may wonder why their loved ones cannot pass away more quickly and peacefully; however, we cannot fully know what lessons a wise Heavenly Father wants our loved ones or us to learn from their suffering: "Ye cannot behold with your natural eyes, for the present time, the design of your God concerning those things which

---

2. "How Gentle God's Commands," *Hymns of The Church of Jesus Christ of Latter-day Saints* (Salt Lake City: The Church of Jesus Christ of Latter-day Saints, 1985), no. 125.

shall come hereafter, and the glory which shall follow after much tribulation. For after much tribulation come the blessings" (D&C 58:3–4).

When we genuinely pray, "Thy will be done," we exercise faith in God, both in His timing and His purposes. We may not know exactly what lessons the Lord has in store for us by extending the life of someone in pain, but we can be confident that He does nothing that is not in our interest or for our benefit (see 2 Nephi 26:24).

My mother experienced paralysis during the last several years of her life as a result of a stroke that affected her right side. As I mentioned earlier, for the last two years she needed care around the clock, and my dear father and a nurse cared for her. One night, a few weeks before she passed away, I knelt at her bedside after a word of prayer, and Mother said, "I would like to go to heaven to see Papa," referring to her father.

She asked, "Why am I going through this pain?"

My response was, "I don't know, Mother. Possibly to learn patience."

"To learn patience?" Mother questioned. Then, with a mother's kind way of teaching, she looked at me and said, "I have learned mine, but have you learned yours?" At that moment, I was sobered by the thought that one purpose of her suffering might have been so that we, her children, could learn patience.

At such moments we begin to understand the "wise and glorious purpose[s]" for which we are on earth, for which we are called upon to go through the transition called death.[3] As those who are dying and those who are living together draw close to the Lord, they realize that the afflictions accompanying death can truly be consecrated to the good of all (see 2 Nephi 2:2).

---

3. "O My Father," *Hymns,* no. 292.

How do we face death as believers in the true and living Son of God, even Jesus Christ? "Wherefore, fear not even unto death; for in this world your joy is not full, but in me your joy is full" (D&C 101:36). As faithful Latter-day Saints, we face death in and through Christ. He is the Holy One who overcame death by love. When we love Him and keep His commandments, we are in Him, and we overcome death as well. "Therefore, let your hearts be comforted concerning Zion; for all flesh is in mine hands; be still and know that I am God" (D&C 101:16).

CHECKPOINTS

✓ How prepared am I to submit my will to God's in all things, including the timing of my departure from this life?

✓ How fully do I appreciate the gift of the Resurrection?

✓ How well do I use my knowledge of the Atonement and the Resurrection to help comfort others in times of grief?

*I am the living bread which came down from heaven:
if any man eat of this bread, he shall live for ever: and the bread
that I will give is my flesh, which I will give for
the life of the world.*

JOHN 6:51

CHAPTER THIRTY-THREE

THE ATONEMENT

I N THIS BOOK I HAVE REVIEWED our mortal journey from our premortal origins to our eternal destiny. I have spoken of this journey in its various seasons and highlighted some of the doctrines and principles that are essential to living valiantly and staying on the path that leads home to Heavenly Father and Jesus Christ, so that we may one day return with honor into Their presence. I have written of how in this life and in eternity, we have agency—the ability to choose between eternal life and death—and that our purpose for existing is to have joy. Yet as I ponder how to conclude, I feel the need to emphasize what we too often overlook in our Heavenly Father's plan: Eternal life and eternal joy are possible only because of our Savior Jesus Christ and His great and infinite Atonement.

Note the italicized phrases in this well-known passage from Lehi's masterful sermon to his sons about God's plan for us:

"Adam fell that men might be; and men are, that they might have joy." So often we quote that verse alone, but the next verse explains how such joy is possible.

"And *the Messiah cometh* in the fulness of time, *that he may redeem the children of men from the fall.* And *because that they are redeemed from the fall* they have become free forever, knowing good from evil; to act for themselves and not to be acted upon, save it be by the punishment of the law at the great and last day, according to the commandments which God hath given.

"Wherefore, men are free according to the flesh; and all things are given them which are expedient unto man. And they are free to choose liberty and eternal life, *through the great Mediator of all men,* or to choose captivity and death, according to the captivity and power of the devil; for he seeketh that all men might be miserable like unto himself" (2 Nephi 2:25–27; emphasis added).

Eternal life and joy are possible because Jesus Christ, the Messiah and great Mediator, redeemed us from death by atoning for our sins. This fact explains the Prophet Joseph Smith's statement that "the fundamental principles of our religion are the testimony of the Apostles and Prophets, concerning Jesus Christ, that He died, was buried, and rose again the third day, and ascended into heaven; and all other things which pertain to our religion are only appendages to it."[1]

I add my voice to the voice of Joseph Smith and all the other latter-day prophets: The center of all that we believe is our Savior, and His work and glory are to bring to pass our immortality and eternal life through His atoning sacrifice. My deepest gratitude is for Him and what He has done for us. The Atonement is the foundation upon which all gospel truths are laid. I wish to pay tribute to Him, the Atoning One of Israel, my personal Savior and yours.

---

1. Joseph Smith, *History of The Church of Jesus Christ of Latter-day Saints,* 2d ed. rev., ed. B. H. Roberts (Salt Lake City: The Church of Jesus Christ of Latter-day Saints, 1932–51), 3:30.

Why the Atonement Matters

Why is the Savior's Atonement the central gospel principle in the Church and in our lives? It is the Atonement that makes our Heavenly Father's plan operative, because "through the Atonement of Christ, all mankind may be saved, by obedience to the laws and ordinances of the Gospel" (Article of Faith 3).

Without the Atonement, death's victory would be final, and we would be in Satan's power. "For as death hath passed upon all men, to fulfill the merciful plan of the great Creator, there must needs be a power of resurrection, and the resurrection must needs come unto man by reason of the fall; and the fall came by reason of transgression; and because man became fallen they were cut off from the presence of the Lord.

"Wherefore, it must needs be an infinite atonement—save it should be an infinite atonement this corruption could not put on incorruption. Wherefore, the first judgment which came upon man must needs have remained to an endless duration. And if so, this flesh must have laid down to rot and to crumble to its mother earth, to rise no more" (2 Nephi 9:6–7).

For the corruption of mortality—physical death and spiritual death, which is sin—to put on incorruption, there must be mercy. This mercy, the scriptures teach us, "cometh because of the atonement" (Alma 42:23). How does the Atonement work? We do not know everything about it, but we do know that it makes resurrection possible by reversing the effects of physical death and decay. We also know that the Atonement makes repentance and forgiveness possible by reversing the effect of sin, which is primarily spiritual death. Christ has willingly overcome both death and sin for each of us—an incalculable gift we claim by coming unto Him and following Him.

In other words, Christ is "the author of eternal salvation unto all them that obey him" (Hebrews 5:9).

I testify that this salvation awaits all of us if we are willing to meet its simple, sure requirements. It is not just a destination. Rather, it is a state of being with privileges and "blessings unmeasured."[2] The Atonement makes that state of being possible because it gives us the power to become like God (see John 1:12), which is the Savior's desire for us and the reason for which we chose to come to the earth.

Without the Atonement it would be impossible for us to return to Heavenly Father's presence. Why? Because no unclean thing can enter the Father's presence, and nothing can be made clean except through the Atonement. There is no other way back. When Jesus taught, "I am the way, the truth, and the life: no man cometh unto the Father, but by me" (John 14:6), he was not stating a personal perspective or preference. He was stating a fact: "I am the door: by me if any man enter in, he shall be saved, and shall go in and out, and find pasture" (John 10:9). "Herein is love," wrote John, "not that we loved God, but that he loved us, and sent his Son to be the propitiation for our sins" (1 John 4:10). Indeed, Isaiah declared, "All we like sheep have gone astray; we have turned every one to his own way; and the Lord hath laid on him the iniquity of us all" (Isaiah 53:6).

The Savior's Unique Qualifications
to Atone for Our Sins

Why is it that only Jesus Christ could atone for the sins of the world?

The Savior was foreordained. Jesus' spirit was born of heavenly

2. "The Lord Is My Shepherd," *Hymns of The Church of Jesus Christ of Latter-day Saints* (Salt Lake City: The Church of Jesus Christ of Latter-day Saints, 1985), no. 108.

parents in a premortal world. He was the firstborn of our Heavenly Father, chosen to be our Savior. Peter taught that Jesus "was fore-ordained before the foundation of the world" (1 Peter 1:20). The Father Himself declared that Jesus was His "Beloved and Chosen from the beginning" (Moses 4:2). Prophets in all dispensations foretold the coming of Jesus Christ and what His mission would be. Jacob taught, "For this intent have we written these things, that they may know that we knew of Christ, and we had a hope of his glory many hundred years before his coming; and not only we ourselves had a hope of his glory, but also all the holy prophets which were before us" (Jacob 4:4). Before we came to this earth, we each knew that Jesus would perform the essential role in our Heavenly Father's plan for us and all of His children.

The Savior was born of a divine Father and a mortal mother. Remarkably, almost incomprehensibly, Jesus performed His role with exactness and honor: He was strictly obedient to the will of His Father. Mary's human heritage made it possible for Jesus to suffer temptation, struggle to avoid sin, have compassion on us, and therefore serve as our mediator before God in the last day. Heavenly Father's divinity made it possible for Jesus to completely resist temptation, never give in to sin and lead a perfect life, and thereby redeem us of our sins at the last day. Mary, being mortal, gave Him the ability to die. His immortal Heavenly Father gave Him the power to overcome death. Because of this unique and vital lineage, Jesus was able to be our Friend, Example, Savior, Mediator, and Master—the only one whereby all mankind could be saved.

The Savior was beloved of His Father and trusted by Him. The scriptures often speak of the joy Heavenly Father has in His Son, Jesus Christ. When Jesus was baptized, the Father said, "This is my beloved Son, in whom I am well pleased" (Matthew 3:17). On the Mount of Transfiguration, "there came a voice out of the cloud, saying, This is my beloved Son: hear him" (Luke 9:35). And when the Savior appeared to Lehi's descendants after His resurrection, the Father again declared, "Behold my Beloved Son, in whom I am well pleased" (3 Nephi 11:7). It particularly touches my heart to read that when Jesus was suffering in the Garden of Gethsemane, out of His great love and compassion for His Only Begotten Son, His Father sent an angel to be with Him to comfort Him and to strengthen Him in the garden.

The Savior used His agency to be obedient. For the Atonement to have its effect, Jesus had to willingly give His life for us. Because of the great love Jesus has for His Father and the love He has for each of us, Jesus said, "Send me" (Abraham 3:27). Unlike Lucifer, who demanded the Father's glory, the Savior volunteered humbly, "Father, thy will be done, and the glory be thine forever" (Moses 4:2). When Jesus said "Send me," He used His agency to be obedient.

Just as the Savior could not have been compelled to come to earth, His life could not be taken from Him in mortality unless He allowed it to be so taken:

"I lay down my life for the sheep. . . . Therefore doth my Father love me, because I lay down my life, that I might take it again. No man taketh it from me, but I lay it down of myself. I have power to lay it down, and I have power to take it again" (John 10:15–18). Paul wrote that Jesus "humbled himself, and became obedient unto death, even the death of the cross" (Philippians 2:8).

Legions of angels could have taken Jesus from the cross if He had desired, and He could have been taken home to His Father sooner. He had His agency. He used His agency to sacrifice Himself for us, to fulfill His mission in mortality, and to endure to the end, thus completing the atoning sacrifice.

The Savior was the only perfect being. Jesus was the only being who was perfect—without sin. Sacrifice in the Old Testament was a blood sacrifice, looking forward to the sacrifice of our Lord and Redeemer upon the cross to fulfill the great Atonement. When a blood sacrifice was made in the ancient temples, it was with a lamb that was unblemished and perfect in every way. The Savior is often referred to in the scriptures as the "Lamb of God"[3] because of His purity. Peter taught that we are redeemed "with the precious blood of Christ, as of a lamb without blemish and without spot" (1 Peter 1:19). The Savior Himself prayed, "Father, behold the sufferings and death *of him who did no sin*" (D&C 45:4; emphasis added).

The Savior endured to the end. As Jesus suffered in the Garden of Gethsemane, the Apostles went to sleep. Three times He found them asleep, and three times He returned discouraged. "And he cometh unto the disciples, and findeth them asleep, and saith unto Peter, What, could ye not watch with me one hour?" (Matthew 26:40).

He had been left alone to complete His mission. Under the weight of our collective sins and sorrows, He had prayed, "O my Father, if it be possible, let this cup pass from me" (Matthew 26:39). He later described His suffering to Joseph Smith this way: "Which suffering caused myself, even God, the greatest of all, to tremble because of pain, and to bleed at every pore, and to suffer both body and spirit—and would that I might not drink the bitter cup, and shrink" (D&C 19:18).

Despite His agony, Jesus added these fateful words to His prayer in the garden: "Nevertheless not as I will, but as thou wilt" (Matthew 26:39). He later proclaimed to the people gathered at the temple in Bountiful, "I have suffered the will of the Father in all things from the beginning" (3 Nephi 11:11). Only when Jesus

---

3. See John 1:29, 36; 1 Nephi 10:10; 11:21; 11:27; 11:31–32; 12:6, 10–11, 18; 13:24, 28–29, 33–34, 38, 40; 14:1–3, 6, 10, 12–14, 25; 2 Nephi 31:4–6; 33:14; Alma 7:14; Mormon 9:2–3; Doctrine and Covenants 88:106.

had endured the trials, suffering, sacrifice, and tribulations of Gethsemane and Golgotha could he finally say, "It is finished" (John 19:30). Jesus had come to earth and retained His righteousness so He could, as an unblemished lamb, perform the atoning sacrifice. He had endured to the end. "Nevertheless, glory be to the Father, and I partook and finished my preparations unto the children of men" (D&C 19:19).

APPRECIATING THE ATONEMENT

How can we show our personal appreciation for this miraculous gift of immortality and the other blessings given to each of us through the Atonement? Jesus said, "If ye love me, keep my commandments" (John 14:15). This is our way to show appreciation for the gift of His overcoming sin and death, for receiving the Resurrection, and for making possible repentance and eternal life. We show our love by repenting through faith in Him and by forgiving ourselves and others.

There are many who were once taught to walk in the ways of God but have rebelled against those teachings. Some may want to repent and turn their lives around to possess the joyful peace of mind that comes when we are living according to the commandments. We often make New Year's resolutions—promises to ourselves or loved ones—which we do not keep. We sometimes even enter into sacred covenants with the Lord, only to fail again and again.

After a number of mistakes and failures to live as we know we should, we lose confidence in ourselves and have a poor self-image of who we are and what we are capable of becoming. We may lose our faith in God, sometimes blaming Him for our unhappiness. We may simply give up, not wanting to once again fail ourselves, others who are close to us, and the Lord. But whenever we give up on ourselves, the adversary has won. We forget that we are a child of God and capable of dwelling in His presence if we will but keep the commandments. And so we must never forget the Savior's invitation: "Look unto me in every thought; doubt not, fear not" (D&C 6:36).

What must we do to gain the strength and courage to be obedient and keep the commandments of God? We are told by prophets that "the Lord surely should come to redeem his people [by the Atonement], but that he should *not* come to redeem them *in their sins*, but to redeem them *from their sins . . . because of repentance*" (Helaman 5:10–11; emphasis added).

For the full blessings of the Atonement to take effect in our lives and allow us to return to live with our Heavenly Father, we must repent of our sins and be faithful in obeying the commandments of God. The redemptive blessings of repentance and forgiveness are an important part of the Atonement, but they are conditional upon our faithfulness in obeying the commandments and the ordinances of God. "For behold, justice exerciseth all his demands, and also mercy claimeth all which is her own; and thus, none but the truly penitent are saved" (Alma 42:24).

Choose to believe in the Atonement of Jesus Christ. Choose to accept the Savior's forgiveness. And then choose to forgive yourself and move forward in a new way, with a new heart, and in a new and perfect brightness of hope. Because of His sacrifice for us, old things can be done away, and all things can become new (see 3 Nephi 12:47). He has the power to remember our sins no more (see D&C 58:42). Now we must do likewise. To refuse to forgive ourselves after fully repenting is to reject the Savior's gift to us, purchased with His blood.

ALWAYS REMEMBER HIM

After we are on the path and are "free to choose" again (2 Nephi 2:27), we must choose to reject feelings of shame for sins of which we have already repented. Choose not to be discouraged about the past and to rejoice in hope for the future. Remember, it is Satan who desires that we be "miserable like unto himself" (2 Nephi 2:27). We must let our desires be stronger than his. We can be happy and confident about our life and about the opportunities and blessings that await us here and throughout eternity.

Perhaps the most effective way to stay on the path is to keep our baptismal covenant to always remember Him. As instituted by the Savior in His Last Supper with His Apostles, we renew this covenant by partaking of the emblems of bread and water, which are symbols of His body and blood. We also promise to always remember Him, to keep His commandments, and to take His name upon us. In doing these things we are given the promise that we will always have His Spirit to be with us—to comfort us, guide us, strengthen us, sanctify us, and bear witness of His divinity to our souls (see Moroni 4–5; D&C 20:77–79).

How we treat our family members, our neighbors, business associates, and everyone we meet reveals whether or not we have made and kept this covenant, for it expresses itself in the extent to which we are becoming like the Savior. How we conduct our lives, all we do and all we say, reflects whether we do, in fact, remember Him.

We show that we remember Him and His Atonement by testifying freely of Him and His Atonement to others. Whatever our calling, our finest teaching will be of our Savior and His atoning sacrifice, for it is the most personal blessing of the gospel we can receive. Naturally, then, the fruits of the Atonement are central to all we do and say, for it is the center of our lives. In this way, we fulfill one of the primary purposes of our lives—to know Jesus Christ as our Savior, having partaken of the fruit of His love, which is sweet above all that is sweet and pure above all that is pure.

I STAND ALL AMAZED

I testify that if we are obedient and desire to have the Spirit bear witness of the divinity of the Savior and His Atonement, that witness will be given to us. We can know.

I cannot tell you when or where or even how that witness will come, but I know that it will. From my own experience and my experience laboring with missionaries, I know that faith will play a key role in your obtaining your own witness. That faith, bolstered by your intense desire, assures that in the Lord's special time and way, you will be granted a sure knowledge that Jesus is indeed the Son of God, our Savior and Redeemer, and that there is a God in heaven who is our Father.

Once each of us receives that precious knowledge, we spend the rest of our days in mortality expressing gratitude in prayer to our Heavenly Father and living each day in such a way that we will be worthy of the blessings of the Atonement in our lives.

Then, with all the believers from the beginning of time, our mission is to go into all the world and preach the Savior's gospel to every creature. The message that has filled our hearts and blessed our lives overflows in everything we say and do. We become a living witness of the message that God lives, that Jesus is the Christ, and that through Him all mankind may be saved.

It is my prayer that we will express our love for our Savior's redeeming, atoning sacrifice in our prayers and that we will acknowledge our love by keeping His commandments. With the people of King Benjamin, may we pray, "O have mercy, and apply the atoning blood of Christ that we may receive forgiveness of our sins, and our hearts may be purified; for we believe in Jesus Christ, the Son of God, who created heaven and earth, and all things; who shall come down among the children of men" (Mosiah 4:2).

I testify that because He came down, we can return home—and return with honor. I testify that God's plan for us is possible because of Him. I bear my witness that our mortal journey is, in fact, the great blessing that is ours because we are God's children, because He is our Father, and His Beloved Son is our Savior and Redeemer. This I know, even as

> *I stand all amazed at the love Jesus offers me,*
> *Confused at the grace that so fully he proffers me.*
> *I tremble to know that for me he was crucified,*
> *That for me, a sinner, he suffered, he bled and died.*

> *I marvel that he would descend from his throne divine*
> *To rescue a soul so rebellious and proud as mine,*
> *That he should extend his great love unto such as I,*
> *Sufficient to own, to redeem, and to justify.*

> *I think of his hands pierced and bleeding to pay*
> *   the debt!*
> *Such mercy, such love, and devotion can I forget?*
> *No, no, I will praise and adore at the mercy seat,*
> *Until at the glorified throne I kneel at his feet.*

Chorus:

> *Oh, it is wonderful that he should care for me*
> *Enough to die for me!*
> *Oh, it is wonderful, wonderful to me!*[4]

---

4. "I Stand All Amazed," *Hymns*, no. 193.

CHECKPOINTS

✓ How well do I understand and appreciate the Atonement?

✓ What do I do in my life to show my appreciation for the Atonement?

✓ How well do I keep my covenant to always remember the Savior?

✓ How often and how clearly do I testify of the Atonement?

INDEX

INDEX